An Historical Study of English

'*An Historical Study of English* breaks new ground in the historical study of the English language. In an impressive display of erudition and expertise, and using insights from sociolinguistics, pragmatics and historical linguistics, Jeremy Smith explores an array of topics in the history of English, ranging from the interpretation of medieval texts to present-day Black English in Britain.'

James Milroy, Program in Linguistics, *University of Michigan*

Through his analysis of selected major developments in the history of English, Jeremy Smith argues that the history of the language can only be understood from a dynamic perspective. In this book, he proposes that internal linguistic mechanisms for language change cannot be meaningfully explained in isolation or without reference to external linguistic factors.

Smith provides the reader with an accessible synthesis of recent developments in English historical linguistics. His book:

- looks at the theory and methodology of linguistic historiography;
- considers the major changes in writing systems, pronunciation, grammar and vocabulary;
- provides examples of these changes, such as the standardisation of spellings and accent, and the origins of the Great Vowel Shift;
- focuses on the origins of two non-standard varieties: eighteenth-century Scots and twentieth-century British Black English.

This book will be fascinating reading to students of English historical linguistics, and will make an original, important and, above all, lively contribution to the field.

Jeremy Smith is Reader in English Language at the University of Glasgow.

An Historical Study of English
Function, form and change

Jeremy Smith

London and New York

First published 1996
by Routledge
11 New Fetter Lane, London EC4P 4EE

Simultaneously published in the USA and Canada
by Routledge
29 West 35th Street, New York, NY 10001

Typeset in Times by Florencetype Ltd, Stoodleigh, Devon
Printed and bound in Great Britain by Biddles Ltd,
Guildford and King's Lynn

British Library Cataloguing in Publication Data
A catalogue record for this book is available from the British Library

Library of Congress Cataloguing in Publication Data
Smith, J. J. (Jeremy J.)
    An historical study of English: function, form and change / Jeremy Smith.
      Includes bibliographical references and index.
    1. English language–Grammar, Historical.   2. English language–History.
    I. Title.
    PE1075.S45   1996
    420'.9–dc20   96–7566

ISBN 0–415–13272–x (hbk)
ISBN- 0–415–13273–8 (pbk)

for Michael Samuels

Contents

Illustrations

FIGURES

PLATES

Preface

Over the last few years, there has been a huge increase in the scholarly effort devoted to the historical study of the English language, represented not only by numerous conferences devoted to the subject but by the appearance of major summations of knowledge, for example the new *Cambridge History of the English Language* (R. Hogg, gen. ed., 1992–). The subject would therefore at first sight appear to be in fine fettle; and since language would appear to be a distinctive and defining characteristic of humanity, and all natural languages change, the significance of the historical study of language within the broad range of the human sciences ought to be widely appreciated.

Yet it remains my impression that this development – at least in Britain and the United States – has not yet had much effect on the teaching of the subject. Student numbers *opting* to take 'history of English' courses at university level remain, with some notable institutional exceptions, comparatively small, and the subject retains a reputation for difficulty and dryness which has tended to deter students from taking it up.

It cannot be denied that there are certain potentially difficult or technical elements in English historical linguistics or philology, although the comparative difficulty can be overstated in the context of the wider discipline of 'English studies': in the world of postmodernism even literary research is no longer (if it ever was) something to be pursued in one's bath. It is true, moreover, that the aims and terminology of the discipline can sometimes be expressed in a language which is almost perversely obscure. But there is a more serious problem. I have found, in several years' experience of teaching the subject, that many students – perhaps more now than in past years – expect some handling of large theoretical questions in advanced historical study, and can be disappointed and impatient if the history of English becomes simply a chronicle, a list of facts and notations for ingesting and subsequent regurgitation at an appropriate examination. And that such situations existed suggested to me that their teachers, too, had some uncertainty about the aims and objectives of their subject.

It therefore seemed to me timely for a new historical study of the English language: not a chronicle, or even an historical narrative – many excellent chronicles and narratives exist already – but a book on how the discipline of English historical linguistics might be pursued, designed primarily for an audience of students who want to engage with some of the broader questions of causation and explanation with which the subject confronts us. As Roger Lass has commented (1976: 220), 'The most important point ... is to know at all times exactly what we are doing'; this statement seems to me extremely wise, and yet it is something which has not always been addressed by linguistic historians. The growth of academic disciplines differs from that of plants, in that it is healthy to disturb their roots at regular intervals; this book is a modest exercise in root-disturbance. Its theme is that a coherent and plausible argument about the factors involved in linguistic change can be offered; as a result the subject may be considered non-trivial, because it has a robust theoretical basis.

Some scholars might feel that such an historiographical goal is entirely comprehensible; but, to others, it might seem over-ambitious. What truth can any such survey achieve, given the limitations of the evidence? Since the historian differs from the chronicler in that the latter does not seek to generalise or to explain whereas the former does, is any history of a language, as opposed to a chronicle, an achievable or worthwhile goal? I myself am of the opinion that it is – it would be dishonest of me to pretend otherwise; but these questions, which query the basis of the entire enterprise, are ones which I should like readers of this book to consider throughout.

It is for this reason that an attempt has been made here to draw some larger patterns from the material presented, while at the same time trying to maintain the focus on individual utterance which is the strength of the philological tradition. I can hardly expect agreement with all (or any) of the approaches or arguments adopted in this book, but I would hope that the material presented should provide enough matter to excite debate. An aspect of the book regarded as important is the inclusion at the end of some annotated suggestions for further reading, so that readers can pursue particular topics and make up their own minds.

The main audience for this book is intended to be those upper-level undergraduate and graduate students who have already acquired a grasp of historical fact from a good standard survey such as Barber (1993) or Millward (1989), some technical vocabulary about phonetics, grammar and lexicology from, for example, Gimson (1989), Leech *et al.* (1983) and Waldron (1979), and a competence in Old and Middle English, using readers such as Mitchell and Robinson (1991) and Burrow and Turville-Petre (1992), and who are now ready to work in a more theoretically sophisticated way. It is hoped, however, that their teachers may also find some points of interest in it, and to that end the results of some original research have been included beside some more familiar material.

Four recent studies, and one rather older one, have attempted something rather similar to this book, although in different ways and with a different orientation, and generally at a more advanced level. Lass (1987) is consistently engaging, stimulating, learned and thoughtful, even though I find it hard at times to agree with the orientation of its argument, restricted as it is to a largely intralinguistic viewpoint within an essentially formalist framework. Milroy (1992) has led me to rethink and clarify a number of my ideas; I believe it to be one of the most important contributions to the historiography of English of the last few years. However, its coverage of material is necessarily selective; it is hoped that the wider approach adopted here will take the argument further. All students of historical linguistics – as in many other fields – owe a huge debt to the work of William Labov; Labov (1994), the first of what is promised to be a multivolume study of linguistic change, represents a major summation of a life's work, which no serious student of the subject can ignore, even though its focus is on using the present to explain the past rather than engaging in detail with a range of historical developments. And finally, Keller (1994) has addressed again the great questions about language change in a philosophical and judicious way which is both convincing and compelling.

The main intellectual debt owed here, however, as will be obvious throughout, is to Michael Samuels's ground-breaking *Linguistic Evolution* (1972), which remains, in my opinion, the outstanding work on the historical study of English. An attempt has been made in this book to address the many questions which have arisen in the subject since 1972; nevertheless, I have generally found that Samuels's work has, even if occasionally cryptically expressed, an answer, or suggestions as to an answer, for these questions. It is one of the intentions of the present volume that it might prepare readers for engagement with some of the advanced issues, both of detail and of philosophy, which are raised by Samuels's book.

This book was completed by the end of 1995. I have therefore been unable, as I should have wished, to take account of two recent publications: C. Jones, *A Language Suppressed: the Pronunciation of the Scots Language in the Eighteenth Century* (Edinburgh: John Donald, 1995), and L. Mugglestone, *'Talking Proper': the Rise of Accent as Social Symbol* (Oxford: Clarendon Press, 1995).

Acknowledgements

There remains the pleasant task of acknowledging the kindnesses of those who have helped me, although it should be emphasised that any faults in the book are entirely my own responsibility and the result of my own ignorance, carelessness or stubbornness. Michael Samuels, Emeritus Professor of English Language at Glasgow, has taken a consistent interest in the work's progress since I undertook it. Many, if not all, of the ideas and insights presented here derive from his work, and I am deeply grateful for the generosity with which he has discussed them with me. It is for that reason that I have dedicated the book to him. Gordon Fulton of the University of Victoria, British Columbia, provided crucial initial input from a systemic–functional perspective; I am grateful both to him and to Kathy Kerby-Fulton for their hospitality towards me during my visit to Victoria, during which time I decided to write this book. A special debt is due to Jane Roberts, with whom I also discussed the project at an early stage. Jim Milroy made a number of invaluable suggestions, especially about the structure of Part I, which I have tried hard to take account of; I am extremely grateful for the orientation these comments gave me. I am grateful to Meg Laing and Angus McIntosh, who made valuable and salutary comments on early working drafts, and to other friends with whom I have discussed issues involved in the writing of the book: in particular, I am conscious (even if they are not) of debts to Sylvia Adamson, Richard Beadle, Michael Benskin, Norman Blake, Derek Britton, David Burnley, Michael Clanchy, Richard Cox, Ian Doyle, Tom Duncan, Beat Glauser, José Gómez Soliño, Kate Harris, John Hines, Jonathan Hope, George Jack, Paul Johnston, Michael Lumsden, Catherine Macafee, Derrick McClure, Bella Millett, Celia Millward, Terttu Nevalainen, Ray Page, Malcolm Parkes, Matti Rissanen, Nikolaus Ritt, Wendy Scase, Patrick Stiles, Irma Taavitsainen, Ron Waldron, Keith Williamson and Laura Wright. I also acknowledge and am grateful for comments on various drafts by anonymous readers.

An exploratory paper on issues engaged with in this book was given at a Cambridge seminar in February 1992, and I am grateful to Susan Wright, who was my host on that occasion; other papers in which aspects of this book received public airing were delivered at conferences and symposia in Boston, Cardiff, Dunfermline, Edinburgh, Glasgow, Hull, Leeds, London, St Andrews, Sheffield, Tenerife (La Laguna), Tokyo (Waseda), Victoria B.C. and York. I should like to acknowledge with gratitude the audiences' comments on all these occasions.

A major part of an early version of Chapter 5 has appeared in *Neuphilologische Mitteilungen*, and portions of Chapter 8 have appeared in *The Glasgow Review* and *Scottish Language*. I am grateful for the permission of the editors of these journals for allowing the material to reappear here. I am grateful to the British Library, and to the Master and Fellows of Trinity College, Cambridge, for their generosity in allowing me to reproduce illustrations of manuscripts in their care. While I have made every effort to contact copyright holders of other material used in this volume, I would be happy to hear from any I have been unable to contact.

I am, as always, deeply indebted to many Glasgow colleagues and students over the years with whom I have discussed the issues raised in the book and who have made numerous useful suggestions. In this connection, I am particularly grateful to Merja Black, Graham Caie, John Corbett, Cathy Emmott, George Head, Carole Hough, Mike MacMahon, Stuart McPherson, Robert Millar, Des O'Brien, Cerwyss Ower, Liz Reay, Seumas Simpson, Damien Walsh and, above all, Christian Kay and Katie Lowe. Katie read through and commented on Part I, and has encouraged me throughout the lengthy gestation of the book. Christian generously shared materials from the ongoing *Historical Thesaurus of English* project, which I have plundered shamelessly in Chapter 6, and she has not only discussed the book with me on many occasions but also read through the complete final draft and made numerous suggestions as to its improvement.

More generally I should like to thank my department for arranging a period of sabbatical leave during which I was able to begin work on the book, and for providing such an encouraging, stimulating and, above all, happy atmosphere in which to teach and do research – a rare achievement in the conditions currently facing British universities.

I have been exceptionally fortunate in my publishers; Julia Hall and her successor Alison Foyle have been consistently courteous, helpful and patient, and I am extremely grateful to them, not only for backing me enthusiastically in what is perhaps a somewhat speculative publication but also for detailed advice and help on the text. I am also very grateful for the efficient editing skills of Claire Chandler and Jenny Potts.

My remaining debts are those traditionally called personal, although this does not mean that they are not intellectual as well: to my wife, Elaine Higgleton, whose knowledge in particular of lexicographical practice has been invaluable, and with whom I have discussed many of the issues raised in the book; to my father and mother, John and Kate Smith, who have always so generously encouraged and supported me; to my brother, Tim Smith; and to my in-laws, Ray and Rita Higgleton, who have given me a

London base on numerous occasions. To my daughter Amy thanks are due of a more general nature, although attentive readers may note a specific contribution, in that her usage occurs as exemplification in one or two places in this book.

Jeremy Smith
Glasgow 1996

Symbols and signs, mainly phonetic

a   Cardinal Vowel no. 4 (front open unrounded vowel)
æ   front unrounded vowel between open and mid-open
ɑ   Cardinal Vowel no. 5 (back open unrounded vowel)
b   voiced bilabial plosive
ç   voiceless palatal fricative
ɔ   Cardinal Vowel no. 6 (back mid-open rounded vowel)
d   voiced alveolar plosive
ð   voiced dental fricative
e   Cardinal Vowel no. 2 (front mid-close unrounded vowel)
ə   unrounded central vowel
ɛ   Cardinal Vowel no. 3 (front mid-open unrounded vowel)
f   voiceless labio-dental fricative
ɡ   voiced velar plosive
h   voiceless glottal fricative
i   Cardinal Vowel no. 1 (front close unrounded vowel)
ɪ   centralised unrounded mid-close vowel
j   palatal unrounded semi-vowel
k   voiceless velar plosive
l   voiced alveolar lateral continuant
ɫ   voiced alveolar lateral continuant with velarisation
m   voiced bilabial nasal
n   voiced alveolar nasal
ŋ   voiced velar nasal
o   Cardinal Vowel no. 7 (back mid-close rounded vowel)
ø   rounded Cardinal Vowel no. 2 (front mid-close rounded vowel)
œ   rounded Cardinal Vowel no. 3 (front mid-open rounded vowel)
θ   voiceless dental fricative
p   voiceless bilabial plosive
r   voiced alveolar trill
s   voiceless alveolar fricative
ʃ   voiceless palato-alveolar fricative
t   voiceless alveolar plosive
u   Cardinal Vowel no. 8 (back close rounded vowel)

ʊ   centralised rounded mid-close vowel
v   voiced labio-dental fricative
ʌ   unrounded Cardinal Vowel no. 6 (back mid-open unrounded vowel)
w   labial-velar semi-vowel
ʍ   voiceless labial-velar fricative
x   voiceless velar fricative
y   rounded Cardinal Vowel no. 1 (front close rounded vowel)
ɤ   unrounded Cardinal Vowel no. 7 (back mid-close unrounded vowel)
ɣ   voiced velar fricative
z   voiced alveolar fricative
ʒ   voiced palato-alveolar fricative
ʔ   glottal plosive (stop)
ː   indicates full length of preceding vowel (i.e. long vowel)
ˈ   main accentual stress or pitch prominence on following syllable
ˌ   secondary accentual stress on following syllable
˔   closer quality
   dental articulation
[ ]   phonetic transcription
/ /   phonemic transcription
⟨ ⟩   orthographic transcription
>   changed to
<   developed from
C   consonant
V   vowel
S   Subject
P   Predicator
O   Object
C   Complement
A   Adverbial
NP   Noun Phrase
VP   Verb Phrase
AjP   Adjective Phrase
AvP   Adverb Phrase
PP   Prepositional Phrase

See further Gimson 1989, Leech *et al.* 1982.

Part I

1   Introduction

THE HISTORICAL STUDY OF LANGUAGE

This book is not a conventional history of English. Rather, it tries to show how the discipline of linguistic history may be pursued – a rather different matter. It does this by using selected phenomena in the history of English to exemplify the dynamic processes of change involved. In so doing it tries to address the question of linguistic change: why does change happen, and why does it happen at the time and in the way that it does?

In answering these questions, this book, rather obviously, holds it as axiomatic that human language is both a cultural and a systematic phenomenon, and that both these characteristics need to be borne in mind when addressing the question of linguistic change. On the one hand, it is held here that the various changes at an intralinguistic level which are held to be the prime concern of writers of linguistic history – changes in writing systems, pronunciation, grammar or lexicon – cannot be mean-ingfully accounted for without reference to the extralinguistic contexts (historical, geographical, sociological) in which these phenomena are situated. Language is plainly a social phenomenon – if societies did not exist, there would be no language – and it follows from this that an asocial approach to its study has a comparatively limited (because formal) interest.

This conclusion applies most uncontroversially to diachronic linguistics (i.e. time-situated linguistics). If we attempt to explain language change entirely intralinguistically, without ultimate reference to extralinguistic factors, then, it is argued here, the explanation will ultimately fail.

But it is also held here that linguistic change can operate intralinguis-tically, that is, without *immediate* reference to external, non-linguistic factors. The key argument in support of this axiom is that linguistic changes, once they have themselves been implemented, interact with each other to produce further change.

To clarify these points, it may be useful to model the structure of natural language diagrammatically. Figure 1.1 is an attempt to schematise the way in which language is used to communicate ideas. The deepest level of language, in this diagram, is semantics, that is, the level of meaning. (There

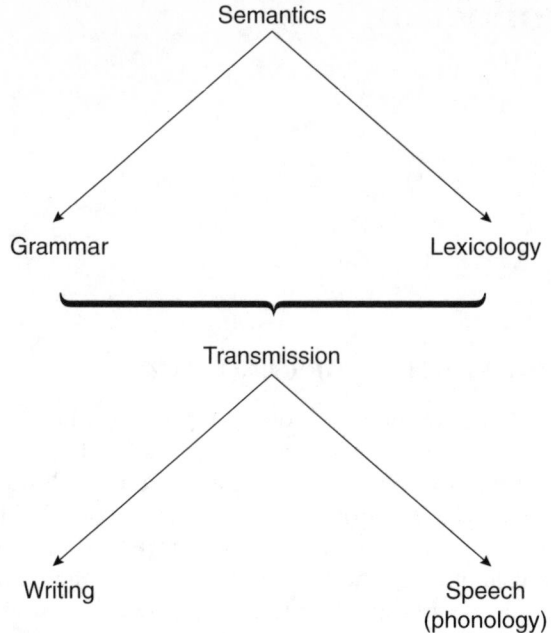

Figure 1.1 The levels of language (hierarchical model)

are philosophical questions as to whether semantics can be deemed properly a part of the linguistic system, but, given that language is about the transmission of meaning (*very* broadly defined) it seems perverse to ignore it here.) Meaning is expressed linguistically through the grammar and lexis of a language; in turn, the grammar and lexis of a language are transmitted to other language-users through speech or (a comparatively recent development in human history) through writing.

The model of language given in Figure 1.1 has its uses, but it is important to be aware of its limitations. It is essentially a static model, a snapshot; it depicts what happens when a single linguistic 'event' (a word, a grammatical construction, a sound or a spelling) takes place. It is hierarchical in orientation, placing semantics at the top of a tree in which transmission occupies a lowly position. Above all for the purposes of this book, it is limited because it does not indicate any point where change might take place.

There are methodological advantages to treating each level of language (written and spoken transmission, grammar, semantics and lexicon) separately, for it is obvious that to attempt to cover every level at once brings with it a threat of incoherence. Nevertheless the approach has dangers. What evidence we have indicates that the human brain uses each level of language in an integrated way, handling them all simultaneously and interactively, and in diachronic study it will frequently, if not generally, be found that change in one level of language relates intimately to change in others. If language is systematic – and it must be, for otherwise it would be impossible to use it to express meaning, however broadly we define that concept – then movement in one part of the system must have an effect or effects on other parts.

Languages, in short, are systems in which everything is connected to everything else (*tout se tient*, in the words of de Saussure, Grammont and their followers; see Grammont 1933, *passim*). This structural notion is the major insight of linguistics since the modern discipline was founded in the nineteenth century, and it is at the heart of the subject's claim for non-trivial status. In sum, we must expect that any given linguistic event is the result of complex interaction between levels of language, and between language itself and the sociohistorical setting in which it is situated. It is therefore necessary, in our modelling of language, to supplement the simple communicative model of Figure 1.1 with a non-hierarchical one, offered here as Figure 1.2 (after Samuels 1972: 141). This latter model allows for the process of change; disruption and subsequent reaction can happen at any point in the system, and thus any model of language reflecting these processes must be of necessity non-hierarchical. (Semantics is omitted from this figure, since meaning can be expressed through Grammar or Lexicon, or even through sound-symbolism, for instance *gr* in *grin*, *grunt*, *grumble*, *grumpy*; see Chapter 6.)

The interactive nature of the phenomenon, of course, makes the investigation of linguistic change a matter of engaging with complexity; and this complexity might lead students of the history of English to despair of finding any generally acceptable truths on which to base their discipline. There is, in fact, a respected and respectable tradition in the linguistic sciences which holds that the only valid goal of diachronic linguistic enquiry is description, and that the discussion of causation is not a proper question for researchers to address.

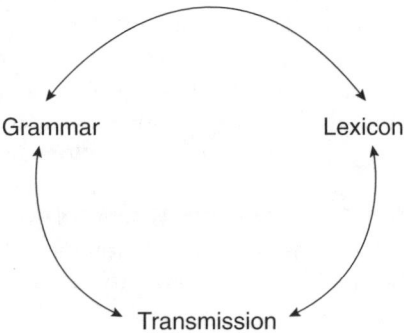

Figure 1.2 The levels of language (dynamic model)

These questions of complexity and explanation will be returned to explicitly in Chapter 3 and (briefly) in Chapter 9, but it is perhaps worth pursuing them a little further at this early stage since the question of causation will be pervasive in the chapters that follow. Since at least the Middle Ages a distinction has been made between a *history* and a *chronicle*: the historian aims to explain past events (and thus to sustain an argument), whereas the chronicler aims to describe the past in as neutral a fashion as possible without attempting to draw causal relationships between events. The outcome of this distinction can be seen in the practice of diachronic linguistic enquiry. Some books are essentially lists of observations, and these may be termed chronicles – not necessarily a hostile criticism, for such collections of observations are the bedrock of deeper understanding. In a sense, the notion of 'chronicle' correlates with the synchronic (i.e. time-independent) approach to linguistic study, in which the purpose of the discipline is to formalise the rules of a given state of language without relating these rules to their antecedents or successors; the true chronicle, with its annalistic approach, may be seen as a series of synchronic snapshots which happen to have been arrayed in chronological order, an ordering which makes no connective reference or causative link to what happens before or after. Most of the readers of this book will have already encountered such annalistic approaches, and may have even formed the impression that such chronicles are what the historical study of English is about. But this conclusion, it is held here, is wrong; the practice of linguistic historiography is to do with the interpretation of these observations, and it is historiography, not chronicle-making, which is the concern of this book.

Since this book sets out to be an historical account, it is orientated in accordance with the practice of historiography as established by tradition: it seeks answers to the question 'why?' through the observation of correspondences. When historians seek to account for a particular event in the past – say, the French Revolution – then they will look for its causes in the state of society within which the event took place: the financial and political bankruptcy of the monarchy, the oppression of the Third Estate, the coexistence of advanced Enlightenment ideas in France with revolution in the United States, and so on. It is by seeking to answer such questions that the discipline of history progresses, although few historians nowadays would claim to have final solutions to the questions which history poses. Similarly, the explanations put forward in this book for changes in the history of English have the validity of historiography; they are attempts to show why certain things happen when they do, argued (it is hoped) rationally from the observation of correspondences, and they are of course falsifiable, that is, open to being superseded by other explanations.

Of course, it is widely accepted by scholars in many disciplines that neutral observation, the goal of the chronicle-maker, is something of a myth, for our position of observation (our point of view) conditions what is observed. Nevertheless, the disabling nature of this so-called 'observer's paradox' can be overstated. Observers of language can strive for neutrality on the basis of shared terms of reference, even if they necessarily fail to achieve absolute objectivity because conditioned by their own intellectual horizons. The answer to the problem is not, it is held here, to cease making observations and hypotheses, but rather to continue to make observations and hypotheses from various points of view. The question has been addressed by philosophers since at least the eighteenth century. (For a resolution of the difficulty in the terms offered here, see further Waldron 1985: 60.)

WHAT IS LANGUAGE CHANGE?

So far, language change has been discussed without further definition or explanation. Yet the question 'what is language change?' has to be confronted at an early stage, for, as we shall see, its definition sets the goals for our enquiry.

The distinction may be made between *potential for change*, *implementation* (itself including triggering or actuation) and *diffusion*. The potential for change exists when a particular speaker or group of speakers makes a particular linguistic choice at a particular time; implementation takes place when that choice becomes selected as part of a linguistic system; and diffusion takes place when the change is imitated beyond its site of origin, whether in terms of geographical or of social distribution. Strictly speaking, the first of these phenomena is not to be included as part of the typology of change. The continual flux of living languages means that new variant forms are constantly being created in a given linguistic state. However, these variants are not themselves linguistic *changes*; rather, they constitute the raw material which is a prerequisite for linguistic change. A linguistic change happens only when a particular variable is selected and a *systemic* development follows. In that sense, language change *begins* with implementation; when implementation of potential for change is for some reason triggered in a linguistic system, then we can speak of a linguistic change. The diffusion of the phenomenon within a particular speech-community is, it is held here, a further process which can be counted as part of the particular change involved; it may, of course, itself have further effects.

In Part II of this book, a number of linguistic events will be examined in the light of this description of change. It will be observed there that the potential for change, the set of 'variational spaces' within a given linguistic system, is always present. However, a particular interaction of processes – extralinguistic with intralinguistic, or intralinguistic with intralinguistic – at a particular time and in a particular place triggers the implementation of change, with subsequent diffusion of that change within and beyond a particular speech-community. Subsequently, other changes can be triggered in turn.

FORM AND FUNCTION

In pursuing the aims described on pages 3–7, two key terms will be used on a number of occasions during the course of this book; it is therefore appropriate to offer some definitions at this initial stage. These are the terms *form* and *function*. These terms are used technically in many disciplines (e.g. in architecture), so it is perhaps worth taking time to define the special ways in which they are used here.

By *function* is meant intralinguistically the role individual linguistic items play within an overall linguistic system, and – and this is an extension of traditional usage, although quite commonplace in sociolinguistic literature – also extralinguistically the role linguistic systems play in society. By *form* is meant the various linguistic items themselves. Thus a pronoun (form) may act (function) as the subject or object of a clause; and a particular usage (form) may signal the role (function) of its user in relation to other users; or, to put matters less abstractly, a particular formal usage such as double negation (*I don't know nothing*), acting functionally in intralinguistic terms as an intensifying marker of negativity, typically functions extralinguistically in contemporary British society as a stigmatising item, signalling membership of a particular (and non-prestigious) social group.

SOCIOLINGUISTICS AND PRAGMATICS

The linguistic discipline which deals with the function of language in society may be subdivided into two related subdisciplines: sociolinguistics and pragmatics. Sociolinguistics is perhaps the better established of these two, in the sense that it has been practised for several decades by a number of major scholars of whom perhaps the most important are William Labov, Peter Trudgill, and James and Lesley Milroy. It deals with the ways in which membership of social groups is signalled through linguistic choices, and it will be observed that insights from sociolinguistics inform many aspects of this book. The work of researchers like Labov, Trudgill and the Milroys has broken new ground in showing how linguistic usages of very delicate differentiation demonstrate membership of distinct social groups, and they have gone on from this insight to develop important perspectives on such matters as the linguistic difficulties suffered by underprivileged groups in society, and the causes and mechanisms of linguistic change.

The sociolinguistic approach is not, however, the only valid one in considering language in use. In recent years, another discipline has emerged which also deals with social interaction: pragmatics. Pragmatics, which has been defined as 'the study of how utterances have meanings in situations' (Leech 1983: x), emphasises how language functions as a means of communication, and various regulative principles have been identified which describe the pragmatic strategies of interpersonal communication which human language-users adopt. One of the most important of these is the philosopher H.P. Grice's Co-operative Principle, which sets out in maxim fashion the constraints which govern conversation. The Principle may be summarised briefly as follows (after Leech 1983: 8):

1 *Quantity*: Give the right amount of information, i.e. (a) make your contribution as informative as required, (b) do not make your contribution more informative than is required.
2 *Quality*: Try to make your contribution one that is true, i.e. (a) do not say what you believe to be false, (b) do not say that for which you lack adequate evidence.
3 *Relation*: Be relevant.
4 *Manner*: Be perspicuous, i.e. (a) avoid obscurity of expression, (b) avoid ambiguity, (c) be brief (avoid unnecessary prolixity), (d) be orderly.

The Co-operative Principle, Grice held, governs all speaker–hearer/writer–reader communications. To communicate with someone else, it is necessary to co-operate with them linguistically; and, to co-operate with someone linguistically, it is necessary to use language they can understand. Thus extralinguistic pressures affect the linguistic usages of those subjected to those pressures.

It would perhaps be more correct to write of the re-emergence of pragmatics as a discipline. Students of the history of linguistic thought have shown that many modern notions of sociolinguistics and pragmatics have their origins in the work of nineteenth-century (and earlier) philologists and philosophers (see Nerlich 1990 and references there cited).

More recent work in the pragmatic and sociolinguistic analysis of speaker-interaction has distinguished between accommodation theory and identification theory, and these notions have significance for a more general theory of language change. Accommodation theory seeks to relate any given linguistic act to the relationship between particular interlocutors, and is a development of the co-operative notions set forth above. Identification is a broader notion which might be taken to comprehend accommodation theory. It tries to span the divide between pragmatics and sociolinguistics; it holds that any particular usage at any particular point in time is the result of an 'act of identity', in which speakers are seen as modifying their behaviour to accommodate to group norms. Thus, 'the individual creates for himself the patterns of his linguistic behaviour so as to resemble those of the group or groups with which from time to time he wishes to be identified, or so as to be unlike those from whom he wishes to be distinguished' (Le Page and Tabouret-Keller 1985: 181). It is an observed fact that speakers use language not just to communicate needs and to transmit information, but also to signal their and others' social standing. Identification theory is functional, in the broad sense used in this book, in that it situates any individual linguistic act in relation to its social setting.

THE LIMITS OF FUNCTIONALISM AND THE ROLE OF FORMAL VARIATION

It is held in this book that the functions of language, both intralinguistic and extralinguistic, are crucial in accounting for linguistic change. To dismiss functional pressure as being at all influential in the direction of linguistic development would be extreme. To take a simple example: the history of the English pronouns shows a steady replacement of many less distinctive native *h*-types (e.g. *hē*, *hēo*, *hīe*, *hiere*, *hiera*, *him*) by markedly distinctive forms borrowed from or influenced by Scandinavian (e.g. *they*, *their*, *them* and, probably, *she*). The shift from native to Scandinavian forms seems to coincide with the rise in importance of pronouns as grammatical 'tracking-devices' as the older inflectional mechanisms fell into decay; and there are therefore both intralinguistic (system-based) and extralinguistic (contact-based) issues involved in explaining the change.

Although functional explanations of such developments, as we shall see, are not in themselves enough – and are certainly not comparable with the predictive explanations considered satisfactory in the physical sciences – it is surely perverse to see them as inherently implausible and philosophically untenable. A parallel can be drawn here with the investigation by palaeontologists of biological evolution: the prehistoric ichthyosaur (a reptile) and the modern dolphin (a mammal), although of quite distinct genetic ancestries, bear a strong resemblance to each other, and biologists accept that both evolved to perform much the same function in the ecosystems within which they lived. A similar ecology has constrained evolution at two periods widely separated in time: function has constrained form.

As has been frequently pointed out, however, linguistic function cannot alone be the determining factor for linguistic choice (for a recent restatement of this point, see Labov 1994: *passim*). The strongly functional argument that linguistic change can be *avoided* because of systemic communicative pressures is untenable, since in that case change would never occur; change, it could be argued, is inherently dysfunctional in communicative terms since it impedes social interaction. For instance, when older generations call for a definition of new terms like *nerd* or *geek* they are demonstrating communicative breakdown with their children, whose choice of these terms is a way of distancing themselves socially from those same older generations.

It is therefore necessary to take account of formal as well as functional factors in discussing linguistic change; and the formal input to linguistic change lies in the field of variation. Usage varies not only from user to user, but also within an individual user's own variety of language (her or his 'idiolect'). Individual items are reflected variously in utterance depending on such extralinguistic factors as the age, sex and social origins of speaker *and* addressee, and on the degree of formality adopted or on the field of human activity within which the utterance occurs. Thus we address an elderly aunt in one way, but a political rally or a husband/wife in others; and the circumstances of delivery of language can vary from an idle conversation over the cornflakes to a formal lecture.

Because of the characteristics of language just described, it is argued in this book that both formal and functional aspects of language need to be taken into account when discussing and explaining linguistic change. Although it is important to distinguish between the two in order to make clear the processes and mechanisms involved, it is nevertheless the case that an approach to the historical study of language which is purely formal or purely functional has severe limitations in explanatory power. The relationship between user and system seems to be a dynamic one, in which complex interaction between formal and functional processes produces linguistic change; it is also open, in the sense that users – and their systems – interact with other users and other systems in situations of linguistic contact. These issues will be returned to repeatedly in subsequent chapters, and will be addressed in greater detail in the last chapter of the book.

THE STRUCTURE OF THIS BOOK

The organisation of this book is designed to take account of the dynamic and open relationship between users and systems which is at the heart of the history of English, and which has been sketched in briefly above. In Part I, a framework for discussion is established, in which the methodology deemed appropriate for the discipline is set out. In Chapter 2, there is discussion of the traditions of linguistic historiography which have informed debate about language change, and there is some consideration of fruitful ways forward for historiographical method – in particular, the relationship between evidence and theory is probed. In Chapter 3 the notion of linguistic evolution is discussed, with reference to extralinguistic and intralinguistic processes respectively. In Part II, changes traditionally assigned to each level of language are used to illustrate and exemplify the notions and approaches set forth in Part I, with discussions and exemplifications of major changes in writing-systems and orthography (Chapter 4), pronunciation (Chapter 5), the lexicon (Chapter 6) and grammar (Chapter 7). Examples discussed in this section of the book include the evolution of script-types during the medieval period, standardisation of orthography and accent, the origins and development of the Great Vowel Shift, the shift from synthesis to analysis and the development of the verb-phrase, and the interaction of Norse and French with and then within the English lexicon. In Part III the diachronic origins of two 'non-standard' varieties, eighteenth-century Scots and twentieth-century British Black English, are examined (Chapter 8); this chapter is concerned to show how these varieties are themselves the result of complex processes of inter-action. The short last chapter of the book (Chapter 9) attempts to take a broader view of the issues raised, and suggests some ways forward for research in the historical study of English.

The general theme of this study may, however, be briefly stated at the outset: it is held here that an adequate history of English must attempt at least to take account of the 'why' as well as the 'how' of the changes the language has undergone; problems of causation must therefore be confronted in any historical account, however provisional the resulting explanations might be.

2 On evidence

THE PRESENT AND THE PAST

Although human beings have changed a great deal in social conditions over the last two thousand years, they are recognisably the same species, and it is therefore plausible to assume that their linguistic behaviour, like their physiology, is in general terms governed by the same principles. This is not to argue, however, that historical linguistics simply entails the transfer to past linguistic states of methodologies appropriate to investigations of present-day language. Historians as a professional body are always fascinated by the detail of the events which they discuss; and there are good reasons for this practice, for data from the past do not come to us directly. Texts are never *simply* illustrative of past states of the language, for every text has a special context which conditions its contents. Thus in an historical study such as this book it is important from the outset to face up to some of the problems with which texts confront us – problems which vary diachronically. It is necessary, in other words, to examine the nature of the evidence for the history of English from various stages in that history; and this chapter demonstrates some typical evidential problems from the three stages of the language conventionally distinguished: Old, Middle and Modern English. (The theoretical problems involved in using the present to explain the past are dealt with much more profoundly than is possible here in Labov 1994, *passim*.)

PHILOLOGY AND LINGUISTICS

Before doing so, however, it must be noted that such a linking of textual analysis to more general linguistic concerns is not a feature of scholarly practice which has been invariably accepted by all linguistic historians. Since the end of the Second World War, two traditions of enquiry into the history of English can be distinguished: the 'philological' and the 'linguistic'. These traditions have from time to time been seen as mutually antagonistic, although there are signs that a scholarly *rapprochement* between them is beginning to emerge.

The term 'philology' has a number of meanings; on the continent of Europe, for instance, it is often used to refer to literary rather than to linguistic studies. Perhaps its most common use, however, is to refer to the close study of the language of individual texts from the past, as opposed to 'linguistics', which may be crudely defined as the scientific study of language, whereby observed facts are placed within a larger conceptual framework. Many scholars have come to see philology as old-fashioned, not concerned with the larger theoretical picture which is considered by some the true domain of historical linguistics, and therefore trivial; traditional philology certainly suffered, at least in British universities, from such atomism, and it is probably for this reason that it has come, at least for the time being, to lose its centrality within the larger domain of English studies in the United Kingdom. Philology seemed to be – or perhaps more correctly seemed to have become – not so much 'theory-free' as 'theory-innocent', and thus ultimately intellectually unsatisfying. Yet it could be argued that a tendency has developed amongst some modern linguists to allow theory to overwhelm data; and the data-centred discipline of philology can be regarded therefore as useful corrective to a tendency to overgeneralise.

The necessity of bringing together these two approaches to the historical study of language is emphasised when we judge the evidence for the history of English. In the Old and Middle English periods, the main sources of information are literary and documentary manuscripts, supplemented to a limited extent by inscriptions on stone, wood, metal or bone, and by place-names, and complex questions of context and transmission surround all these texts. In the Early Modern English period, things seem at first sight more hopeful; the evidence of the manuscript is supplemented not only by that of the printed book but also by that offered by the first serious writers on the English language: the spelling-reformers, the early phoneticians and grammarians and the early lexicographers. Many of these scholars were excellent observers of the language of their time; however, their evidence always needs to be judged in the light of contemporary prescriptive attitudes to speech and writing. Only in the nineteenth and twentieth centuries, with the rise of the scientific study of contemporary language, does the evidence become in any sense complete; but, even then, there are problems to do with the sheer quantity and range of the material collected, and with the theoretical assumptions which governed its collection. The direct evidence for past states of the language, therefore, survives in patchy and fragmentary ways; and, although this direct evidence can be supplemented by the indirect evidence to be derived from processes of linguistic reconstruction, these latter methods not only present problems of their own but also themselves depend on the historical record. Unlike the modern sociolinguist or dialectologist, historical linguists cannot choose their informants for their social class or geographical setting; we have to make do with what the vagaries of time have left us, and, very frequently, we depend on the merest hints to help us construct our hypotheses about past states of the language.

It is therefore important not to draw linguistic conclusions from textual data without first subjecting the texts to careful examination. 'Every text has its own history' could be taken as the key axiom which underlies – or should underlie – philological practice. To refer simply to diatopic ('through-space', i.e. geographical) and diachronic ('through-time', i.e. historical) variation in texts is not enough; texts need to be contextualised, so that the true status of the information they contain may be ascertained.

WRITING AND SPEECH

Perhaps the most important point to make about the evidence for past states of the language is that, until the very end of the nineteenth century, direct (as opposed to reconstructed) evidence is to be found solely in the written record. Thus the most important act of evidential contextualisation needed in an historical study of English is a clarification of the relationship between the written and spoken modes of language. For most of the language's history, the written mode is all that survives; and this fact raises problems of how far writing maps onto speech. It is, of course, obvious that the writing-systems of the world used today do not have any clear relationship to the sounds which, often at some removes, they represent: the relationship between symbol and sound is arbitrary, not necessary. Thus, in alphabetic scripts, Cyrillic ⟨Ш⟩ 'means' [ʃ], whereas Roman ⟨w⟩ 'means' [w] in English (but [v] in German), and so on. This complexity is compounded by the appearance of conventional uses based upon distributional distinctions (e.g. ⟨y⟩ has two different phonic significances in Present-Day English *yacht, many*), and by diachronic variation. As an example of the latter, the representation of [ʃ] might be examined, for this sound has been represented very variously in spelling during the history of English. An examination of the *Linguistic Atlas of Late Mediaeval English* (1986) yields a broad range of forms for Present-Day English *sh-* in 'shall' as recorded in manuscripts from the period 1350–1450, for instance *chal, scal, schal, shal, ssal, sȝal, xal*; with the possible exception of the initial *x-* in *xal*, none of these spelling-variants seems to signify any sound other than [ʃ]. At a more general level, the written mode is traditionally taken to represent a more formal register than the spoken mode: thus the distinction between language appropriate for, say, a conversation and, for example, a learned article.[1]

On the other hand, and despite the existence of conventional usages (e.g. 'silent ⟨e⟩' or 'silent ⟨gh⟩' in forms such as *life, knight*), it is plain that English alphabetic script has evolved so that the symbols ⟨a, e, i, o, u⟩ *generally and typically* represent vowels of some kind, whereas ⟨b, d, g, v, z, p, t, k, f, s, m, n, l, r⟩ etc. are used *generally and typically* to represent consonants. And there are obviously areas of discourse where the distinction between formal written language and less formal speech becomes hard to draw, such as in the academic lecture.

There are two important points to make here. One is that the modes of speech and writing should be treated by historians of a language as distinct manifestations of that language, with important implications for the methodology of linguistic historiography. The second point, however, is equally valid: there is an obvious connection between the written and spoken modes, because both are manifestations of (i.e. transmission-mechanisms for) the 'same' language. Thus, for example, although we need not necessarily agree with those scholars who have claimed from time to time that Present-Day English spelling is optimal in the way in which it represents Present-Day English sounds, it is obvious that alphabetic orthography reflects, very roughly speaking, phonemic distinctions; in other words, letters correspond *in principle* to phonemes, the smallest speech-units that distinguish one word from another in terms of meaning. Thus, in Present-Day English, the letters ⟨b⟩ and ⟨p⟩ disambiguate the words *pat* and *bat* in the same way that the phonemes /b/ and /p/ disambiguate in meaning the minimal pair /pat/, /bat/. On the other hand, an orthographic distinction to show the difference between [l] and [ɫ] in [lɔŋ], [ɫɔŋ] as realisations ('allophones') of /l/ in /lɔŋ/ *long* is unnecessary; no change of meaning results from the different allophonic variations and thus no orthographic distinction is needed in the written mode. Spelling-systems, it would appear, are maximally efficient when they are economical for the purposes of distinguishing meaning, and thus 'broad' in their reflection of the spoken mode. But there are constraints on the economy of spelling, for a written language with too few distinctions would risk unintelligibility. We will be returning to this balance between least effort and intelligibility later in this book.[2]

The relationship between these two modes of language may be illustrated diagrammatically (see Figure 2.1, after Samuels 1972: 6). In this diagram, axes A and B represent the spoken and written modes of language changing over time, while lines C and D represent the forces interacting between the two modes. The relationship between speech and writing is close, but there are lags in the effect of one upon the other. The spoken mode may be affected by the written mode, for example the traditional pronunciation ['wɛɪkɪt] for *waistcoat* has been generally replaced by 'spelling-pronunciations' such as ['weɪst ˌkəʊt]; more important for our purposes, in the written mode there are forces of conservatism at work which maintain spellings such as *knight* long after the pronunciation has changed from Middle English [knɪxt] to Present-Day Southern British English [naɪt]. Such traditions of spelling, whether derived from a monastic scriptorium (as seems to have been the case in the early Middle Ages) or a nationwide educational system (as in Present-Day English), need to be taken into account at an early stage of an investigation of the language's history.

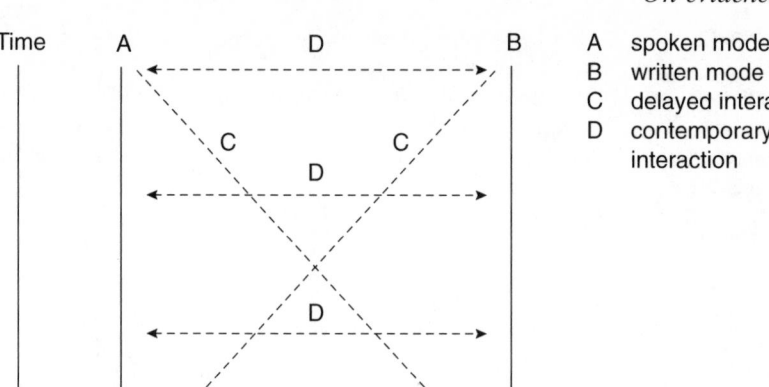

Time   A   D   B   A   spoken mode

B   written mode

C   delayed interaction

D   contemporary interaction

Figure 2.1 The interaction of written and spoken modes over time (after Samuels 1972: 6)

EVIDENCE FOR ENGLISH

The problem of evidence for the history of English is at its most acute for the period up to *c.* 1250, that is, the Old English and post-Old English periods. It is usual to classify the extant Old English texts as belonging to four dialect-groupings: Old Northumbrian and Old Mercian (which are usually grouped together as Anglian), West Saxon and Old Kentish. We will be returning to the meaning of these labels shortly; but, before we do so, we might note that the evidence for each of these dialect-groupings varies in extent very considerably, both diachronically and diatopically. Figure 2.2 is a table showing the surviving texts in terms of (a) date and (b) dialect-grouping. It includes the major inscriptions in runes, the ancient Germanic alphabetic system.

The virtue of the table in Figure 2.2 is that it shows up the massive gaps in the written record, and that the pattern of gaps and entries does seem to correlate with historical events. Thus the seventh and eighth centuries, the period of Northumbrian hegemony in England, are unsurprisingly also the time when most texts traditionally called 'Old Northumbrian' survive; in the eighth and ninth centuries Mercia held primacy amongst the Anglo-Saxon kingdoms, and 'Old Mercian' texts predominate; and, in the tenth and eleventh centuries, the period of the supremacy of Wessex, by far the largest number of texts are 'West Saxon'.

The table has obvious flaws, however, and these need to be spelt out rather carefully. First of all there is the question of what we mean by the labels 'Northumbrian', 'Mercian', 'Kentish' and 'West Saxon'. For a

Figure 2.2 Evidence for Old English: surviving major texts

Northumbrian	Mercian	Kentish	West Saxon	Date (century)
Ruthwell Cross; early texts of Cædmon's *Hymn*; Bede's *Death Song*; Auzon Casket	Corpus glossary	–	–	seventh/eighth
Liber Vitae names	Epinal/ Erfurt glossaries; *Vespasian Psalter Gloss*	*Codex Aureus*; *Charters*	Early WS texts (e.g. *Parker Chronicle*)	ninth
Lindisfarne Gospels Gloss; *Ru²*	*Ru¹*; *Chad*; (ancestor of AB-language)	*Psalms*; *Hymns*; *Glosses*	Late WS texts (e.g. certain MSS of *Ælfric*)	tenth/eleventh

Note: For the background to all these texts, see in the first instance Campbell 1959, Hogg 1992a.

number of scholars, these terms are abstractions which do not have any clear geographical significance; but this view seems to beg some important questions. It is obvious, from their descendants in the much better attested Middle English period, that these various Old English dialects can be given a roughly geographical ordering, even if the placings can scarcely be as accurate as that achieved in detailed surveys of present-day varieties of English. It is perhaps best to see these terms as typological expressions, useful ways of expressing broad diatopic relationships between bodies of texts.

Just how rough these expressions are, however, is indicated when we move to a second caveat about the table: the way in which it places each text in a clear-cut relationship of descent and difference. The trouble is that many – if not most – of these texts are situated in quite complex linguistic and textual networks. Thus the Erfurt glossary was almost certainly copied by a scribe whose first language was not English, with all the implications that has for the status of the text as linguistic evidence. The *Vespasian Psalter Gloss*, although the major ninth-century Mercian text, was copied in Canterbury, possibly by a non-Mercian scribe working from a Mercian original. The ninth-century *Kentish Charters* differ from the tenth-century *Kentish Psalms* in that many of the former show (so it is often, if controversially, claimed) the impact of Mercian orthographic tradition while the latter are influenced by West Saxon (see Toon 1983, King 1992a, Lowe forthcoming (a)). In the Early West Saxon texts, as A. Campbell (1959: 8) remarks, 'West Saxon is fighting against the strong tradition of Mercian spelling'. The whole question of the relationship between the corpora of Early and Late West Saxon texts is a complex one; it has been traditional to refer to the writings of King Alfred's day (the late ninth century) as exemplifying 'Early West Saxon' whereas those of Abbot Ælfric's time (the early eleventh century) are often termed 'Late West Saxon', yet the relationship between Early West Saxon and Late West Saxon is distorted if the material remains which make up the latter are taken as descended straightforwardly from the former. The relationship between the *Lindisfarne Gospels Gloss* and the Mercian portion of the *Rushworth Glosses* ('*Ru*[1]') is an intricate one; but this did not stop Farman, the Mercian glossator of this part of the *Rushworth Gospels*, feeling and reflecting the impact of what must have been an incipient West Saxon standardised written language. This list of special cases could be greatly expanded.

Finally, the table in Figure 2.2 might seem to indicate some broad coverage across the country. Such an impression is quite fallacious. Apart from West Saxon, the dialect materials from Anglo-Saxon England are slight and fragmentary, and major parts of the country are almost entirely unrepresented (e.g. East Anglia).

It seems that what the written evidence of Anglo-Saxon England supplies us with is a set of snapshots of individual usages, of varying evidential value, giving us an idea of the kinds of language found in a few regional centres of the period. This picture corresponds with what we know of Anglo-Saxon writing abilities in the vernacular: something restricted to the monastic scriptorium. It is in this sense that some distinguished scholars have spoken of the impossibility of Old English dialectology, if our aim is to produce something comparable to the modern *Survey of English Dialects*; and it seems certain, despite some researchers' gallant attempts, that quantitative surveys comparable to those carried out by modern sociolinguists are not an appropriate methodology for the study of the language of this period – the material remains to allow for statistical analysis of the kind favoured by such investigations are simply not to be had. However, it is possible to make some interesting typological statements, and the investigation of scriptorial practices remains a valid goal of enquiry.[3]

A similar situation may be found when we turn to the manuscript-evidence for the post-Old English/transitional Middle English period, that is, from the Norman Conquest up to *c.* 1250. Until the middle of the thirteenth century, manuscripts in the vernacular continued to be produced in England; a remarkable fact is that more manuscripts in what is conventionally called 'Old English' survive dating from after the Norman Conquest than from before it. But these texts were generally produced under a conservative scriptorial system which survived in only a few regional centres, for instance Worcester, and which could enforce a normative spelling-system; in less geographically and politically peripheral

Figure 2.3 Evidence for post-Old English (1100–1250) and Early Middle English (1250–1350): localised and localisable texts (provisional placings; see Laing 1991, 1993)

scriptoria, such as Canterbury, the vernacular was replaced much earlier by Latin as the language of written record.

Even in the West Midlands, this scriptorial system had broken down by the middle of the thirteenth century as a result of wider vernacular literacy and demand for books; it has usually been argued that, sustained by the close supervision associated with monastic discipline, the system could not survive in the looser institutional structures needed to produce books rapidly. And in some parts of the country, such as the North or the extreme South-West, conditions were such that vernacular literacy to all intents and purposes seems to have disappeared for much of the Middle English period. The map in Figure 2.3 (after Laing 1991: 43–46) shows that the evidence for post-Old English remains patchy. Moreover, the manuscripts which do survive raise textual problems in many ways similar to those raised by the Old English evidence; for instance, the texts associated with and derived from the much-copied early-thirteenth-century handbook for solitary religious women, *Ancrene Wisse*, make up a very high proportion of the texts located on this map. Without them, a large portion of the evidence for transitional Middle English would disappear. And yet there is evidence that these texts were in some sense and at some point in their transmission standardised, that is, focused on a conventionalised usage, traditionally localised at the North Herefordshire religious house of Wigmore Abbey (but see further Chapter 4 below).

The evidence for the central period of Middle English (1250–1450) is much fuller. The most important source of information for much of this period, as for Old English, continues to be the corpus of surviving manuscripts. But whereas the manuscript-remains from the period up to 1250 are comparatively scanty, the manuscript-evidence for Middle English after that date is very considerable indeed. Moreover, its evidential value is qualitatively distinct. Middle English is 'dialectal' rather than 'standardised'; a debased vernacular for much of the period, English did not achieve the status of availability for all possible registers until well after the end of the Middle Ages – arguably, not until the nineteenth century, when French was replaced by English as the language of acts of parliament.

The reason for this debasement of English is historical. Although there is good evidence that the Norman aristocracy learnt English fairly quickly after the Conquest – a trend encouraged by the events of 1204, when the rulers of England lost control of Normandy and those barons who owned land in both countries (as many did) had to choose between their English and Norman estates – nevertheless French remained the language of prestige and sophistication during the Middle Ages. Since no general norm of written English was taught until at least the fifteenth century, the written mode of Middle English reflects the diatopic variation of the spoken medium more clearly than ever since. (On the roles and functions of the various languages of Britain in the Middle Ages, see notably Clanchy 1993 and references there cited.)

Despite this plethora of evidence for contemporary linguistic variation, however, it was until comparatively recently (and, in some circles, remains) scholarly practice to confine the discussion of the dialectal manifestations of Middle English to a rather small set of texts considered to be of first-class evidential value: thus the primacy in this scholarly tradition of authorial holographs, which are supposed to give precise information about the language of a (comparatively) fully contextualised individual. During the Middle English period, such texts are unhappily few: Dan Michel's *Ayenbite of Inwyt* (Canterbury, 1340) is one such, as are the holograph writings of the poet and scribe Thomas Hoccleve (early fifteenth century), or much of the fascinating late-medieval collection of papers and letters collected by and for the Paston family of Norfolk. To these might be added – albeit somewhat controversially – the English poetry of John Gower, William Langland and possibly even Geoffrey Chaucer himself, all of whose usages may be reconstructed from the evidence of manuscripts copied around or just after the time of the poets' deaths. Any discussion of the language of these authors, especially in the field of phonological reconstruction, has in the past been usually restricted to the analysis of poetic rhyming or metrical practice.

Such an emphasis on authors derives from the traditional primary philological goal of textual criticism: the construction of the 'critical edition', whereby the authorial text could be presented to a modern audience free from an assumed overlay of scribal accretion and corruption. However, the completion of the *Linguistic Atlas of Late Mediaeval English* (*LALME*) in 1986 has meant a massive addition to the body of localised and localisable texts for the period 1350–1450, and hence a liberation from the restricted corpus hitherto studied. The focus of *LALME* is on individual scribal usage rather than on that of the author – thus scribes are granted equal importance to authors in terms of their status as linguistic informants – and on the written language as an object of interest in its own right rather than as indirect evidence for the spoken mode. The research which produced *LALME* will be described at greater length below. Figure 2.4 is a map derived from *LALME*, showing the coverage achieved by this survey.

LALME covers the period 1350–1450, and the reasons why it ends at the later date are obvious: it is from that time that standardisation of the written mode obscures the earlier pattern of richly recorded dialectal variation. By the sixteenth century, in England at least, the public written mode of the vernacular had become standardised – focused – in a way which points forward to the fixed and educationally enforced standard of present-day written English. The use of printing for reproducing English texts from the end of the fifteenth century provided prescriptive norms for contemporary manuscript-usage, a development which correlates with the contemporary growth in vernacular literacy. Printing was introduced into England, it seems, as the result of popular demand for the rapid production of books. Its invention correlates with the growth of a larger distinct reading public, that is, notably in London and the rest of the prosperous South and East, a literate, upwardly mobile, urban middle class. It is worth recording that upper-class readers still demanded lavishly decorated manuscripts for presentation to them; printed books were essentially aimed at the emerging middle classes, for whom the traditional workaday manuscripts were a poor second-best. During this period, the origins of Present-Day English society, with its modern class-gradations, may be detected; and these class differences are marked by linguistic standardisation in both written and spoken modes (see further Chapters 4 and 5 below).

Figure 2.4 Survey points (localised and localisable texts) used for the *Linguistic Atlas of Late Mediaeval English* (1986) (after Vol. I, p. 568)

For information about the spoken mode during the Early Modern English period we depend not so much, as in the Old and Middle English periods, on the evidence supplied by variant spellings and grammatical forms in written texts (although informal writings from the period do sporadically reflect contemporary speech-habits in ways which are disguised in contemporary printed books, and deserve more attention than they are often given). Rather, students of Early Modern English speech depend on the interpretation of contemporary statements about the language: the works of the orthoepistical writers and the early English grammarians and lexicographers. Even here, it is important to note that the evidence of these early commentators cannot itself be taken at face value. A number of writers claim usages as authentic which are at obvious variance with the facts, misled by their own conception of what is more or less prestigious practice (see, for instance, Dobson 1968: 245).

Helpful extra information about pronunciation is given by rhyming practices and, even, puns; and there is also the evidence provided by, for instance, writers of the time attempting to represent, frequently for the purposes of parody, the variousness of contemporary spoken language; good examples of the latter are to be found in Shakespeare's representation of non-standard speech, such as in Edgar's 'countryman's' language in *King Lear*. However, these practices, too, can be affected by the growth of prescriptive norms, and a degree of formalisation cannot be ruled out even (perhaps especially) in parodic writing – just as present-day stage Glaswegian is not to be too closely identified with the actor's target for imitation, 'real' Glaswegian. Rhymes and puns, archaistic grammar or vocabulary, can be conventional, and not a true reflection of the spoken mode of the time.

It is therefore important, in studying the language of this period, for a third source of evidence to be brought into consideration: the evidence of Present-Day English itself. Present-Day English is made up of many varieties; and many of these varieties themselves contain residualisms which illuminate the earlier history of the language.

RECONSTRUCTION

So far in this chapter, we have been concerned with the analysis of direct, that is extant, evidence for the historical study of English. There is, of course, another, indirect source of evidence for states of the language in the past, which has proved particularly useful when engaging with pre-historic matters (i.e. discussion of linguistic events which take place before the period of written records). This source lies in the well-established methodologies associated with comparison of recorded language-states and subsequent reconstruction of common unrecorded ancestor-forms.

A simple example of *comparative reconstruction* (as it is called), that is, reconstruction based on the data of more than one related language or variety, is given by Lehmann (1992: 142–143), who cites the contrast between British, Australian and North American pronunciations of the words *atom*, *bitter* and *little*. In some varieties of American English (AE), the medial -*t*- is voiced, so that *atom* and *Adam*, *bitter* and *bidder* are pronounced alike (i.e. they are homophones); this usage contrasts with that of British English, where *atom*, *bitter* have medial /t/ beside medial /d/ in *Adam*, *bidder*. Pronunciations like those of British English (BE) are also found in other varieties of English, for example in Australia (AusE). Such comparisons enable the linguist to reconstruct a *proto-form* or *etymon*, as in Figure 2.5.

The implication of this diagram is that American English had undergone an innovation not experienced by the other varieties in question.

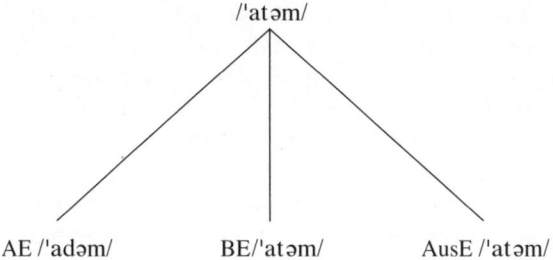

Figure 2.5 Comparative reconstruction (after Lehmann 1992: 143)

This simple reconstruction is supported by an examination of words made from the same base in American English, such as *hitter* American English /'hɪdər/ beside *hit* American English /hɪt/. The voiceless /t/ in the verb suggests that the American English pronunciation of *hitter* with /d/, the derived noun, not shared by British English and Australian English, is an innovation.

Beside comparative reconstruction, historical linguists also have had recourse to *internal reconstruction*. Internal reconstruction, as its name suggests, uses data from within one variety – which itself might be reconstructed – for reconstructing its ancestor. Again, Lehmann (1992: 163–164) gives a simple example of this procedure. He notes that an earlier American English /t/ became /d/ in certain environments, such as those italicised in Figure 2.6.

Lehmann points out (1992: 164) that 'the method of internal reconstruction is applicable because sound change does not take place in specific morphological categories. . . . Rather, it takes place in phonological sets. If these can be identified, we can posit the earlier situation. . . . Future students of English will . . . suspect any /d/ found after a stressed vowel and before an unstressed vowel, especially if it maintains an interchange with /t/.'

Both methods are well established in scholarship, and have proved themselves to be a valuable resource of indirect evidence for historical study. However, there are problems about these methods which, when the disciplines of reconstruction were first established during the nineteenth century, were perhaps not addressed as fully as they might have been. In

Figure 2.6 Internal reconstruction (after Lehmann 1992: 163)

tick	sin	bid	hit
ticker	sinner	bidder	*hitter*
ticking	sinning	bidding	*hitting*
ticks	sins	bids	hits
red	black	fast	fat
redder	blacker	faster	*fatter*

essence, these problems centre on the question of uniformity, that the proto-language represents a uniform state from which subsequent varieties have diverged. The evidence of present-day and historically recorded languages is that such uniformity is a fiction; any single language is a congeries of varieties which have emerged through processes of complex interaction with each other.

Furthermore, the techniques of reconstruction can be taken only so far back. It has been a presumption of most linguists that all human languages have an ultimate common ancestor, but the reconstruction of this ultimate proto-language has not proved possible. As will be further discussed in Chapter 3, languages borrow material from other languages as well as inherit it from their ancestors, and the further back the reconstruction is taken, and the more languages there are for comparison, the smaller the amount of inherited material there is.

In such circumstances, it is worth reminding ourselves that any set of reconstructed proto-forms is an abstract representation of an underlying system, not reflecting the surface variation of which natural languages consist; a useful formalisation, but limited if our aim is to use such formalisations as evidence for the processes involved in linguistic change. It is for this reason that this book, although it deals with a few problems where reconstruction of some kind is necessary, has avoided dealing with language-states such as Proto-Germanic, where only reconstructed forms can be adduced as evidence. It is worth noting, moreover, that reconstructions of proto-languages depend on the earliest historical data available; and the earliest data for English from the Anglo-Saxon period themselves need textual analysis before they in turn can be used for reconstruction.

PROBLEMS OF TEXTUAL ANALYSIS

At the beginning of this chapter, reference was made to the necessity for textual analysis before linguistic deductions can be legitimately made. In what remains, some textual problems characteristic of the various periods of English conventionally distinguished will be discussed, exemplifying the kinds of difficulty which the diachronic linguist needs to confront.

AN OLD ENGLISH PROBLEM

The first example will be taken from the Old English period, that is the period roughly from the arrival of the Anglo-Saxons in England up to the Norman Conquest of 1066. A typical linguistic innovation, observable in Present-Day English and referred to from time to time elsewhere in this book, is that which scholars refer to as 'misadaptation' or 'hyper-adaptation' or, sometimes, 'hypercorrection'. Hyperadaptation is charac-teristic of socially mobile, upwardly aspiring people; such folk are weakly tied to the social network they are attempting to leave, and similarly weakly tied to the target-class at which they are aiming. A good example in Present-Day English is the spread of initial [h] by habitual '*h*-droppers' to environments where it is not used in 'standard' speech and where it has no etymological justification, for instance [haɪ] for 'I'.

Such innovations can become objects of mirth and parody. But they are of interest to linguists because they display the classic features of an innovation, being produced by a group of upwardly aspiring people with weak ties in the community both to their social origins and to their social target.

Such hyperadaptations can be found early in the history of English. MS Oxford, Bodleian Library, Auct. D.2.19, an eighth/ninth-century copy of the Gospels in Latin, was given an Old English interlinear gloss in the tenth century by two scribes whose names are recorded in the manuscript: Farman and Owun. The book belonged in 1650 to John Rushworth, deputy clerk to the House of Commons, and he donated it to the Bodleian; it is therefore known as the *Rushworth Gospels*. Farman's portion consisted of the gloss to Matthew, Mark 1–2, and a small portion of John (18. 1–2); Owun wrote the rest. The colophon indicates that Farman wrote 'æt harawuda', usually identified as Harewood near Leeds in Yorkshire. Owun seems to have been a Northumbrian. The two scribal contributions are traditionally known as Ru^1 and Ru^2 respectively.

It has long been recognised that Farman's glossing differs linguistically from the Old Northumbrian of Owun, but accounting for the difference was controversial before R. Menner's study of 1934. Until that date, it was a persistent belief that Ru^1 was 'a kind of mixture of Mercian and West Saxon' (Menner 1934: 1); and some scholars had concluded that this mixed variety existed because Farman was copying a West Saxon gloss and interlarding it with his own (Old Mercian) forms.

Menner showed convincingly that Farman was a translator of the exemplar before him. The basis of his proof was that, in his glossing of Mark, Farman used as his exemplar the Old Northumbrian gloss to the *Lindisfarne Gospels*, which still survives: 'this is obvious ... from his frequently copying the variant glosses and even a marginal expansion (Mark 1, v. 6) from Lindisfarne' (Menner 1934: 5); the gloss to Matthew, however, was derived independently. Careful comparison of the two sets of glosses in Ru^1 shows few linguistic differences between them (see Menner 1934: 10). What differences there are can be explained in terms of what has been called 'constrained usage':

> One may ... risk the deduction that in copying another gloss Farman would avoid a word that did not belong to his own dialect, but might on the contrary follow his original in the use of words that would not be his choice in an independent translation.
>
> (Menner 1934: 11)

Although Menner vindicated Farman's usage as his own, his work left a number of questions unanswered. In terms of the traditional Old English dialect typology, Farman's language remained mixed in appearance, and his writing included a number of forms which seemed not to be etymologically justified.

The key work on Farman's usage remains Kuhn's study (1945) of *e* and *æ* in *Ru*[1]. Kuhn demonstrated that Farman's peculiarities could be accounted for in terms of hyperadaptation (although Kuhn did not use the term) in the direction of West Saxon, a dialect which, in the generations after Farman, became prestigious and was therefore imitated in the written mode outside its area of origin.

Probably the clearest instance of this behaviour, fully documented by Kuhn, is Farman's use of *æ* for the isolative development of both West Germanic *a* and West Germanic *e*. As a Mercian, Farman might have been expected to share the development of these sounds found in the chief Old English 'Mercian' text, the ninth-century gloss to the *Vespasian Psalter*; but there are some interesting differences. Because of a prehistoric Old English sound-change known as 'second fronting', the gloss to the *Vespasian Psalter* has *e* for West Germanic *a* where West Saxon has *æ* (e.g. *deg* 'day' instead of West Saxon *dæg*). Farman, however, generally has *æ*; beside *dæg*, other common forms are *æfter*, *fæder*, *hrægl* etc. He uses *e* only rarely, for instance *hweþre*. Kuhn shows that Farman uses *æ* to *e* as the reflex of West Germanic *a* in the proportion 25:2.

Farman's usage here may seem unexceptionable; we know little enough about the true geographical extent of second fronting in the Old English period, and it could be argued that the sound-change simply did not reach 'æt harawuda'. However, this position cannot be sustained when we examine the reflexes of West Germanic *e* in Farman's glosses. Unless affected by neighbouring sounds, the reflex of West Germanic *e* has been astonishingly stable in the history of English, and *e* is the usual form in all Old English dialects. Yet Farman uses *æ* for *e* in West Germanic *e*-words in the proportion of 5 *æ* to 9 *e* – a remarkable statistic. Thus forms such as *æfne*, *cwæþende*, *stæfn*, *þæc*, *þægn*, *wær* appear (cf. 'normal' Old English *efne*, *cweþende*, *stefn*, *þec*, *þegn*, *wer*). A. Campbell (1959: 111 n. 1) objected to a 'general identification of *æ* and *e*' in Farman's idiolect, and drew attention to the restricted set of words in which *æ* for *e* occurred. Campbell did not, however, make as clear a distinction as he might have done between writing and speech; and this held him back from accepting Kuhn's explanation of these forms, even though he felt that the 'cause of these abnormal spellings requires investigation'.

Kuhn, having found similar behaviour in the eleventh-century *Worcester Chronicle*, explained Farman's usage as follows:

> [Farman] was a Mercian whose native speech must have been essentially the same as that of the scribe who glossed the *Vespasian Psalter*, but

whereas the latter was writing with a minimum of outside influence, Farman was trying to imitate the language of his temporal and ecclesiastical superiors. As a consequence of this imitation, he introduced numerous Saxonisms into his glosses, among them *æ* instead of *e* for [West Germanic] *a*. He, like the Worcester scribe, carried the imitation too far, and wrote *æ* frequently for [West Germanic] *e*.

(1945: 641–642)

In other words, Farman hyperadapted in the written mode. His hypercorrection, moreover, can be accounted for in terms of what may be termed weak cultural ties; Farman was not a West Saxon, but aspired to West Saxonism. This makes him a typical innovator; but it also makes his evidence for Old Mercian problematic.

A MIDDLE ENGLISH PROBLEM

Until quite recently, Middle English scholars generally held to the dictum, perhaps most clearly enunciated by J.R.R. Tolkien (1929), that the language of a Middle English text was a reflection of its textual transmission. Since Middle English was the age when dialectal variation was reflected in the written mode, and therefore scribal idiolects varied very considerably, and since most Middle English texts other than authorial holographs were the result of scribes copying the work of other scribes whose idiolects almost necessarily differed to a greater or lesser extent from their own, it was assumed that any given scribal copy was written in what became called a *Mischsprache*, a 'mixed language', to which each scribe involved in transmitting the text had contributed some element. It was therefore assumed that texts other than holographs – which were felt to be in some sense 'pure' – were of very limited linguistic value.

The publication of *LALME* has, however, revised scholarly opinion on this matter. It is now held that the problems of interpretation raised by scribe–author interaction in the copying of Middle English texts can be overcome.

The means by which this has been done have been set out in a series of ground-breaking articles (McIntosh 1963, 1973, Benskin and Laing 1981, also *LALME*, Volume I), which established a typology of scribal practice. This typology, which is clinal, divides the habits of copyists of Middle English manuscripts into three categories:

1 *literatim*-copying, whereby a scribe reproduced, letter-by-letter, the forms of an exemplar;
2 translation, whereby scribes converted the language of their exemplars into their own language;
3 something between these two poles.

Examples of all three kinds of behaviour are not hard to find in Middle English texts:

1   The Cotton text of *The Owl and the Nightingale* (MS London, British Library, Cotton Caligula A.ix), although copied by one hand throughout, is written in two distinct spelling-systems which fall into two distinct sets of stints (see Atkins 1922).

2   A comparison of William Caxton's text of Malory (printed 1485) with Caxton's own prose shows that, in this instance, the printer had imposed his own spellings on whatever exemplar was being presented to him. This was not Caxton's usual practice, as is demonstrated by his retention of particular spelling-usages characteristic of especially prestigious text-descent, e.g. his prints (in verse) of John Gower's *Confessio Amantis* or (in prose) of Nicholas Love's translation of the *Mirror of the Blessed Life of Jesus Christ* (Smith 1986, 1988a, forthcoming b).

3   The Titus manuscript of *Ancrene Riwle* (MS London, British Library, Cotton Titus D.xviii) seems to be written in a mixture of 'AB-language' and North-West Midland Middle English; even if the manuscript were still written by a *literatim*-copyist, it suggests very strongly that a mixed language lies somewhere in the ancestry of the text.

M. Benskin and M. Laing, as well as engaging with the mechanisms involved here, distinguish subcategories, for example progressive translators, who begin as *literatim*-scribes but become translators as copying proceeds, or constrained scribes, whose repertoire of forms is partially but not wholly activated by their exemplars. They conclude that, during the period covered by *LALME*, 2-type scribes, or scribes who tended towards 2-type behaviour, were by far the most common kind. This insight makes scribes as well as authors legitimate objects of investigation.

The processes involved in scribal translation may be illustrated by an examination of four texts of a major Middle English poem, the *Cursor Mundi*. This lengthy (about 30,000 lines) spiritual history of humanity from the Creation to the Day of Judgement survives in nine fourteenth-century manuscripts or manuscript-fragments in a number of Middle English dialects. Short parallel passages appear in Figure 2.7, derived from four manuscripts. All contractions have been silently expanded, but the texts are otherwise as they appear in the manuscripts. The four texts chosen are MS London, British Library, Cotton Vespasian A.iii, written in the dialect of the West Riding of Yorkshire in the early fourteenth century (hereafter referred to as C); MS Oxford, Bodleian Library, Fairfax 14, copied in a Lancashire dialect of *c.* 1400 (hereafter F); MS Goettingen, University Library, Theol. 107, which contains a mixture of Lincolnshire and Yorkshire forms (hereafter G); and MS Cambridge, Trinity College R.3.8, copied in the language of Staffordshire in the late fourteenth century (hereafter T). A translation of the text C is also supplied. A comparison of these four texts soon reveals quite wide dialectal differences, in orthography and (by reconstruction) phonology, in grammar and in lexis; a selection of formal differences is discussed below.

Figure 2.7 Parallel passages from *Cursor Mundi* (after Morris 1876)

C: *The Cursor o the world*

Man yhernes rimes for to here,
And romans red on maneres sere,
Of Alisaunder þe conquerour;
Of Iuly Cesar þe emparour;
O grece and troy the strang strijf,   5
þere many thosand lesis þer lijf;
O brut þat bern bald of hand,
þe first conquerour of Ingland;
O kyng arthour þat was so rike,
Quam non in hys tim was like,   10
O ferlys þat hys knythes fell,
þat aunters sere I here of tell,
Als wawan, cai and oþer stabel,
For to were þe ronde tabell;
How charles kyng and rauland faght,   15
Wit sarazins wald þai na saght;
[Of] tristrem and hys leif ysote,
How he for here becom a sote,
Of Ioneck and of ysambrase,
O ydoine and of amadase   20
Storis als o ferekin thinges
O princes, prelates and o kynges;
Sanges sere of selcuth rime,
Inglis, frankys, and latine,
to rede and here Ilkon is prest,   25
þe thynges þat þam likes best.

(TRANSLATION: One likes to hear rhymes and romances read in various ways
– of Alexander the conqueror, of Julius Caesar the emperor; the fierce war of
Greece and Troy, where many thousand lose their lives; of Brutus, that warrior
bold of hand, the first conqueror of England; of King Arthur who was so
powerful, whom none in his time was like, of marvels that happened to his
knights, whose many adventures to defend the Round Table I hear tell of, such
as Gawain, Kay and other sturdy knights; how King Charles and Roland fought
– they wanted no peace with the Saracens; of Tristram and his beloved, Isolde,
how he became a fool because of her; of Yonec and of Ysambrase, of Ydoine
and of Amadase; stories also of various [*serekin*; MS *ferekin* is a scribal error,
confusing *f* for *s*] things – of princes, prelates and of kings; various songs of
different rhyme, English, French and Latin. Each one is eager to read and hear
the things that best please them.)

F: *Þis is þe best boke of alle: þe cours of þe werlde men dos hit calle*

Men couettes rimes for to here
And romance rede of mony maner
of Alisaunder þe conquerour
of Iuly cesar þe emperour
Of grece and troy þe grete strife   5
þer mony þousande lost þaire life
of brute þat was bolde of hande
first conquerour of Ingelande.
of kyng arþorow þat was rike
In his tyme was nane hym like   10
of ferles at þer kynges felle
of mony aunters I here of telle
of wawen cay and oþer stabil
for til kepe þe rounde tabil
how charles þe kyng and roland faȝt   15
wit sarasynes walde þai noȝt saȝt
of tristram and his lefe Isot
how he for hir bicome a sot
of Ionek and of isombrase
of ydoine and of amadase   20
storis als of mony þinges
of [prin]ces prelates and of kynges
sa[nge]s sere of selcouþe rime
Ingeles frenche and latine.
to [re]de and here ilkan ys prest   25
þe þinges þat ham likes best.

G: *Þe tretis þat men cals cursor mundi*

[Me]n ȝernis iestis for to here,
And romance rede on maner ser,
Of alexander þe conquerour,
Of Iuli cesar þe emparour
[Of grece & Tr]oye þe strong strijf,   5
[þere many thosand lesis] hir lijf,
[O brut þ]at berne bolde of hand
[First Conqu]erour of meri ingland;
[Of] king arthour, þat was so riche,
[W]as non in his time funden suiche;   10
Of ferlijs þat his knigh[t]es fell,
[Of] auntris did i here of tell,
[Of] wawain, kay and other stabil,
[For] to were þe runde tabil.
Hou king charlis and rouland faght –   15

Wid sarazins ne wald þai neuer be saght; –
O tristrem, and ysoude þe suete,
Hu þai wid luffe first gan mete;
Of king ionet and ysumbras,
Of ydoyne, and of amadas;   20
Storijs of diuers thinges,
Of princes, prelates, and of kinges,
Sangys sere of diuers rime,
Engliss, franss, and latine,
To rede and here, ilkon is prest,   25
Of thinges þat þaim liked best.

T: *Here bigynneþ þe boke of storyes þat men callen cursor mundi*

Men ȝernen iestes for to here
And romaunce rede in dyuerse manere
Of Alisaunder þe conqueroure
Of Iulius cesar þe emperoure
Of greke & troye þe longe strif   5
þere mony mon lost his lif
Of bruyt þat baron bolde of honde
Furste conqueroure of engelonde
Of kyng Arthour þat was so riche
Was noon in his tyme him liche   10
Of wondris þat his knyȝtes felle
And auntres duden men herde telle
As wawayn kay & oþere ful abul
For to kepe þe rounde tabul
How kyng charles & rouland fauȝt   15
Wiþ Sarazines nole þei [neuer be] sauȝt
Of tristram & of Isoude þe swete
How þei wiþ loue firste gan mete
Of kyng Ion and of Isombras
of Idoyne and of amadas   20
Storyes of dyuerse þinges
Of princes prelatis & of kynges
Mony songes of dyuerse ryme
As englisshe frensshe & latyne
To rede & here mony are prest   25
Of þinges þat hem likeþ best

MS C has a number of features which characterise it as Northern. Late
Old English *ā* is reflected as ⟨a⟩ in *strang* 'strong' 5, *bald* 'bold' 7; the
weak adjective ending -*e*, which was lost early in Northern England, has
disappeared in *the strang strijf* 'the furious strife' 5, even though the stress-
pattern of the verse indicates that it probably appeared in the authorial

original, and the present plural ending is -*is* in *lesis* 'lose' 6; Norse-derived pronominal forms, *þer*, *þam* 'their', 'them' appear in 6, 26, and *sere* 'various' 12, 23 is also of Scandinavian derivation.

MS F is similarly marked by Northern forms. Late Old English *ā* appears as ⟨a⟩ in *nane* 'none' 10 (cf. MS C *non*; but cf. also MS C *bald* 'bold' 7, MS F *bolde* 7); -*e* seems no longer to reflect any phonetic fact, and thus appears unhistorically, for example *þousande* 'thousand' (cf. MS C *thosand*); the present plural ending in -*s* appears in *dos* 'do' (rubricated heading); a Norse-derived form, *þaire* 'their' 6 appears beside native *ham* 'them' 26; *sere* 'various' is replaced by native *mony* 12, but retained as *sere* 23. Probable Norse-derived forms in MS F but not in MS C include *til* 'to' 14 (cf. C's *to*).

MS G is something of a mixture. Late Old English *ā* appears as ⟨o⟩ in *strong* 5, *bolde* 7, *non* 'none' 10. The weak adjective is no longer inflectionally marked: *þe strong striff* 5, but this practice is more widespread in late-fourteenth-century Middle English than it was earlier in the century. However, *men cals* 'men call' in the rubric at the head of the passage shows the characteristic Northern present plural ending, *þaim* 'them' 26 appears, and *sere* 'various' 23 is retained.

MS T is in a markedly distinct dialect from the other three manuscripts. Old English *ā* appears as ⟨o⟩, ⟨oo⟩ in *longe* 5, *bolde* 7, *noon* 'none' 10 etc. There is some evidence for the retention of the weak adjective as a living feature of the language: *þe longe strif* 5; and the present plural is the Midland -*en* in *callen* (rubric), *ʒernen* 'desire' 1, *duden* 'did' 12. *hem* 'them' 26 appears for MS C's *þam*, and *mony* appears instead of *sere*.

It is from the evidence of such texts, both localised by internal reference and localisable by subsequent deduction, that *LALME* was created. The coverage it achieved is illustrated in the map already referred to (Figure 2.4), which indicates the locations of every localised and localisable text used in the published atlas. The distinction between 'localised' and 'localisable' is methodologically important; localised texts form a group of materials, largely documentary and thus usually brief, which are firmly identified with a particular locality. They supply the anchors to which other longer texts, generally literary, may be 'tied' or 'fitted' typologically (both terms frequently used in the literature).

The following hypothetical and simplified example may illustrate the process. A short document, which we shall call Text Z, contains *a* for 'he', *meche* for 'much', *scholle*(*n*) for 'shall'. Another, much larger literary text, Text Y, contains the same features, and thus may be associated with Text Z; but the larger text by its very nature yields a good deal more information about other items and their forms as well as *a*, *meche*, *scholle*(*n*). Thus the information gained from the exercise is greatly increased. The fit-technique, as it is known, is typologically governed; thus a further text, Text X, may have *a*, *meche* but not *scholle*(*n*), and is therefore to be placed at some remove from Texts Y and Z in the direction of other texts which do not have *scholle(n)*. Once fitted, the literary texts localised in this way may themselves be used for further localisations; a typological matrix has been established within which other texts as yet unstudied may be placed.

As with the Old English example of Farman, however, it is sometimes dangerous to take Middle English texts at face value. MS Manchester, Chetham's Library, A.6.11 (6696) is an early-sixteenth-century copy of John Gower's late-fourteenth-century poem, the *Confessio Amantis*. At the end of the manuscript appears the name 'Notehurste'. This word also appears in another manuscript, MS Glasgow, University Library, Hunterian V.2.8, a copy of the alliterative *Gest Hystoriale of the Destruction of Troy*, and it refers to Nuthurst in South Lancashire, where the Chetham family lived. Both manuscripts were copied by the same scribe, Thomas Chetham (*c.* 1490–1546), probably for his own use.

The Glasgow *Gest Hystoriale* is localised entirely plausibly by *LALME* to the South-East Lancashire/Cheshire border; but the linguistic evidence presented by the manuscript needs to be judged with some care. Figure 2.8 is a table comparing a selection of forms from the *Gest Hystoriale* with two other texts: the Chetham Gower, and MS Oxford, Bodleian Library, Fairfax 3, another copy of the *Confessio Amantis* whose language has been shown to be as good as that of an authorial holograph (Samuels and Smith 1981).

A number of forms in the Chetham Gower differ from the equivalent forms in the Glasgow *Gest*. Of these, the following (group (a) in Figure 2.8) would appear to be accommodations, to a greater or lesser extent, to the kind of language represented by the Fairfax manuscript: *she, yei, suche, thoughe, ȝit, dede, stede, moche, -ed*. However, for the following items (group (b)), Chetham uses in his Gower the same form he uses in the *Gest*: *mony, any, shuld, hundreth, but*.

Figure 2.8 Constrained variation: a Late Middle English example

Fairfax	Chetham Gower	Glasgow *Gest*
Group (a)		
þei	yei	yai
sche	she	ho
such(e)	suche	suche/soche
þogh	thoughe	yof
ȝit	ȝit	yet
dede 'did'	dede	dyd
stede	stede	stid
moche	moche	miche/myche
Group (b)		
many	mony	mony
eny	any	any
sholde	shuld	shuld
hundred	hundreth	hundreth
bot	but	but

It seems probable that Chetham's behaviour here is of the kind called 'constrained'. In such an interpretation, *mony* etc. would represent Chetham's core repertoire of forms – forms which he will always use, because others are outside his linguistic 'horizon' – while his variation between, for example, *she* when copying Gower and *ho* in the Glasgow *Gest* shows the activation of one of two possible variables in his repertoire when one of them appears in his exemplar. If this hypothesis is correct, it reminds us of the vagaries of textual survival; if the Chetham Gower had not survived, then we would not be aware that Chetham's repertoire of possible variation covered such a comparatively wide spectrum of forms.

A MODERN ENGLISH EXAMPLE

In Middle English phonological studies, the evidence of rhymes has long been used as a primary source of information. Comparison of rhyming forms with distinct etymologies enables the investigator to reconstruct authorial pronunciation as well as localise the place of origin for the text.

Of course, this procedure depends on an assumption: that Middle English authors attempted exact rhyme. Although this assumption has sometimes been challenged, it is nevertheless plausible in medieval conditions. Middle English poets were closer to oral traditions of verse than those of the present day; verse was, we know, commonly rather than rarely read aloud; and thus a forced rhyme would be stylistically foregrounded more obviously than would now be the case.

In the postmedieval centuries, however, a practice of 'conventional' rhymes developed, whereby poets rhymed forms which had once been entirely acceptable acoustically but which sound-change had made no longer current. Thus, for instance, William Blake rhymes *mine* : *join* in a poem of 1783, even though these words (as in most varieties of Present-Day English) almost certainly no longer contained the same vowel in his variety.

Similarly, the practice of 'eye'-rhyme, whereby written similarity outweighs spoken distinction, seems to have become common from approximately the same date; thus Robert Burns, in his Augustan (as opposed to Scots) verse, can make play with the similar visual appearance of *rough* and *plough/bough*, even though the rhyming elements of the three words were differently pronounced in the incipient standardised forms of spoken English (both English and Scottish) at the time. A good example of this practice, discussed further in Chapter 8 below, appears in *The Brigs of Ayr*, published in 1787:

> The simple Bard, rough at the rustic plough,
> Learning his tuneful trade from ev'ry bough.
>
> (1–2)

In these lines there is an ironic contrast between the Augustan register of language (in which the three words are eye-rhymes but not ear-rhymes) and the rustic Scots register (where the three words are even in the twentieth century good ear-rhymes). Eye-rhymes are signs of the way in which 'linguistic acceptability ... is ... increasingly vested in the visual rather than the aural' (Mugglestone 1991: 58), reflecting a shift from the world of orality to that of the literary poet with a literate reading public. Burns, of course, a man keenly conscious of the interaction of social settings, is playing on this historical development in *The Brigs of Ayr*, contrasting the oral and quasi-mythical Scots world of the 'simple Bard' with the literate, Augustan English of the opening of the poem.

The problem of conventionality in rhyming practice, and what that means for the phonological interpretation of poetic usage, is acutely presented by the rhyming practice of John Keats. Keats suffered at the hands of his first reviewers, and one of the grounds of their criticism was his habit of rhyming such pairs as *higher* : *Thalia*, *thorns* : *fawns*, *thoughts* : *sorts*, indicating that his accent was non-rhotic (i.e. 'non *r*-pronouncing'; cf. Southern English beside Scottish and some US pronunciations of *bar*). In Present-Day English, of course, non-rhotic accents are (in the United Kingdom, if not invariably in the United States) prestigious, being associated with Received Pronunciation, but at the beginning of the nineteenth century such rhymes were regarded by many people as 'Cockney', and therefore inappropriate for serious literary discourse. Thus John Lockhart in *Blackwood's Edinburgh Review* criticised Keats as without 'learning enough to distinguish between the written language of Englishmen and the spoken jargon of Cockneys' (cited Mugglestone 1991: 59). It is significant, in the light of page 36 above, that Lockhart criticises Keats for deviance from a norm derived from *written* usage. And as late as 1877, Thomas Hood the younger considered that 'such atrocities as "morn" and "dawn", ... "fought" and "sort", are fatal to the success of verse' (cited Mugglestone 1991: 60).

It has been shown, however, that Keats's lack of rhoticity was not wholly stigmatised by contemporaries. B.H. Smart, for instance, in his prescriptivist *A Grammar of English Sounds* (1812), comments that 'the smooth *R*, is often pronounced with so little force, as to be, in fact, nothing more than the vowel sound AH' (cited Mugglestone 1991: 61; 'smooth R' in Smart's usage seems to be the realisation of *r* in postvocalic and final positions, as opposed to initial 'rough R'). Although in his earlier *A Practical Grammar of English Pronunciation* (1810) Smart seems to have regarded non-rhoticity as something Londoners were 'too liable' to exhibit – since the written mode was seen by him as offering a guide to correct pronunciation – nevertheless he seems to accept it as characteristic of quite large numbers of persons whose social status is not in doubt. And an analysis of the rhymes of, for example, P.B. Shelley (educated at Eton and, albeit briefly, Oxford) shows that poets of impeccably upper-class descent were fully capable of using non-rhotic rhymes without receiving any comparable attack from contemporaries. L. Mugglestone has pointed out that part of

Lockhart's venom may be due to his Scottish origins; the accents of Present-Day Scots and Scottish English are still rhotic, and Lockhart's attack on Keats's usage may have been an assertion of the value of a Scottish accent as well as of the primacy of writing over speech. Vocalisation of *r* may have been sporadically stigmatised, as a failure to pronounce a letter sanctioned in writing; but, in general, the disappearance of postvocalic *r* in upper-class nineteenth-century speech, and not just in that of Cockneys, is clearly attested. Thus the attack on Keats by Lockhart and others is not a simple attack on some linguistic deficit; it is rather the use of any tool to hand to aid a knocking review.

CONCLUSION

The three examples discussed above – Farman, the Chetham Gower, Keats – all demonstrate how textual analysis and an understanding of context help our understanding of linguistic output. A theme of this study is that an understanding of texts in relation to their contexts is essential to an adequate theory of diachronic linguistics; thus philology and linguistics are ideally complementary disciplines for students of the history of a language, and not competitive paradigms. In the next chapter, a theoretical paradigm for the historical study of English will be sketched in, based upon a linking of philological and linguistic traditions.

3 Linguistic evolution

THE EVOLUTIONARY MODEL

Since the beginnings of the discipline, historical linguists have, like other scholars, used models to explore and explain the nature of their object of enquiry. By far the most popular of these models, in use since the nineteenth century, has been an evolutionary model based upon Darwinian notions of divergence between species.

Given the rapidity with which Charles Darwin's work came to dominate the intellectual paradigm of his time, it is not surprising that many nineteenth-century linguists were quick to adopt what they perceived to be Darwinian concepts and adapt them for the examination of linguistic evolution. Within a few years of the appearance of Darwin's *The Origin of Species* (1859), linguists such as Auguste Schleicher (*Die Darwinische Theorie*, 1863) and Max Müller (*Lectures on the Science of Language*, 1861–1864) had used Darwinian ideas for their own purposes; and by the end of the century evolutionary notions had become central to linguistic enquiry. Thus Hermann Paul, in the 'Neogrammarian bible' of late-nineteenth-century philological study *Prinzipien der Sprachgeschichte* (*Principles of the History of Language*, trans. H.A. Strong 1888), held that linguistic change was to do with 'the greater or lesser fitness of the forms which arise' (1888: 13); in other words, the Darwinian – or perhaps, more correctly, sub-Darwinian – notion of 'the survival of the fittest' could be adapted for the use of historical linguists.

'The survival of the fittest', of course, is a phrase which has been widely reinterpreted by thinkers subsequent to Darwin. For Paul, the phrase meant survival of variant forms of highest frequency in a particular speech-community. Thus, he would hold that, when the *p* of Proto-Indo-European 'became' the *f* of Proto-Germanic, the former sound survived in some languages such as Italian (e.g. *padre*, *pesce*) but evolved in others (e.g. Present-Day English *father*, *fish*) because the Germanic community had determined (unconsciously, over many millions of usage-occurrences) that an *f*-type realisation of an earlier *p* was appropriate, and that other realisations were eccentric and thus insufficient for the clear expression of meaning.

That this notion was itself insufficient was demonstrated by Ferdinand de Saussure; the Neogrammarians, in the opinion of de Saussure and his followers, did not emphasise sufficiently the role of *system* in the operation of language. De Saussure pointed out that views such as Paul's did not distinguish clearly between what he called *langue* and *parole* (see de Saussure 1974: 7–17 and *passim*). *Parole* is linguistic substance, the forms which survive over time, but forms perform different functions at different times in their history depending on the *langue*, or system, within which they work. Thus Proto-Indo-European *p*/Proto-Germanic *f*, although the latter developed historically from the former, are distinct because the two sounds had different functions within the two *langues*, Proto-Indo-European and Proto-Germanic; the *p* > *f* shift took place because of system-change during the divergence of Proto-Germanic from the other Indo-European dialects. In Saussurean terms, simple variation is not change; linguistic change occurs when a systemic development takes place. However, this insight did not entail a dismissal by de Saussure of the Darwinian model; rather, de Saussure's ideas on variant forms acquiring useful functions (and discarding unneeded ones) as *langue* changed were closer to true Darwinian theory than Paul's, and placed linguistic Darwinism on a firmer theoretical footing. The Saussurean model has remained a dominant one for historical linguists ever since. However, Darwinian theory has not remained static, and developments of evolutionary theory over the last hundred years or so have implications for linguistic modelling.

BIOLOGICAL MUTATION AND SELECTION

Darwinian theory, as developed by the late twentieth century, rests upon an understanding of two basic mechanisms: (1) biological mutation and (2) natural selection. *Mutations* are spontaneous, random errors in genes transmitted from one generation to another; their effect is to produce a pool of variation within a given biological 'community' – a beak becoming a little longer here, a claw becoming a little shorter there. These mutations are non-teleological, in the sense that they are not directed *preferentially* towards any particular improvement from generation to generation. What appears to be direction is what Dawkins (1986) has referred to as 'the blind watchmaker': *natural selection*, operating on a pool of available genetic material.

> Natural selection is a relentless slight bias in death rates, or a slight bias in reproductive rates, among the individuals within a species. Given enough time, small changes in lineages accumulate into large differences between species. Given even more time, lineages diverge yet further until we have descendants as different as elephants from moles, or squid from warthogs.
>
> (Dawkins 1994: 15)

Recent study of this process in evolutionary biology is exemplified by the recent work of P. and R. Grant on the Darwin's Finches of the Galapagos Islands of the Eastern Pacific. These birds all appear to descend from a single lineage which arrived in the Galapagos a few million years ago – perhaps blown off course by an unusual storm. Since that time they have diverged into thirteen separate species, each one specialised for a particular way of life on the islands. One incident in the evolution of the finches is of particular relevance:

> 1977 was a drought year in the Galapagos, and 1983 a year of unprecedented floods. After the drought, a higher proportion of large-beaked finches were found to have survived. After the floods, small-beaked finches predominated, presumably because they were better equipped to pick up the smaller seeds that wet weather favours. Reversals of this kind are common. Long-term evolution will result only if there is a sufficiently drawn-out trend in a particular direction – as there often is, especially when evolving enemies such as predators or parasites are involved rather than just the caprices of the weather. ... The drought of 1977 did not induce beak-enlarging mutations, nor did the floods of 1983 provoke opposite mutations. The mutations had already happened, regardless of the weather. Droughts and floods enter the story only afterwards. In [sic] the role of non-random selecting agents.
>
> (Dawkins 1994: 15)

In other words, certain tiny mutations in form, easily within the range of natural variation, are favoured for functional reasons by the environment in which they are situated; and these mutational choices, which Dawkins has elsewhere referred to as the 'small-change' of evolution (1986: *passim*), steadily accumulate to produce such a shift in form that it is possible to speak of the emergence of some new species of creature. The process described here is slow, since Darwin's Finches reproduce only annually; but biologists have found empirical support for Darwinian theory in studying the evolution of such creatures as fruit-flies, where many generations can emerge within a few days, and through the use of computer-based modelling (see further Dawkins 1986).

PROGRESS IN LANGUAGE

It is held here that the model of evolution established in biology is also at least partially applicable to linguistic evolution. To describe linguistic change as evolutionary is, of course, in one way a metaphor, since the notion of evolution was first established in biology and has simply been transferred to linguistic study by analogy. The 'language instinct' certainly appeared in humans as a result of evolution, and bears all the hallmarks of having emerged through straightforward evolutionary processes. As proof of this, we might notice, for instance, how – typically in biological evolution – the articulators used for human speech, such as tongue, teeth, nasal cavity and so on, had physical functions to do with eating and breathing before they developed secondary, speech-forming functions (cf. animals with tongues, teeth etc. but without speech); in biology, this process has been termed *exaptation*, and the term has recently been applied to linguistic evolution as well (see Lass 1990).

It may be permissible, however, to argue that historical linguistics is *literally* an evolutionary discipline, since the mechanisms of change with which the subject engages seem to work in evolutionary ways (see further Waldron 1985). Most notably, linguistic evolution seems to work through a 'blind watchmaker', or (using another frequent metaphor) through a 'hidden hand' (Keller 1994).

There remain, however, two important differences between biological and linguistic evolution. The first difference is one which is more apparent than real. Some early evolutionary biologists interpreted Darwin's theory to mean that there was an overall direction in evolution, in which more 'advanced' creatures succeeded more 'primitive' ones. This view is no longer held in quite the same terms by modern evolutionists, although it remains part of the popular understanding of the theory; it is now felt by evolutionists that an amoeba (for instance) does a perfect job *for the environment in which it exists*, and in such an environment a human being (for instance) would not be nearly as efficient. Dinosaurs were magnificent and complex creatures, comparable with many twentieth-century organisms, but the environment in which they lived changed and they became extinct. Much of the appeal of the modern ecology or 'green' movement lies in the way in which it has engaged with this notion of the 'equality of species'.

The older view of evolutionary progress had a certain vogue in the nineteenth century, correlating with contemporary ideas about the perfectibility of humankind, and it is therefore not surprising to find some nineteenth- and early-twentieth-century linguists extrapolating from this misunderstanding of Darwin's theories and introducing notions such as 'progress' or 'decay' into their linguistic speculations. Thus O. Jespersen wrote in 1922 that in 'the evolution of languages the discarding of old flexions goes hand in hand with the development of simpler and more regular expedients that are rather less liable than the old ones to produce misunderstanding' (cited Aitchison 1991: 6–7).

It is now generally held that linguistic evolution does not work in this way, however. It is no longer believed by serious linguists that any language, at any point in its history, is any more or less 'primitive' or 'advanced' than any other; the language of the 'primitive' Bushmen is just as complex (or simple) in grammatical, phonological or lexical terms as the language of an 'advanced' European, and thus the adjectives *complex* and *simple*, *difficult* and *easy* are really inappropriate as neutral descriptors of natural languages. After all, many readers of this book may find Old

English difficult – but the Anglo-Saxons, eleven hundred years ago, evidently did not.

The second difference is a more significant one. In biological evolution, species diverge from each other so that it is possible to classify them as separate; they do not *genetically* come together again. For example, the three orders of nature known as *birds*, *insects* and *mammals* undoubtedly share a common ancestor, a proto-form, which lived many thousands of millions of years ago; but it is possible to classify birds as a group separate from mammals and insects because all birds share a common ancestor which differs from the distinct common ancestors of *mammals* and *insects*. Languages do not behave precisely in this way. Present-Day English is a Germanic language, descended, like Present-Day German, Swedish, Dutch etc., from a common ancestor. But English has also, during its history, taken on characteristics from non-Germanic languages with which it has come into contact, such as French. It is an important principle of biological classification ('cladistics') that separate orders, species etc. cannot overlap in evolutionary terms, and this distinction might be expressed notationally thus: (birds) (mammals) (insects). However, languages cannot be separated in this way; were we to express the relationship between German, English and French using a similar notation we would arrive at a formula something as follows: (German (English) French). It follows from this formula that, unlike in biology, acquired characteristics in language *can* be inherited, for – for instance – English speakers can take on French vocabulary and integrate it into a system which can be then passed on to their successor language-users (see Dawkins 1986: 292). We shall be returning to this distinction on pages 49–50 below.

LINGUISTIC VARIATION AND CONSTRAINT

Corresponding in language to the minute mutations of biological evolution are linguistic variants. All living languages vary – the only ones which do not are dead ones, such as Latin, or formal ones, such as mathematical or logical notations. For instance, a single speaker can vary quite radically in the way he or she realises an individual linguistic item on different occasions – at its simplest, exemplified by the way in which many speakers of English have in their repertoire of usage two pronunciations of the stressed vowel in the item *either*, or different stress patterns for the word *adult*. Most obviously, languages vary diatopically, that is, through geographical space, and we therefore distinguish between, for instance, Scottish and English accents or grammatical and lexical usage. However, variation can also arise within dialects or even individual linguistic repertoires because of such factors as age, social class and the level of formality adopted. Such variation is a property of all natural languages, and – as was indicated briefly in Chapter 1 above – it lies at the heart of linguistic change, for change depends on the availability of different choices. When a particular variant–innovation becomes adopted systematically by other speakers and used 'conventionally to communicate particular forms and meanings' (Labov 1994: 311), it is possible to speak of linguistic change having taken place.

Since Weinreich *et al.* (1968), three stages in the operation of linguistic change have been generally distinguished by linguists: actuation, implementation and diffusion. It may be recalled from Chapter 1 above that a slightly modified version of this categorisation is adopted here: the *potential for change*, the *triggering and implementation of change*, the *diffusion of change*. The potential for change exists in the particular linguistic choices made by particular language-users at a particular time; such choices may be compared with the constant process of biological mutation; it is constantly taking place, for it exists in the perpetual ebb and flow of linguistic variation. When linguists refer to linguistic change, they tend to refer to implementation and diffusion, that is, the systemic development.

Corresponding to natural selection in language are the constraints which govern communication within a given speech-community and therefore regulate the processes of implementation of change. These are the constraints of pragmatic interaction and of social setting; thus usage can only vary in so far as it remains broadly meaningful to the interlocutor, and there are powerful forces to do with social stigmatisation which constrain expression in other ways. These functions of language were discussed in Chapter 1 above.

In pragmatic terms, it makes sense to use as little effort as possible to express meaning. However, this effort cannot be too little; the production of differentiated meaning is clearly a matter of speaker–hearer interaction, and the demands of communicative efficiency are such that a whole series of cues, not just one, must be offered to the hearer by the speaker. Languages need such redundancy, for no two speakers have the same usage, and to attempt to distinguish meaning on the basis of single cues would risk unintelligibility. But if too much redundancy is maintained, or if the cues which are chosen are contradictory (e.g. an intended statement is expressed with intonation appropriate to a question), the system undergoes pressure. Such an opposition correlates with functionalist views of language, in which a 'principle of least effort' is balanced against a 'principle of maintaining intelligibility'. Notions such as these are well established in the literature (see e.g. Jespersen 1941).

A key notion in this context is that of *variational space*. Variation is possible because individual linguistic items occupy fairly broad slots in the *langue* within which they are situated, and their realisations in *parole* can therefore vary quite widely. Variational space is relevant to all levels of language. Thus, for example, Figure 3.1 (a schematisation of Lieberman 1984: 160) shows the realisations of the vowel-phoneme /ɪ/ produced by seventy-six different speakers in terms of recorded sound-frequencies. These speakers all considered that they were producing the 'same' sound;

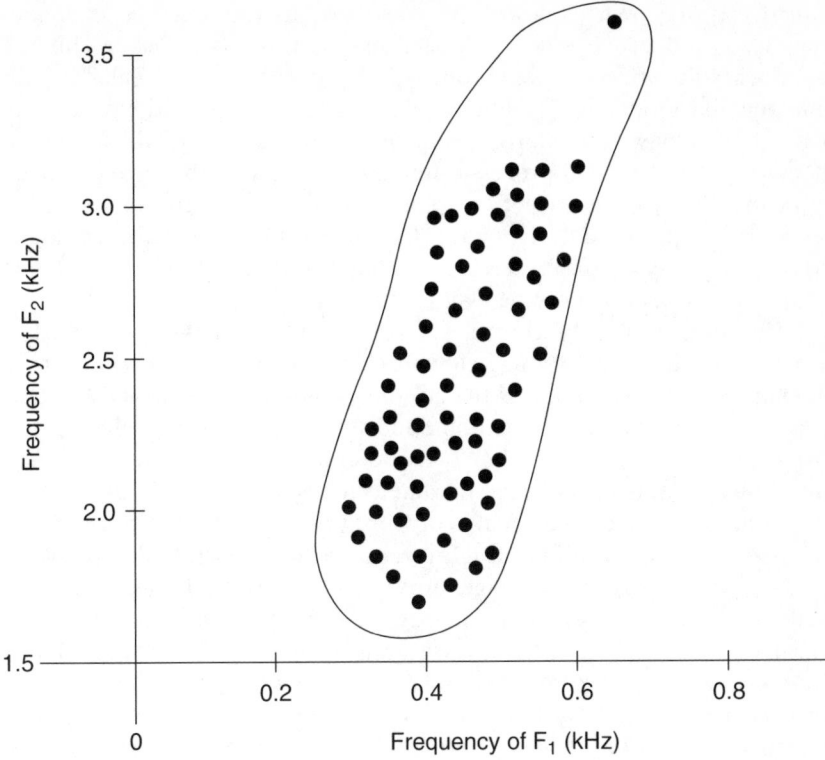

Figure 3.1 Realisations of the vowel-phoneme /ɪ/ produced by seventy-six different speakers in terms of recorded sound-frequencies (see further Lieberman 1984: Chapter 7)

but the records show that, although there are clearly defined limits for these realisations, there was nevertheless considerable phonological space within which they could take place. This variation is not inefficiency, but communicatively necessary. Any two speakers will have, to a greater or lesser extent and as the result of slight physiological and social differences, a differing set of realisations for a particular phoneme, and it is therefore important for communicative purposes for each speaker to have a fairly wide tolerance of others' usages. Moreover – and this point will be returned to in Chapters 4–7 below – variational spaces can overlap, and such overlaps are typically the sites of change in the linguistic system.

Similarly, in grammar, formal and informal usages can exist side by side within the same variational space, for instance *isn't* and *is not* occupy the same slots in the sentences *That isn't right* and *That is not right*, and, although one usage is more formal than the other, there are situations when either is suitable. Other sources of variation in grammar are to do with stress, and with analogy. The most obvious examples of analogous usage are produced by children acquiring linguistic skills. When children say *mouses* for *mice*, or *singed* for *sang*, or *mines* (cf. *yours, hers, his*) for *mine* they have observed certain regularities in language and have extrapolated by analogy to regularise historically inherited forms which seem to them irregular. A similar process is found in 'non-standard' English spoken by adults; thus *foots* for 'feet', a common usage in children's speech, has been recorded in adult language by dialectologists in (for instance) Present-Day East Suffolk, *buyed* for 'bought' in Present-Day Devon, and *badder* for 'worse' in Present-Day Cumberland.

All such examples, of course, are commonplace in those varieties of speech which are comparatively unconstrained by the pressures of formal and normative education. It is the custom of modern parents and teachers to correct such analogical creations, and for adult users of such forms to suffer social stigmatisation; but, with reference to earlier times, before prescriptive norms of language became established, it is easy to conceive of a situation where analogical reorganisations would have been widely imitated. Thus, Present-Day English *those*, a form entirely acceptable in the modern prestigious language, arose in the late Middle Ages through analogy: a prototypically plural inflection, *-s(e)*, was added to earlier *tho* (from Old English *þā*), and the resulting form has been accepted into Present-Day English prescribed usage. The new, analogically produced form *those* seems to have been favoured in the standard language because it corresponds to an ancient contrastive usage ('ablaut'), whereby front vowels correlated with nearness (thus *these*) and back vowels with distance (thus *those*).

On the other hand Present-Day English *yous* ('you' pl.), a more recent analogical creation found in many varieties of the language, providing speakers with a potentially useful singular/plural distinction in the paradigm for the second-person pronoun and correlating with other grammatical markers such as the form of the verb *to be*, has not been so accepted; it appeared after the emergence of prescriptive norms, and has thus been stigmatised. (See further Milroy and Milroy 1993: *passim.*)

As for the lexicon, it is a proven fact that words mean different things in different contexts, and therefore have a fairly broad variational space. For instance, the expression *to let the cat out of the bag* has both a literal and a metaphorical significance: literally, a feline is liberated, but metaphorically, a truth (usually unwelcome) has been revealed, and this metaphorical usage would seem – in my own variety, at any rate – to be now more commonplace. Another source of variation is to do with linguistic register: thus, two words may denote the same referent – for example, *begin* and *commence* – but have very different connotations (in this example, to do with levels of formality). This second example shows what happens when two words from different language-families – here, Germanic (*begin*) and Romance (*commence*) – are brought together within the same language: the two words, because first heard in different (and socially charged) circumstances, develop different connotations. A similar example is the contrast between *destroy* and *break up*, to be discussed further in Chapter 7 below. Yet another kind of variation is demonstrated by the difference in connotation of the words *ordure* and *shit*; the usage of these words in Present-Day English exemplifies the contrast between technical and taboo usage (cf. the colloquial expression *The shit hit the fan*, beside a potentially more formal if less likely **The ordure hit the fan*). *Ordure* and *shit* refer to the same natural object, but they plainly have developed distinct connotations.

It should have become clear how such variation within variational space corresponds to the mutations of biological evolution; and, as in biological evolution, these linguistic mutations are constrained by the setting in which they exist. The main constraint on (phonological, grammatical, lexico-logical) variational space within a given variety of a language relates to the systemic properties of language in general. Thus, for instance, analog-ical change in the history of a language may proceed further than the rest of the system requires, so further regulation becomes necessary. If language is systematic, then the rules of language are interconnected, and change in one can be assumed to have implications for others. Space can be 'squeezed', that is, variables may start to overlap with each other to an unacceptable extent, introducing loss of information content and subse-quent reorganisation; or space can be 'expanded', leading to an excess of redundancy (see page 44 above). The interaction between variation and systemic constraints will be returned to frequently in subsequent chapters.

CONTACT BETWEEN LINGUISTIC SYSTEMS

The attentive reader will have noticed a flaw in the argument as presented in the previous section. If variation is constrained by a system, and that system reacts therapeutically, then there will in theory come a point in time when the system reaches an optimum position where all elements of which the system consists are in stasis; the variational spaces for each linguistic item will be stable, and the potential for the implementation of linguistic change will not be realised. In such a situation, and given the existence of the mechanisms of linguistic evolution sketched so far, change should cease to occur. However, it is a matter of observation that no living language is unchanging.

It is therefore necessary to distinguish a third factor in the operation of linguistic change: contact. Contact is most obviously manifested linguis-tically in the changing lexicon, when words are borrowed into English from other languages, but it can be more subtle: not only words, but also grammatical structures and even sounds can be transferred between languages, or from variety to variety within a language, for all sorts of reasons (e.g. for reasons of social prestige). Moreover, the effects of linguistic contact need not be simply a matter of transference of forms; languages or varieties can affect each other in more subtle ways, as will be seen later in this book.

Contact is a crucial factor in linguistic change because no language or variety of language exists in a vacuum. Speech-communities come into contact with other speech-communities in all sorts of situations, and the subsequent interaction between these communities causes linguistic change. Some languages and varieties of language certainly change more slowly than others, and the reasons for the variable speeds of linguistic change are easy to determine, through the observation of extralinguistic correspondences. Languages such as Icelandic and Lithuanian have changed slowly over time because they are spoken by relatively homo-geneous speech-communities which are comparatively isolated – either by geography or by historical hostility – from the groups of people around them. Thus rural varieties of English tend to change slowly in comparison with their urban counterparts not only because people in the countryside have fewer folk to interact with, but also because those folk who are there interact more closely. In all these cases, there are strong social ties between the users of these languages or varieties, necessary in communities where the environment is hostile or where a strong communal sense is necessary for the efficient functioning of society.

In urban settings, such limited change is demonstrated by those who stick closely to one social group without interacting greatly with those out-side their immediate circle (e.g. the core members of certain urban 'gangs', who sustain their linguistic norms through exceptionally strong social ties).

Other languages, or varieties of language, change more quickly, and here, too, the social correspondences are well attested. Change is pecu-liarly liable to occur when large-scale immigration, invasion or social revolution takes place; it also tends to happen more quickly in towns, where large numbers of people, many with quite distinct linguistic systems, interact with each other. The term used to describe the social relationships between such folk is 'weakly tied', that is, having comparatively loose social ties with those around them. Typically, a person with weak social ties will be 'class-mobile', attempting to leave one class and enter another, or feeling uneasily poised between one social group and another. It is an interesting fact that the modern discipline of dialectology/sociolinguistics has tended to move away from the study of strongly tied individuals (e.g. the notorious NORMS, 'non-mobile older rural males' who have preserved traditional usage because their language tends not to change, reflecting their tight social networks) towards weakly tied persons whose language, because it is liable to show a wider range of variation, exemplifies the processes of linguistic change discussed above.

There is a parallel in biological theory for 'variable-speed' evolution in language: so-called 'punctuationism' (for which see Eldredge 1985 and Gould 1982), which, to put it crudely, holds that evolution takes place more quickly at some periods than at others. Some who have written on these matters have unfairly taken the work of the punctuationists to represent a rejection of Darwinian theory. However, it has been shown quite conclusively that punctuationism, or more properly the 'theory of punctuated equilibrium', can be comfortably accommodated within the Darwinian paradigm; Dawkins (1986: 223–252) points out that to take punctuationism as a rejection of Darwinian theory 'is as if the discovery that the Earth is not a perfect sphere but a slightly flattened spheroid were given banner treatment under the headline: COPERNICUS WRONG. FLAT EARTH THEORY VINDICATED' (1986: 251–252). The notion of variable-speed change in language has been interestingly pursued by Labov (1994: 23–24).

MONITORING

The three mechanisms of linguistic change distinguished above – variation, systemic regulation, contact – are not to be taken as totally separate causes of the phenomenon; rather, they interact in complex and, except in the most general terms, practically unpredictable ways to produce dynamic change in the history of a given language. To sum up the argument so far: new variants are produced, and are imitated through contact; but they are constrained by the changing intra- and extralinguistic systems of which they are a part.

The description of change given above might be considered somewhat mechanical, but it can easily be restated in more human terms. Human beings are social creatures, and not simply transmitters (speakers) or receivers (hearers); they are both. When humans speak, they are not only producing sounds and grammar and vocabulary; they are also monitoring what they and others say by listening, and evaluating the communicative efficiency of their speech for the purposes for which it is being used: communicative purposes which are not only to do with the conveying and receiving of information, but also to do with such matters as signalling the social circumstances of the interaction taking place. And what humans hear is constantly being monitored, that is, compared with their earlier experience as speakers and hearers. In any given speech-community there may be broad agreement as to the prototypical core-value of a given linguistic item, but, when speech-communities interact with each other, the overlap will not be exact, and this 'rough fit' is the source of linguistic variation. Such individual microlinguistic events, the choices of individual speakers, can (although they need not) develop into those macrolinguistic events which we term 'linguistic change'.[1]

This principle of monitoring, or feedback as it is sometimes called (Lyons 1968: 111), is crucial to an understanding of language-change. Individual and group-usages are all systems which overlap to a greater or lesser extent, each system consisting of a range of allowable variation – variation which can be found at every linguistic level.

The range of allowable variation within any individual system makes up the 'givens' from which each new utterance proceeds: the linguistic input to a new speech-act. Givens may be considered to be either inherited or borrowed; speakers use variants which are native to their own variety, or they select variants which are available to them through contact with other varieties or even with other languages. This process whereby givens are transmitted is not of course genetic, for there does not seem to be any genetic transmission of language-*specific* features. Rather, the process comes about through immersion in a particular speech-community. The truth of this argument is indicated, for example, by the fact that children of immigrants often adopt not their parents' language or variety but that of their peers in the same age-group.

Linguistic givens exist at every level of language – lexicon, grammar, graphology, phonology – and in all they exist as the set of inherited and borrowed choices. They provide the language-setting from which any particular linguistic choice made at a particular time must proceed.

TREES AND WAVES

The last section concluded with a reference to the notions of inheritance and borrowing, and these notions are central to the historical study of language. Two descriptive models have traditionally been used to illustrate the processes of inheritance and borrowing respectively: the tree model and the wave model. Both models derive from nineteenth-century scholarship, and stem from comparisons with what were (and in some quarters still are) perceived to be more 'mature' sciences: the tree model relates to the phylogenetic tree used in evolutionary biology, and the wave model relates to theories of action and reaction developed for the discipline of physics. At one time the two models were seen as mutually exclusive, but most linguists since the end of the nineteenth century have considered them to be complementary.

These models are relevant in both micro- and macrolinguistic contexts. According to the tree model, children attempt to reproduce the language of their parents; according to the wave model, children borrow linguistic features from their peers. These models are also relevant on a macro-linguistic scale: languages descend from earlier ancestors (thus French and Spanish descend from Latin), or they borrow from neighbouring languages (thus Finnish, a non-Indo-European language, contains many Indo-European lexical items borrowed from Swedish). (See also Figure 3.2.)[2]

LANGUAGE AND CHAOS

But the two models, even when considered together, lack an important component: they do not allow for the element of apparently chaotic

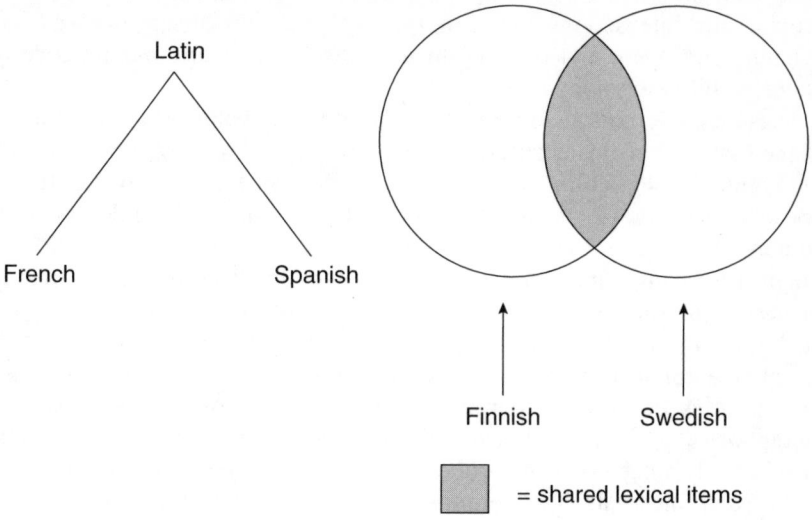

Figure 3.2 Trees and waves

dynamicity in the operation of language, whereby the complex interaction of changing systems produces yet further change.

Relevant here is recently fashionable 'chaos theory' – which, of course, is not so much about the chaotic nature of the world as about the ways in which order emerges from apparently chaotic processes (see further Gleick 1988). M.A.K. Halliday (e.g. 1987) is probably the most prominent of those linguists who have used fruitfully the chaotic model of language (although he has not yet applied it to historical linguistics; see, however, Lemke 1992, and most recently Croft 1995). Halliday's views on the nature of a 'dynamic open system' are directly relevant to the argument of this book:

> Dynamic open systems have the property that they are metastable: that is, they persist only through constant change; and this change takes place through interactive exchanges with their environment. In the course of such interaction, the system exports disorder; and in the process of exporting disorder, and so increasing the entropy of its environment, the system renews itself, gains information, imports or rather creates order and in this way continues to function.
>
> (1987: 139)

Languages working through time would seem to be a perfect example of such a system. Speaker-innovations constantly interact with their intra- and extralinguistic environment, which forms a system; and these interactions can cause system-wide changes. Thus a theory of historical linguistics must take into account both speaker and system, and have the ability to provide for interactions between the two. The processes involved are dynamic and open, and this insight needs to be built into our practice of linguistic historiography.

These chaotic notions do not conflict with the evolutionary orientation of the first part of this chapter. Chaos theory holds that order comes from the complex interaction of apparently random factors. Of course, this is not to argue, metaphysically, that there is some ultimate intended goal for human language in general or the history of English in particular. Linguistic change may rather be regarded, in a comparison already suggested at the beginning of this chapter, as driven, like biological evolution, by a 'blind watchmaker': apparent direction is the result of interactive reinforcement between variables at every level of language. This process of interactive reinforcement is also sometimes described, metaphorically, as a 'hidden hand', or a 'conspiracy', or (perhaps most satisfactorily, since no element of consciousness is to be supposed) a 'snow-ball'. Such snowballs are common in linguistic evolution, and will be exemplified in Part II below.

Some of the more general issues raised by these last points will be returned to in the last chapter of this book. In these first three chapters, the intention has been to establish a theoretical framework for the historical study of English. In Part II, this theoretical framework will be tested and exemplified through the examination of a number of major linguistic developments in English during the last two thousand years. In each case examined, outcomes which have been traditionally assigned to one linguistic level – writing-system, phonology, lexicology, grammar – are shown to be the result of interaction between intralinguistic developments (i.e. developments in other parts of the linguistic system, not just restricted to the level in which the development in question is assigned) and extra-linguistic events (i.e. social and historical change). This interaction, which may be termed *dynamic*, demonstrates a fact well attested in many of the natural sciences but even now not yet fully accepted in the humanities: that a given event can be the result of more than one cause. It is held here that this perception of multi-factorial causation is crucial for understanding linguistic change.

Part II

4　Transmission I: change in writing-system

THE LEVELS OF LANGUAGE

In Part I, a framework for discussion has been established in which the mechanisms of linguistic change have been identified. In Part II the interaction of these mechanisms will be exemplified by looking at selected developments in all four levels of language conventionally distinguished: writing-system and sound system (often linked together as 'transmission'), grammar and lexicon. In each case, outcomes traditionally assigned to one of these categories will be shown to be the result of dynamic interaction between intra- and extralinguistic processes. Thus, for instance, the Great Vowel Shift (the main example discussed in Chapter 5) will be shown to be the result of dynamic intralinguistic interaction between grammatical, phonological and lexical developments within an overall extralinguistic framework of sociohistorical change.

The theme of these four chapters, therefore, is to do with the interaction of linguistic levels with each other and/or with the world in which they are situated. Now the precise dividing-lines between the levels of language conventionally distinguished, of course, are extremely controversial amongst linguists. But for the present purposes it is convenient simply to take a fairly traditional view, whereby meaning ('semantics') is expressed through words ('lexicology') and grammatical rules ('grammar') themselves conveyed by sounds ('sound-system' or 'phonology') or writing ('writing-system'). The limitations of this model were already discussed in Chapter 1, and do not need repeating here. But there is one advantage: this communicative model draws attention to the truth that there are special relationships between lexicon and grammar on the one hand and between writing and speech on the other. Semantics would appear to have an independent, underlying status.

WRITING-SYSTEMS

Many scholars would exclude consideration of writing-systems from their discussion of linguistic matters, either ignoring it completely or considering it part of a separate discipline; after all, the written mode undoubtedly follows speech chronologically, and many languages have never developed a written equivalent to speech. But it is worth recalling that the word *grammar* derives from Greek *grapho* 'write', and that, in a number of cultures – including English – the written mode has developed a considerable prestige; thus non-linguists frequently assign higher social value to speech which is closer in grammatical form to the normative usages established in writing. Moreover, most of the history of English is mediated to us not through mechanical or electronic recordings – a comparatively recent technological development – but through writing. It therefore seems necessary to take account of the historical evolution of writing-systems in this book. It is an interesting scholarly development of recent years that the discipline of palaeography, the study of the evolution of handwriting, has shown itself to be highly amenable to the application of notions hitherto considered the domain of linguistics; see, for instance, McIntosh 1974, Parkes 1992, Lowe (forthcoming b).

By 'writing-system' is meant here two components of written transmission: (1) handwriting, and (2) spelling. In this chapter, examples of each component of the English writing-system will be examined to show how the principles outlined in Part I have been active in determining their evolution.

THE METALANGUAGE OF HANDWRITING

Until the arrival of printing in Britain in the fifteenth century, handwriting (including the carving of inscriptions) was the only means whereby written language could be mediated. Handwriting differs from printing in that, like spoken language, every user's practice is idiosyncratic, even if people are taught to write in similar fashions; with printing, fonts are not personalised in the same way.

Palaeographers have often (although not always consistently) in their discussions distinguished between *hand* and *script*. *Script* may be defined as the particular model of handwriting at which a scribe aimed, for instance Secretary, italic, gothic, whereas *hand* is the actual realisation of this script achieved by the scribe. The parallel between the *script/hand* distinction and the distinction between, for instance, *phoneme* and *allophone* might seem an obvious one to readers of this book (see further Parkes 1979).

The parallels between handwriting and other levels of language can be further developed. For instance, practitioners of handwriting frequently distinguish between formal and informal writing styles – which distinction corresponds to the linguistic notion of *register* – and, even within one register of handwriting, individuals can have variant forms depending on the position of the letter-form in question in relation to other forms, and on whether or not the scribe had a fixed idea of the script being aimed at (many did not). It is thus, at least potentially, possible to develop a terminology of description for handwriting which parallels that used for phonetics and phonology.

Such a descriptive terminology does exist, but it has caused a good deal of scholarly controversy. There is perhaps room for a usage of greater delicacy than has been hitherto achieved.

The terms *grapheme* and *allograph* are often used with reference to the written mode, in order to parallel the notions 'phoneme' and 'allophone' in the analysis of speech. The grapheme/allograph distinction works well enough if it is considered that all hands are attempting, albeit with varying degrees of success, to represent one letter-shape; and it is useful, in many medieval scripts, to be able to distinguish, for instance, between allographs of the grapheme ⟨s⟩ which appear in complementary distribution in different environments. For instance, *б*, *ʃ*, ʃ are three realisations of the grapheme ⟨s⟩ regularly found in single hands writing in the late-fourteenth-century English script *Anglicana Formata*. However, a difficulty is that there is what might be termed a 'second-order goal' at which scribes aim: the model letter *in their particular script*. Thus the ⟨w⟩ aimed at in (say) italic script differs from the ⟨w⟩ aimed at in (say) Anglicana script.

The most convincing speech/writing parallel to be made here would seem to be between these second-order goals and spoken *varieties* or distinct *languages*. Just as a particular speaker of English aims at (say) Received Pronunciation or General American, so it could be argued that a particular writer aims at (say) italic or gothic or Textura or Secretary. Thus the individual usage of a particular scribe would correspond to the individual usage ('idiolect') of a particular speaker.

There seems to be no accepted *linguistic* (as opposed to palaeographical) term for this second-order level of language-transmission in writing. For this reason, the term *grapheme* will here be used to refer to the general letter aimed at: thus (for instance) italic ⟨g⟩, Textura ⟨g⟩ and Secretary ⟨g⟩ are all attempts to realise the grapheme ⟨g⟩. But the term *allograph* will be avoided, except when talking about complementary distribution of letter-forms for the same grapheme (e.g. the 'long' and 'short' ⟨s⟩, which are characteristically distributed medially and finally respectively in many varieties of script). Instead, the palaeographical terms *script* and *hand* will be adopted, as defined on page 56 above: *hand* is the product of an individual, *script* is the second-order level at which the individual aims.

Given the model of linguistic evolution outlined in Chapter 3 above, we might expect to find the origins of linguistic change in the variational habits of individual hands, with the systemic adoption of particular variants being the equivalent in handwriting to linguistic change in the spoken mode. This indeed is what seems to happen.

Interaction between registers, and thus linguistic change, can be seen very clearly in the history of handwriting during the Middle English period. A simple example may be observed at the outset of the period, in the way that graphemes hitherto restricted to Latin manuscripts (e.g.

⟨q⟩) start to appear in vernacular texts (e.g. *quarterne* for Old English *cweartern* in MS Oxford, Laud Misc. 636: *The Peterborough Chronicle*, annal for the year AD 1137). This development reflects a revival of Latin learning in England during the course of the twelfth century, and the gradual atrophy of the old monastic vernacular tradition represented, in late Anglo-Saxon England, by writers such as Ælfric and Wulfstan. What written English there was would increasingly be copied by scribes more used to writing in Latin than in the vernacular, and thus liable to transfer habits gained in copying Latin texts to English ones. The change is systemic, because the alphabetic system used in Anglo-Saxon times was replaced eventually by that used in the later Middle Ages.

This example may be incorporated within the model outlined in Part I above. The scribe of the *Peterborough Chronicle* was evidently weakly tied to the cultures from which he drew. The old traditions of Anglo-Saxon England were dying out, but were still strong enough to cause him to continue copying annals in the time-honoured way, in the vernacular; the new traditions, in which Latin would take over from English for the purposes of historical record, were only just appearing. Being situated between two cultures, the scribe was not fully part of either; and it is therefore not surprising to see him transferring usages from one system into the other. Both usages would be variants within his writing-system brought there by contact; the choice of one rather than the other would reflect the adoption of a new usage which was probably felt to be more prestigious because more up to date. The selection of usages, therefore, reflects historical developments.

A CASE STUDY: THE EVOLUTION OF HIERARCHIES OF ENGLISH SCRIPTS, 1100–1500

More linguistically interesting processes in the history of handwriting can be demonstrated by the interaction of registers (i.e. script-types); and the example used to illustrate this process will be the evolution in script-hierarchies which took place during the period 1100–1500. The standard work on this subject is by M.B. Parkes (Parkes 1979), and his account is followed here, although with slight modifications in terminology and orientation to correlate his descriptions with the linguistic themes of this book.

The reasons behind the evolution of script-hierarchies – the use of different scripts to reflect register distinctions between texts – during the Middle Ages are essentially two: 'the increasing demand for books, and the increase in the size of the works to be copied' (Parkes 1979: xiii). Parkes relates these demands to contemporary social developments:

> The secularization of learning and the rise of the universities created a voracious demand for texts and commentaries. At the same time

improving standards of literacy led to a demand from a wide range of
patrons for books of a more general nature. The size of the commen-
taries upon the Bible, the 'Sentences', and the civil and canon law
increased as each new generation enlarged upon the work of its predecessors; and, in poetry, works like the 'Cursor Mundi' (some 30,000
lines) and the 'Roman de la Rose' (some 20,000 lines in its final form)
imposed heavy demands upon the time and energy of the scribes who
copied them.

(Parkes 1979: xiii)

To meet this demand, scribes felt compelled to develop new scripts
which could be written more rapidly than the old, non-cursive scripts of
Anglo-Saxon England, where letters were formed individually without
running connections between them. But pragmatic considerations, to do
with scribe–reader interaction, constrained this development. Some book-
users, such as priests celebrating the sacraments, wanted texts for litur-
gical, display purposes; for them, speed of copying was a secondary
consideration. For such users a special, calligraphic, non-cursive script was
developed: Textura (sometimes known as 'Text Hand'). Other users,
however, wanted books for reading rather than display, and for them a
new, cursive handwriting was eventually developed, where the pen was
not lifted from the page in the formation of words and where curved
letter-strokes, more easily controlled when writing rapidly, replaced the
straight ones used in non-cursive scripts.

By the middle of the thirteenth century, a major new cursive script had
emerged in England: Anglicana. This script was first used in the copying
of documents, now becoming of more importance in medieval society as
older, oral methods of governance began to be replaced by ones depending
on written communication (see Clanchy 1993; *passim* for a discussion of
this process). It soon began to be used in the copying of books but, as it
did so, something new happened to it: it began to develop more and less
formal registers. The more wealthy patrons required books to reflect their
own magnificence, and formal versions of the current cursive script
appeared, in which letters were written with an eye to calligraphy. This
formal version of Anglicana, Anglicana Formata, became usual in more
dignified scribal productions, whereas informal Anglicana was used in the
production of cheaper vernacular texts. Scribes could handle both scripts,
as is evidenced by the appearance of texts where the main body of the
work is written in Anglicana Formata but where the same scribe uses
plain Anglicana (sometimes known as 'Anglicana Facilis') in supplying the
catchwords, used for the benefit of the binder who put together the quires
of the book. An ⟨a⟩ in Anglicana Formata appears thus: ⟨𝔞⟩ .

During the fourteenth century, a version of Anglicana even took over
largely from Textura, the old display script for use in texts where speed
of production was of less significance. Although Textura continued to be

copied, it appeared more and more rarely as the Middle Ages progressed, and in many of its functions it began to be replaced by so-called Bastard (or 'hybrid') Anglicana, in which certain non-cursive 'noble' Textura features were blended with the 'base' cursive script. An ⟨a⟩ in Bastard Anglicana can appear thus: 𝖺 .

Anglicana, as its name suggests, was a native development. During the late fourteenth century a new cursive script appeared in England: Secretary. This new script, which seems to have originated in Italy, was brought to England via France, and had advantages over Anglicana in terms of ease of effort and speed of writing. Blend-texts soon began to appear, in which Secretary and Anglicana letter-forms appear side by side. Ultimately, Secretary replaced Anglicana, first in documents and subsequently in the copying of books. An ⟨a⟩ in Secretary appears thus: 𝖺 . Secretary script even developed a Bastard or hybrid variety in which elements of Textura style are often rather clumsily assimilated to Secretary letter-forms, for example 𝖺 ⟨a⟩.

A little thought soon suggests that the development in scripts described above may be easily restated in linguistic terms. Key principles involved in the evolution of script are those of 'least effort' and 'maintaining intelligibility'; *systemic* pressures are therefore obviously a central mechanism in script-evolution, as they are in the evolution of language. To these principles may be added the notions of more and less formal register; stylistic *variation* in every level of language is a source for subsequent structural changes, and that is the case with handwriting. And the new variety, Secretary, appears in English texts as the result of *contact* between English and continental culture. The central factor governing the whole process is to do with extralinguistic context: scripts emerged as part of the interplay between the demands of readers and the strategies of supply adopted by scribes. All these notions, of course, correlate with the mechanisms of linguistic change described in Chapter 3 above.

The previous paragraphs in this section represent a 'broad-brush' account of the evolution of script-hierarchies, and the main impulses which governed the replacement of one script by another can from this description be clearly distinguished. However, it is important to realise that the process did not simply consist of one variety of script replacing another wholesale, for at a number of points in the development it would appear that two scripts of apparently equal status in the hierarchy described above could exist side by side. As a result, individual hands frequently show mixtures of scripts – just as speakers can sometimes feel the magnetic pull of two prestigious usages and therefore produce blended idiolects. However, the outcome of this blending process was often not simply to produce a mixture; sometimes the two scripts were distinguished in function by the scribe, who could choose from a repertoire of available forms to reflect register-distinctions.

Good examples of the kinds of mixtures which can appear in the usages of individual scribes are not hard to find; an illustration of mixture in a Latin manuscript of the fifteenth century is the handwriting of Thomas Colyngborne, which is illustrated by Parkes (1979: 24). Colyngborne mingles Anglicana and Secretary forms indiscriminately in one text, and it is therefore hard to classify his hand as one or the other variety.

Perhaps more typical of 'mixed' scribes are those who use the various scripts within their repertoire for distinct purposes. A good example of such a practice is the hand of the well-known Ellesmere manuscript of Chaucer's *Canterbury Tales* (MS San Marino, Huntington Library, 26 C 9), who uses Anglicana Formata for the main body of his text, Bastard Anglicana for the headings, but Anglicana with sporadic Secretary forms (notably the single compartment 'a') in the glosses and catchwords with which the manuscript is supplied. The scribe is known in other manuscripts, notably the Hengwrt manuscript of the *Canterbury Tales* (MS Aberystwyth, National Library of Wales, Peniarth 392), and a copy of Gower's *Confessio Amantis* in Trinity College, Cambridge (MS R.3.2). In his copy of Gower, it is noticeable that the habit of using occasional Secretary 'a' has crept into the main body of the text.

Even more interesting is another early *Canterbury Tales* scribe, the copyist of MSS London, British Library, Harley 7334 and Oxford, Corpus Christi College 198. This latter scribe, one of the most prolific yet detected from the English Middle Ages, developed at least three varieties of script: a normal usage based upon Anglicana Formata, which appears in his copies of Chaucer; a slightly more formal usage which he adopted in two of the seven early manuscripts of Gower's *Confessio Amantis* with which he was involved (MSS Oxford, Bodleian Library, Bodley 294 and London, British Library, Egerton 1991 – the other five are written in his normal usage); and an informal usage, which appears in many of the catchwords and directions to the artists who were involved in decorating and illuminating the manuscripts. In all, although to a varying extent, a number of Secretary-script features appear beside the usual Anglicana forms, but the appearance of Secretary forms becomes rarer as the register of the hand becomes higher. For example, an obvious distinguishing feature between Anglicana and Secretary is in the formation of the letter 'a'. It will be recalled that, in Anglicana, the latter appears as a two-compartment form, somewhat like modern 'printed a', whereas in Secretary it appears as a single-compartment form. The Secretary form for this letter appears only in the scribe's informal 'catchword' usage, but not in the other two registers. Similarly, the Secretary form of the letter 's', β, appears in catchwords and in normal usage, but only rarely in the most formal usage adopted in the Bodley and Egerton MSS of the *Confessio Amantis*. (See Plate 1.)

Quite a lot is now known about the scribe referred to in the previous paragraph. First identified by Doyle and Parkes (1978), he is known to have been active in London at the beginning of the fifteenth century,

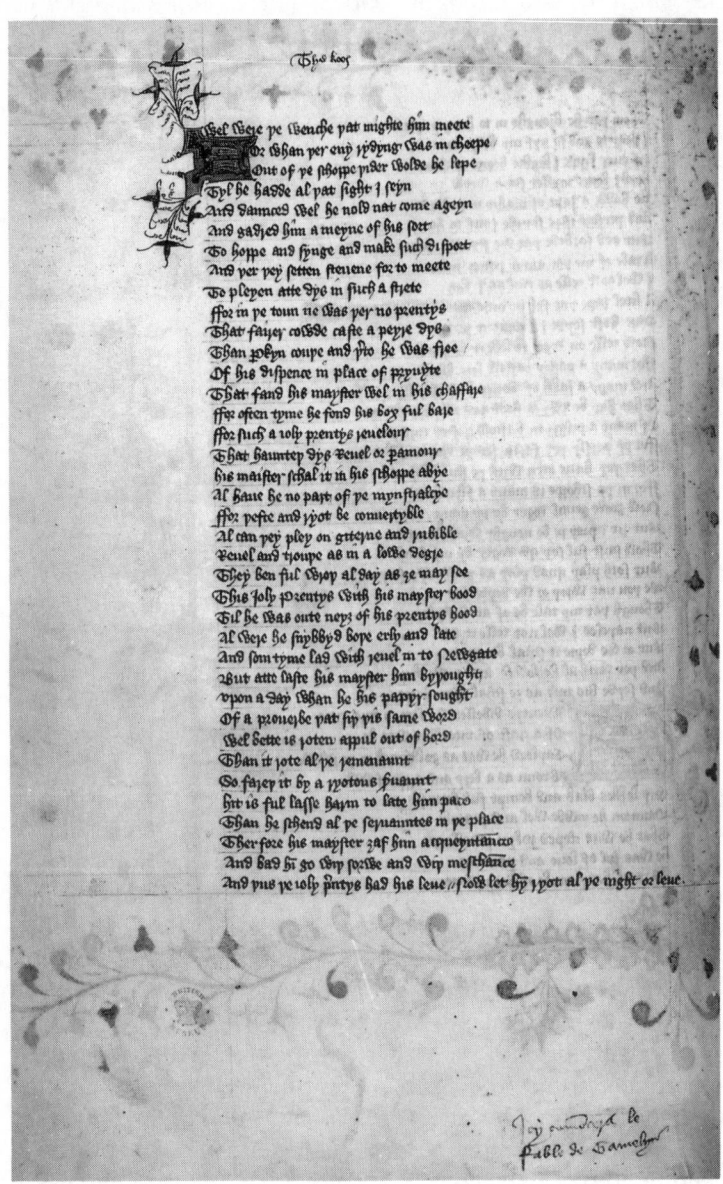

Plate 1 MS London, British Library, Harley 7334, fol. 58r. By permission of the British Library.

probably working on a bespoke, 'commission and sale' basis in the traditional stationers' quarter around Old St Paul's Cathedral. Yet he was not a native Londoner; analysis of the language of his output shows him to have originated in the Worcestershire region, and to have emigrated to London subsequently. As an immigrant, it may be suspected that his social ties were comparatively weak; it is therefore in turn not surprising that he started to introduce features from other scripts into his Anglicana-based usage. Such mixtures between scripts in the output of single hands are quite commonplace (for further study of this scribe, see Smith 1988b).

Thus the potential for change in individual usage existed, as exemplified by the usage of the Ellesmere and Harley scribes, and the shift to Secretary hand was under way during their lifetimes. Both hands appear together in the Trinity Gower referred to above. Three other hands also appeared in that text; two are as yet unknown in other manuscripts, but the fifth hand is well attested elsewhere. This fifth hand is that of the poet and civil servant Thomas Hoccleve, who made a number of copies of his own texts as well as documents produced as part of his duties as a Clerk of the Privy Seal. Hoccleve wrote regularly in Secretary hand, and follows this practice in his copying of Gower. Internal references date the Trinity Gower to after 1408; the death of Hoccleve, which is known to have taken place in 1426, gives the *terminus ante quem* for the manuscript. Hoccleve must therefore have been a near-contemporary of the Ellesmere and Harley scribes; yet he feels able to use the 'newer' Secretary script in many more functions long before they do. The Trinity Gower would therefore seem to demonstrate neatly in one place the process of linguistic change, whereby a script originally assigned to a less formal usage starts to infiltrate more formal registers (in the Secretary elements in the stint of the Ellesmere scribe) and finally replace the earlier usage altogether (as in Hoccleve's practice). (See Plate 2.)

THE METALANGUAGE OF ORTHOGRAPHY

Whereas the terminology *grapheme/allograph* needs a little modification when studying handwriting, the study of orthography during the Middle Ages is, terminologically at least, rather more straightforward. The relationship between phoneme and grapheme in alphabetic writing-systems was discussed in Chapter 2 above, and it was pointed out that phonology and spelling have a close relationship. It is therefore possible to speak of graphemes in writing as corresponding to phonemes in speech; and spelling is to do with graphemic analysis.

However, it was also pointed out in Chapter 2 that the relationship between phoneme and grapheme can be obscured by sound-change on the one hand and written conservatism on the other. Although graphology is related to phonology in that both are levels of language through which the other linguistic elements – lexis, grammar – are transmitted in their

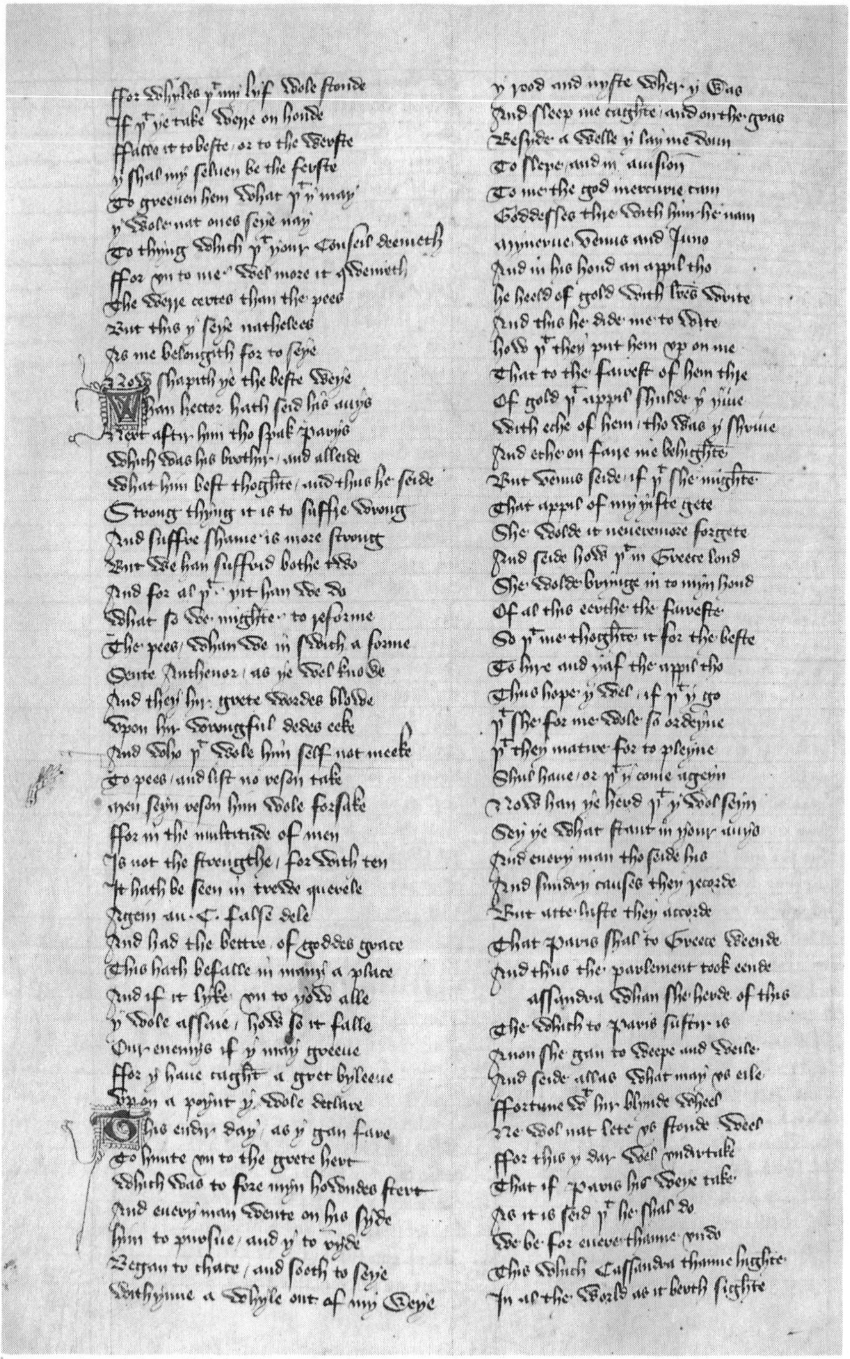

Plate 2 MS Cambridge, Trinity College R.3.2, fol. 83v: hand of Thomas Hoccleve. By permission of the Master and Fellows of Trinity College.

respective modes, nevertheless they can develop in different ways at different speeds. This difference is demonstrated most clearly in the process of *written standardisation*, a process whereby extralinguistic and intralinguistic pressures interacted to produce Present-Day English orthography.

Before discussing this process, however, it is worth examining some of the terminology used to describe it. First of all, the term *standard language* needs further definition. In Present-Day English studies the expression has two meanings. In the written mode it refers to the fixity of spelling, lexicon and grammar which derives from the work of the prescriptivist writers of the eighteenth century. To use written Standard English is to signal competence in a set of established rules enforced by a normative educational system; to use non-standard forms in writing is a way of marking oneself off from other users of language in terms of prestige, or of literary artfulness (e.g. in so-called dialect poetry, such as that of the nineteenth-century Dorset poet William Barnes, or, although a much more complex case, some of the verse of Robert Burns).

With reference to the spoken mode, standard language is an extremely complex and notoriously loaded term. A frequent definition of standard spoken English is that it is a prestigious system of grammar and lexis which can be used by any speaker in communities where English is the first language, available for any register of language (as opposed to varieties which are often termed 'restricted' or 'dialectal'). In the British Isles, it can be, but need not be, expressed in Received Pronunciation, a prestigious accent of English associated with, but not restricted to, the South-East of England. Thus it is possible to speak Standard English with a Scottish, Welsh, American, Australian or Yorkshire accent. Other linguists will refer to Received Pronunciation as a 'standard' or 'reference' accent, in the sense that it is a prestigious accent no longer tied to a specific locality, and they will refer to 'Standard English' with a Received Pronunciation accent as a 'standard language'.

It is clear that there is a good deal of confusion over this issue; the present writer holds that this confusion is the result of transferring written-mode notions of fixity to the spoken mode without modification.

In this context, it is worth looking again at the notion of Received Pronunciation. Although, as was pointed out above, Received Pronunciation is what linguists call a reference accent (that is, a comparatively well-known accent which is useful as a basis for comparison with and between other accents), it is even now not fully described. One of its defining characteristics is that it is not a clear-cut set of fixed shibboleths, but rather what the nineteenth-century scholar A.J. Ellis, who first described it, called 'a sort of mean': a kind of prestigious magnet of pronunciation towards which prestige-seeking accents tend. In some parts of the British Isles there are competing magnets of prestige, such as the accent component of 'Scottish Standard English', and most people feel the force of other

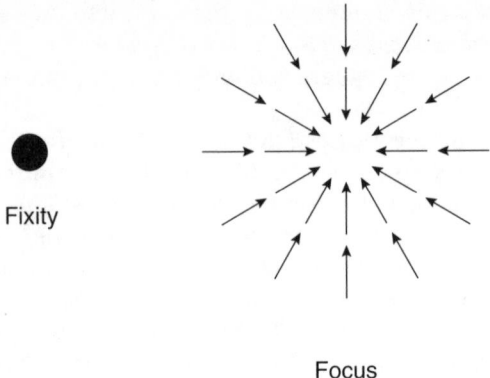

Fixity

Focus

Figure 4.1 Fixity and focus

more covert magnets which derive from class- or district-solidarity. Received Pronunciation may be defined, therefore, as an abstraction, rather like the phoneme; individual speakers may produce utterances which tend towards or deviate from this 'mean'.

It is therefore perhaps better to consider Received Pronunciation in terms of focus rather than fixity; in other words, individual speakers tend to a greater or lesser extent to conform to Received Pronunciation usage, but no one of them can be said to demonstrate every characteristic of the accent. Thus Received Pronunciation may be considered to be *standardised* or focused rather than *standard* or fixed: a centripetal norm towards which speakers tend, rather than a fixed collection of prescribed rules from which any deviation at all is forbidden. (See Figure 4.1 for a schematisation of this situation.)

DIALECT AND STANDARD IN THE HISTORY OF ENGLISH ORTHOGRAPHY

The distinction between standard/fixed and standardised/focused language is important when we turn to past states of English orthography. Until rather late in the history of English, spelling varied to a greater or lesser extent depending on the prestige of the vernacular at the time when the language was being used. As was discussed in Chapter 2, towards the end of the Anglo-Saxon period one variety of Old English, Late West Saxon, appeared in texts copied outside Wessex, the area where this dialect originated. Scholars have often dubbed this variety 'Standard Old English'. This variety lost prestige, however, in the transition from Old to Middle English; the revival of Latin learning on the continent of Europe, and the arrival of a new French-speaking aristocracy in England, meant that

English became a debased vernacular, without any national standing. As a result, it began to exhibit marked dialectal diversity in the written mode as Latin and French took on the functions hitherto met by 'standard Old English'. This situation only changed towards the end of the Middle Ages as the role of the vernacular rose in prestige; as a result of this new prestige, English began to develop new varieties, at first based on London usage, which have again often been termed 'standards' by modern scholars.

Yet it is wrong to consider these medieval 'standards' as identical to their modern written equivalent. Medieval written standards seem to have worked in the same way as spoken Received Pronunciation does in Present-Day British English: they are a sort of mean towards which scribes tend. It is therefore perhaps more correct to refer to standard*ised* or to focused written language; such usages remind us that we are dealing with a process of normative focusing rather than with a fixed set of forms.

Thus, before the Late West Saxon written mode is directly paralleled with Present-Day English standard written language it is worth making two points:

1 Close examination of the written record soon reveals that 'Standard West Saxon' admitted of a good deal more variation than standard written Present-Day English. Not only are there certain lexical habits which are restricted to certain monastic scriptoria, but also there seem to be persistent orthographic distinctions between the various scriptorial outputs. Codification of these latter features remains an important task for Anglo-Saxonists.

2 There are indications that other literary 'standards' existed in Anglo-Saxon England, even if they were overshadowed by Late West Saxon. The similarities between, for instance, the ninth-century *Vespasian Psalter Gloss* and the thirteenth-century 'AB-language' of the Corpus manuscript of *Ancrene Wisse* (Cambridge, Corpus Christi College 402) and the homilies and saints' lives of Oxford, Bodleian Library, Bodley 34, combined with the evidence of the *Life of St Chad* in Oxford, Bodleian Library, Hatton 116, attest to a continuity of non-West-Saxon-centred writing traditions in the West Mercian region from Old to Middle English times. Similar, if more tenuous, cases could be made for the existence of Northumbrian or Kentish literary traditions. These alternative traditions form another set of magnets: weaker than Late West Saxon but nevertheless to be taken account of in studies of this period.

In the transition to the Middle English period, the role of the vernacular changed, and many of its functions were carried out using the 'up-to-date' practices of the continent of Europe (that is, by using Latin and French). As a result, the vernacular became in general parish- rather than nationally or regionally focused and, in turn, wide variation in the written mode of English – when English was written at all – became the norm. Since the function of written English had become particular and local, it was open to modification to reflect spoken-language changes peculiar to the individual dialect-areas, and this practice was encouraged as the ability to write in the vernacular became more widespread. Even in the comparatively conservative South-West Midlands of England, where there was a persistence of old traditions of text-production, there was a gradual dissimilation of usages as individual scribes modified the traditional spelling-systems of their areas to reflect more closely the spoken mode of their own particular localities. Thus even a so-called 'literary standard' such as 'AB-language' is on closer inspection revealed to be simply a particular dialect, to be placed typologically beside other varieties from the South-West Midlands which have remodelled spelling-practices based upon the traditional Old English usage of the area.

THE STANDARDISATION OF WRITTEN ENGLISH, 1350–1550: FOCUS AND FIXITY

As a result of this development of parochial spelling-practices, the Middle English period is, notoriously, the time when linguistic variation is fully reflected in the written mode. To exemplify this, we might examine the range of Middle English spellings for the item 'THROUGH'. *LALME* (1986) records something like 500 ways of spelling this item, ranging from fairly recognisable *thurgh*, *thorough* and *þorowe* to exotic-seeming *drowgȝ*, *yhurght*, *trghug* and *trowffe*. The remainder of this chapter will discuss how this – to modern eyes – bizarre degree of written-language variation was suppressed in favour of standard forms. In doing so, the monitoring principle referred to at the beginning of this chapter will be returned to on a number of occasions.

The processes of standardisation of the written mode in the fourteenth and fifteenth centuries have been much studied over the last thirty years, especially by contributors to *LALME*. The classic study still remains that by Samuels (1963), who first distinguished 'types' of 'incipient standard' from the fourteenth and fifteenth centuries. It is significant that the origins of a number of these types correlate with the parts of the country where population had undergone a considerable increase since the Conquest; these areas were the source of the immigrants to London who brought the advancing forms with them to the capital. These types are as follows:

Type I, which was in use from the middle of the fourteenth century onwards, is found in the majority of manuscripts attributed to Wycliffe and his followers, although it is not restricted to them. Otherwise (perhaps a little misleadingly; see page 70 below) known as 'Central Midlands Standard', its importance is testified by the large number of texts, not only religious, which have survived in it. Characteristic texts in Type I use a mixture of forms common in the Central Midland counties in Middle English times, for example *sich* 'such', *mych* 'much', *ony* 'any', *silf* 'self', *stide* 'stead', *ȝouun* 'given', *siȝ* 'saw'.

Type II is found in nine mid-fourteenth-century texts from the Greater London area, including the well-known Auchinleck manuscript. It replaces earlier London English, as represented by Henry III's Proclamation of 1258, which was basically Southern English with a marked influence from Essex. Characteristic Type II texts display forms from Norfolk and Suffolk, such as *-ande* (pres. part.), the word *þerk* 'dark' etc.; these forms seem to correlate with the pattern of mid-fourteenth-century immigration into the capital, which shows a marked influx from East Anglia. Other characteristic forms include *werld* 'world', *þat ilch(e)*, *ilch(e)* 'that very', *noiþer*, *noþer* 'neither', *þei(ȝ)* 'though', *þai, hij* 'they'.

Type III, which appears in texts copied in London from the late fourteenth century, is the language of the best Chaucerian manuscripts (e.g. the Ellesmere and Hengwrt manuscripts of the *Canterbury Tales*), and of various documents pertaining to London affairs in the period. Its characteristic features reflect a shift in immigration patterns at the end of the century, whereby newcomers to the capital originated in the Central Midlands and brought their forms with them. Frequently attested forms – many of them the same as in Present-Day written English – include *world, thilke, that ilk(e)* 'that very', *neither, though, they, yaf* 'gave', *nat* 'not', *swich(e)* 'such', *bot* 'but', *hir(e)* 'their', *thise* 'these'.

Type IV is the language used in the mass of government documents after *c.* 1430, for which reason it has been labelled 'Chancery Standard'. It shows the impact of yet further waves of immigrants from the Central Midlands, who included in their linguistic repertoires some originally North Midland forms. Characteristic forms include *gaf* 'gave', *not* 'not', *but, suche(e), theyre* etc. 'their', *thes(e)* 'these', *thorough/þorowe* 'through', *shulde* 'should'.

Of these four types, only I and IV appear to have been widely copied outside their area of origin and thus were standardised written languages comparable to Late West Saxon. Type III seems to have had a limited impact outside London as a 'literary' language appropriate for art-poetry, and its influence can be traced even in certain Middle Scots texts (e.g. MS Cambridge, University Library, Kk.1.5, a text of the anonymous *Lancelot of the Laik*; see Gray 1912). Type II is simply a standardised form of the language found in the capital in the mid-fourteenth century; its appearance in the Auchinleck manuscript, a book probably associated with the court of Edward III, does not necessarily mean that any special prestige was associated with this variety. The roughly contemporary author of *Sir Gawain and the Green Knight* produced a text which, although apparently composed as well as copied in a North-West Midland dialect, yields nothing in courtly sophistication, and thus in the status of its likely audience, to the contents of the Auchinleck romances.

As with Late West Saxon, it is important to bear in mind that these four types represent focused or 'standardised' forms of language, not fixed 'standards' (thus expressions such as 'Central Midlands Standard', 'Chancery Standard', which commonly appear in the scholarly literature, are potentially confusing if not given careful qualification). As a number of scholars have pointed out, these types are not uniform in the same way that Present-Day written Standard English is uniform; rather, 'seen against the perspective of Middle English dialects overall, each type comprises closely similar samples from the cline that is the total range of dialectal variation' (Sandved 1981: 39). In other words, the types represent standardisation in the written mode in the same way that, for example, Received Pronunciation represents standardisation in the spoken mode in Present-Day English: a norm to which particular users tend rather than a set of shibboleths from which any deviation is stigmatised. The types are therefore distinct from the Present-Day English written mode, where usage is fixed and prescribed through the normative practices of the educational system.

The focused – as opposed to fixed – nature of Types I and IV, the two varieties which achieved broadest diatopic spread, may be demonstrated by the analysis of relevant texts. To illustrate the range of variation within Type I, six texts will be chosen:

1   various Wycliffite texts collected by Hudson (1978): (i) a sermon on the ecclesiastical hierarchy (Text 15) from MS London, British Library, Royal 18.B.ix; (ii) a short treatise on the wickedness of miracle plays (Text 19) from MS London, British Library, Additional 24202; and (iii) an extract from the tract *The Lanterne of Liʒt* (Text 22) from London, British Library, Harley 2324;
2   a polemical text attacking the friars, known as *Jack Upland* (Heyworth 1968), from London, British Library, Harley 6641;
3   two manuscripts containing groups of Lollard sermons (Cigman 1989): (i) MS London, British Library, Additional 41321 (first hand's stint) and (ii) MS Oxford, Bodleian Library, Rawlinson C.751 (Sermon 12 only).

All the above texts are associated with the Wycliffite or Lollard movements; all represent the kind of text associated with 'Central Midlands Standard'. The table in Figure 4.2 lists the forms for five items in these texts: 'SUCH', 'MUCH', 'ANY', 'SELF', 'GIVEN'.

If we compare the forms presented in Figure 4.2 with the set of 'Central Midlands Standard' forms described as characteristic of Type I, it will soon be apparent that none of the texts analysed here has all five characteristics. Rather, it is possible to order the texts typologically, in which ordering Additional 24202 and Harley 2324 are nearest to, but not at, the focal

Figure 4.2 Focused repertoires of spellings in Middle English (Type I)

	SUCH	MUCH	ANY	SELF	GIVEN
Royal 18.B.ix	suche	moche	ony	silf	ʒouun
Add. 24202	siche	myche	ony	silf	ʒyuen
Harley 2324	suche	miche	ony	silf	ʒouun
Harley 6641	suche	myche, moche	ony	silf	ʒouun
Add. 41321	suche	myche, miche	any, ani	self	ʒouen
Rawl. C.751	suche	myche	ony	self, selfe	ʒouen

point and Additional 41321 furthest away, with Royal 18.B.ix, Harley 6641 and Rawlinson C.751 somewhere in between. In other words, it could be argued that the complex of 'Central Midlands Standard' texts represented here are focused on a central model, but not fixed.

Type IV is often characterised as 'Chancery Standard', and, to illustrate the range of usage available in this variety, a short selection of texts will be analysed here, emanating from offices of state in the early fifteenth century. It should be noted that there are difficulties in the selection of these texts, since those lodged in the various departments of government at the time often represent not some 'house-style' of orthography but rather an attempt to reproduce the language of a regionally produced original; thus, although the material gathered together by, for example, Fisher *et al.* (1984) is of interest linguistically, it does not necessarily form a coherent body of texts representing 'Chancery Standard' (see further *LALME* I: 47–49).

For that reason – and also because research into this topic is still in progress, notably in forthcoming work by Professors Benskin and Sandved – only a brief example of the variation available within Type IV will be offered. In 1436, the office of the Privy Seal recorded, in the name of the young Henry VI, a summons to arms to suppress a revolt by 'he þat calleth him Duc of Bourgoigne oure rebell with his puissance of fflemmenges Picardes Bourgoignons and oþer' (cited from Fisher *et al.* 1984: 161). Three versions of this summons survive (MSS London, Public Record Office E28/57A, E28/57B and E28/57C); E28/57B is somewhat damaged, but the other two texts are complete. All three appear in Fisher *et al.* (1984: 161–164), as documents 132–134.

Texts of the first paragraphs of E28/57A and E28/57C appear as Figure 4.3. The two texts are fairly good representatives of Type IV, but even a superficial survey reveals a degree of variation between them that would not be acceptable in Present-Day written Standard English: for example variation between *i* and *y*, the addition or omission of final *-e*, consistent differences in the spelling of common words (e.g. *you*, *yowe*). The variation is not as large as was possible within the Middle English dialect continuum, but it is nevertheless there. In other words, the texts contain a focused form of language which is nevertheless not a fixity. Spelling variants

Figure 4.3 Focused repertoires of spellings in Middle English (Type IV)

London, Public Record Office, E28/57A (a Privy Seal document of 1436: Summons to Arms, first version (part))

Trusty and *welbelouyd ffor* as moche as he þat calleth him Duc of *Bourgoigne* oure rebell with his puissance of *fflemmenges* Picardes Bourgoignons and oþer is come ouer þe water of Grauelyng and hatyh *pighte* his tentes with Inne oure Pale of þe marches þere willyng and disposyng him to gete oure *Toune* of caleys and *alle* oure strengthes in þe marches þere þe which if so were þat god defende *shulde* be vn to vs *you* oure *Reamme* and *subgitt3* to grete an hurte and a *perpetualle* shame we þerfore willyng to resiste þe malice of þe *saide* callyng him Duc dispose vs in persone for to *go* to oure Citee of Caunterbury for þe rescous to *oure said Toune* and marches Wherfore we desire and *praye* oure oþer feod men þat in *alle* þe *haste* þat ye maye ye make *you* redy and *alle þe* defensable *people* þat ye can and *maye* and drawe *you þeder* to ward vs *So* þat ye be þere at þe ferþest on mary *Maughdelenes* day next redy in *your* beste *arraye* for þe said rescous with oþer of oure feod men and trewe *subgitt3* to whom we write *sembly* for þe good of vs you oure Reaume and *subgitt3* of þe same And in no wise *faylleth her* of as oure singuler *truste* ys in *yowe*: yeuen vnder oure priue *sealle* at *Westminster* þe *laste* day of Iuyn

London, Public Record Office, E28/57C (a Privy Seal document of 1436: Summons to Arms, third version (part))

Trusty and *welbeloued for* asmoche as he þat calleth hym Duc of *Bourgoine* oure rebell wyth his puissance of *fflemynges* Picardes Bourgoignons and oþer is come ouer *the* water of Gravelyng and hath *pight* his tentes with Inne oure pale of *the* marches *there* willyng and disposyng hym to gete oure *tovne* of caleys and *all* oure Strengthes in þe marches þere *the* which if so were þat god defende *shuld* be vnto vs *yowe* oure *roialme* and *subgettes* to grete an hurte and *perpetuall* shame: we þerfore willyng to resiste *the* malice of *the said* callyng hym Duc dispose vs in persone for to *goo* vnto oure Citee of Caunterbury for *the* rescous to *owre seid tovne* and marches wherfore we desire and pray yow hertly as oure feod man in wise as at this tyme we desire and *pray* oure oþer feod men þat in *all* þe *hast* ye may ye make *yowe* redy And *all the* defensable *poeple* þat ye can and *may* And drawe *yowe thider* toward vs *Soo* þat ye be *there* at *the ferthest* on mary *Magdelan* next redy yn *youre* best *array* for *the seid* rescous with oþer of oure feod men and trewe *subgettes* to whom we write *semblably* for *the* good of vs you oure reaume and *subgett3* of *the* same and yn no wise *faileth here* of as oure singuler *trust* ys yn *you* yeuen vnder oure priue *seal* at *westminstre the last* day of Iuyn between the two texts, none of which has any dialectal significance, have been italicised.

SELECTION, CODIFICATION, ELABORATION AND ACCEPTANCE

Some scholars have held that the appearance in prestigious government documents of a standardised written language, like Type IV, was itself the mechanism whereby written Standard English emerged. However, recent scholarship indicates that the process was a little more complex. If 'Chancery Standard' was simply adopted wholesale as a result of its contemporary prestige, then we would expect a simple pattern of replacement of regional by 'Chancery' forms as the fifteenth century progressed.

This pattern is not what is found, however. To illustrate this fact, the manuscripts of Chaucer's *Canterbury Tales* will be examined. The manuscript-tradition of the *Canterbury Tales* seems to have been produced within a generally prestigious social milieu; Chaucer, a Londoner, was not only an important royal servant but also a courtier, much of whose poetry seems to have been written with a royal audience in mind. Ownership of the manuscripts of the *Canterbury Tales* during the fifteenth century demonstrates that the poem continued to be admired either by the nobility or by those (a distinct group) aspiring to the status of nobility. Thus it might be expected, were the shift to Type IV simply a matter of the replacement of regional by prestigious usage, that the texts would show the impact of Type IV; but this does not appear to have been the case. Figure 4.4 shows the presence or absence within a range of *Canterbury Tales* manuscripts of 'Chancery Standard' forms for a selection of common items: (1) 'these', (2) 'not', (3) 'but', (4) 'such', (5) 'their', (6) 'given', (7) 'through', (8) 'should' (cf. 'Chancery' *these, not, but, such(e), th*-type forms for 'they', *geuen, thorough* etc., *shuld(e)*). The table indicates that, in these manuscripts, there has been a slight general movement towards Chancery Standard forms; but it also shows that the process is neither complete nor decisive (see Figure 4.4).

It is perhaps more significant that a large number of the *Canterbury Tales* manuscripts are written in a 'colourless' dialectal mixture, that is, a mixture of non-'Chancery' forms which shows no special dialectal distinctiveness, the forms in question having a wide distribution in Middle English. Such colourless regional usages come about

> when a writer replaces some or all of his distinctively local forms by equivalents which, although still native to the local or neighbouring dialects, are common currency over a wide area. The result is not a series of well-defined, regional standards . . . but a continuum in which the local element is muted, and one type shifts almost imperceptibly into another.
>
> (*LALME* I: 47)

Figure 4.4 Reflection of Type IV forms in manuscripts of Chaucer's *Canterbury Tales*

This table is based upon an analysis of the fifty medieval copies of the *Pardoner's Tale* printed by the Chaucer Society at the end of the nineteenth century (Zupitza and Furnivall 1892–1898). Texts are ordered according to date, the dates for each manuscript being taken from Manly and Rickert (1940), still the standard survey of the manuscripts. The names for each manuscript are abbreviated; for full names and descriptions see Manly and Rickert 1940, esp. Vol. 1. In this table, the presence of a 'Chancery' form in the text in question is marked by +; non-appearance of the Chancery form in the text in question is marked by a –; 0 means that the form is missing in the text open for analysis.

Form	(1)	(2)	(3)	(4)	(5)	(6)	(7)	(8)
1400–1425								
CUL Dd 4.24	–	–	+	–	–	–	–	+
CUL Gg 4.27	–	+	+	+	–	–	–	–
Corpus Oxon 198	–	–	+	+	–	–	–	–
Ellesmere	–	–	+	–	–	–	–	–
Harley 7334	–	–	+	+	–	–	–	–
Hengwrt	–	–	+	+	–	–	–	–
Lansdowne	–	–	–	+	–	–	–	–
Petworth	–	+	+	–	–	–	–	+
1425–1450								
Add. 25178	–	–	+	+	–	–	–	+
Add. 35286	–	+	+	–	–	–	–	–
Bodley 686	–	+	+	–	–	–	–	+
CUL Ii 3.26	0	+	+	+	–	–	–	+
Egerton 2726	–	–	+	–	–	–	–	–
Egerton 2863	–	+	+	+	–	–	–	–
Helmingham	+	–	+	+	–	–	+	+
Laud Misc. 600	0	+	+	+	–	–	–	+
Lichfield	–	+	+	+	–	–	0	+
Lincoln	–	+	+	–	–	–	–	+
Paris F.A. 39	0	+	+	0	–	+	–	+
olim Phillips 8137	+	+	+	+	–	–	–	–
Royal 18.c.ii	–	+	+	+	–	–	–	–
Sloane 1685	–	+	+	+	–	–	–	+
1450–1475								
Addit. 5140	–	–	+	+	–	–	–	+
Barlow 20	–	+	+	+	–	–	–	–
Bodley 414	–	+	+	+	–	–	–	+
Cbg. Trinity R.3.3	–	–	+	0	–	0	0	0
CUL Mm 2.5	–	+	–	+	–	–	–	+
Christ Church	–	+	+	+	–	–	–	+
Delamere	–	–	+	–	–	–	–	+
Devonshire	+	+	+	+	–	–	–	+
Egerton 2864	+	–	+	+	–	–	–	+
Glasgow	0	–	+	+	–	–	–	+
Harley 1758	–	+	+	+	–	–	+	+
Harley 7333	–	+	+	+	–	–	+	–
Harley 7335	0	+	+	–	–	–	–	+
Hatton Donat 1	–	+	+	–	–	–	+	+

Form	(1)	(2)	(3)	(4)	(5)	(6)	(7)	(8)
McLean 181	+	+	+	+	–	–	+	+
Morgan 249	–	+	+	+	–	–	–	+
Northumberland	0	–	–	+	–	–	–	+
Oxon, New Coll. 314	–	+	+	+	–	–	+	–
Oxon, Trinity 49	–	+	+	–	–	–	–	+
olim Phillips 8136	–	+	+	+	–	–	–	+
Physicians 13	–	–	+	–	–	–	–	+
Rawlinson poet. 149	–	+	–	–	–	–	–	+
Rawlinson poet. 223	–	–	+	+	–	–	–	+
Selden B.14	+	+	+	+	–	–	–	+
1475–1500								
Cbg, Trinity R.3.15	0	+	+	+	–	–	–	+
Laud Misc. 739	–	+	+	+	–	–	–	+
Royal 17.d.xv	–	–	+	+	–	–	–	+
Sloane 1686	–	+	+	+	–	–	–	+

The evolution of colourless usage can be discerned if we look more closely at, for example, Herefordshire usage between the thirteenth and the fifteenth centuries. Although this period is comparatively short in terms of the history of the language, it is clear that grossly provincial Herefordshire usage is in recession. To exemplify this pattern, I have chosen the reflection of five items – 'these', 'them', 'their', 'many', 'was' and 'little' – in three texts:

1 MS Oxford, Jesus College 29, the well-known miscellany containing (amongst other texts) *The Owl and the Nightingale*, dating from the mid-thirteenth century: *þeos, heom, heore, mony, wes, lutel*;
2 MS Longleat, Marquess of Bath 5, Wycliffite sermons, dating from the late fourteenth/early fifteenth century: *þeose/þese, hem, her(e)/hure, many/mony(e), was, luytul*;
3 MS Cambridge, St John's College B.1, Gower, *Confessio Amantis*, dating from the beginning of the fifteenth century: *þese, hem, heore, mony, was, lytel/lytul*.

Although text 3 above, the St John's manuscript of Gower, is undoubtedly a Herefordshire text, it is also true that its usage is not so grossly deviant from contemporary usages elsewhere as to make it markedly inefficient in basic communicative terms; the forms cited are, individually, quite widely distributed amongst the Middle English dialects, and no experienced reader of Middle English would have had any difficulty with them. Middle English scribes could expect, when copying writing other than their own, to encounter a wide range of linguistic variation. It is clear that many of them became used to this gross range of variation in writing, although there are often interesting errors in scribal copying which show that misunderstanding between dialects was quite common (see further Smith 1994a).

The question remains, however, as to why such colourless usage was itself eventually displaced by a variety based upon 'Chancery Standard'. A range of variation which allows 500 ways of spelling the item 'THROUGH' is obviously communicatively dysfunctional in terms of meaning, but this problem would be solved by the adoption of colourless English. The answer must be something as follows: the advantages offered to a writer of a focused usage are not only communicative but also socio-linguistic (should a distinction need to be drawn between the two). The further step towards the adoption of a written Standard English based upon 'Chancery' usage must have taken place because it had become *socially* as well as communicatively dysfunctional to use non-standard forms at a time when a perception of 'better' and 'worse' ways of spelling was beginning to develop.

Such an explanation would account for the sequence of evolution which has been described above. As the use of the vernacular reasserted itself in English during the latter part of the Middle Ages, grosser provincialisms such as *trghug* were discarded and those of wider currency were allowed to remain – producing a colourless language which allowed a fair range of variation. This colourless usage survived for a long time, especially in private letters (see, for instance, the private as opposed to the public usage of Dr Johnson in the eighteenth century; I owe this reference to Professor N. Blake). The role of this colourless writing in paving the way for the ultimate wide acceptance of a variety based upon 'Chancery Standard' as a national norm has recently been emphasised, and it is in this context that the spellings of the *Canterbury Tales* manuscripts must be viewed.

With the growth of literacy and the assertion of prescriptive ways of writing in the vernacular, however, a usage based upon Chancery Standard ultimately displaced this colourless language. As the usage of Chancery Standard, on which the early printers had based (more or less) their practice, became imitated throughout the country, remaining spelling-variation became more obviously dysfunctional in social as well as communicative terms; it became sociolinguistically stigmatised to use non-Chancery forms.

> Once the printers fixed their spellings, a norm was provided for private spelling, and after 1550 we find a gradual improvement in the quality of private education reflected in greater stability and regularity of spelling in private documents.
>
> (Scragg 1974: 68)

The process whereby focused usage became fixity may be swiftly described. Written Standard English in the modern sense may be said to have developed in accordance with the set of criteria for standardisation listed by E. Haugen: *selection, codification, elaboration* and *acceptance* (quoted in Hudson 1980: 32–34). Chancery Standard, with its basis in the language used in the capital, was *selected* as power became increasingly centralised and concentrated in London; it was *codified* and thus *fixed* (never by an academy, as in seventeenth-century France, but by the enforcement of prescriptive educational norms deriving from widespread reading, associated with the Protestant Reformation, of printed books such as the Bible); it was *elaborated*, in that it became the usage accepted for English in every function; and it was ultimately *accepted* as the only acceptable usage in written discourse.

A FAILURE OF STANDARDISATION: THE CASE OF OLDER SCOTS

The 'success' of Chancery English may be contrasted with the 'failure' of another national standardised written language in the same period: standardised written Older Scots, the Old-English-derived variety used in the Lowlands of Scotland during a period roughly corresponding to later Middle and Early Modern English (see further Chapter 8 below). There is good evidence that Older Scots was proceeding towards standardisation along the same path as Late Middle English; the pressures and processes were the same as in England, in that the vernacular was beginning to take on new functions in the fifteenth century, and that wide regional variation within the (admittedly comparatively small) Scots dialect-region was beginning to be suppressed. But, whereas Chancery Standard became the ancestor of Present-Day written Standard English, the process was interrupted in the evolution of Scots.

There were two connected historical reasons why this variety did not succeed in the same way as Chancery Standard did, that is, develop into a prestigious written norm not restricted to its place of origin. On the one hand, throughout the time of its widespread use it evidently had an uneasy relationship with English south of the border. Up until the late fifteenth century, the term used for the Old-English-derived language spoken in the south of Scotland was *Inglis* (the term *Scottis*, up to the same date, was reserved for Gaelic). That there was intimate cultural contact between English and *Inglis* is illustrated by the close connection between the flowering of Scottish vernacular literature, associated with the poets Robert Henryson and William Dunbar, and the slightly earlier English pantheon of Chaucer, Gower and John Lydgate. The strength of these cultural connections is demonstrated by the curiously blended language of texts such as *Lancelot of the Laik* in MS Cambridge, University Library, Kk.1.5 (see page 69 above), or the anglicised spellings which appear in the early prints of, for instance, Dunbar's 'high-style' verse (i.e. ceremonious poetry for court use, characterised by latinate diction and complex syntax; see further Agutter 1989).

The second – and probably stronger – reason for the ultimate failure of standardised written Older Scots was the collapse of real Scottish political autonomy in the wake of the disaster of the battle of Flodden (1513), followed quite soon afterwards by the Protestant Reformation. The Union of the Crowns in 1603 meant a decisive shift south in the centre of Scotland's political gravity; and, as Murison (1977: 5) has pointed out, despite the existence of Scots Bibles such as the adaptation of the Wycliffite Bible (1513–1522) by Murdoch Nisbet, the Authorised Version of the English Bible's 'language became familiar to the people as the language of solemnity and abstract thought ... while Scots remained in the language of ordinary life'. Devitt (1989: 71) has shown that the linguistic shift from standardised Older Scots to English between 1520 and 1659 worked its way through written genres in an interesting and ordered way which correlates with the impact of religious discourse:

> The genre that had the greatest use of Anglo-English [*sic*] variants was religious treatises, followed by official correspondence, private records, personal correspondence, and national public records.

The process is well illustrated by the two versions of King James VI and I's prose treatise, *Basilikon Doron*. The first, manuscript version is written in Middle Scots, and demonstrates this fact by such characteristically Scots forms as *aulde* 'old', *quhilke* 'which', *haill* 'whole', *hes ... cumd* 'has come' etc.; but, when printed in 1603, the Scottish features have been replaced by their contemporary English equivalents: *olde, whiche, whole, hath ... come* etc.

Thus the standardisation of written Scots was cut short. It has been suggested that Older Scots in the early sixteenth century was developing a standardised variety in the sense that Central Midlands Standard in the fourteenth century and Chancery Standard in the fifteenth were standardised; but Scots never took the extra step, which Chancery English and its successors did, into becoming a prescribed and normative standard written language taught in schools. To be successful and to proceed from focus to fixity, a written standard must be linked to broad-based and continuing social prestige. This prestige Chancery Standard acquired, but its parallel Scottish equivalent failed to sustain it.

The general lesson from this last example is clear: the evolution of orthography can be understood only when the dynamic interaction between extra- and intralinguistic processes and pressures is brought into consideration. In the next chapter, a similar conclusion will be drawn from the study of phonological change.

5 Transmission II: sound-change

PHONEME AND ALLOPHONE

In Chapter 3, it was observed that linguistic variation arose in two ways: through divergence from a common inherited ancestor, and through contact with other varieties or languages, that is, through the interaction of intra- and extralinguistic phenomena. In the last chapter, the standardisation of written English in particular was placed within its extralinguistic and intralinguistic context. In this chapter, the attention shifts to the transmission of the spoken mode, that is, phonology and phonetics, and it will be observed that dynamic interaction between extra- and intralinguistic processes is similarly of key importance. In short, it is argued here that a given sound-change is the result of a number of factors, both intra- and extralinguistic, acting in combination.

Historical linguists have traditionally focused their attention on sound-systems – that is, phonology – rather than phonetic detail, and there are good reasons for this. If we leave aside the science of phonological reconstruction, the history of sounds, before the widespread use of mechanical and electronic methods of recording language in the twentieth century, has to depend on the study of written language. As was noted in Chapter 2, alphabetic writing-systems, such as that in which English is and has been recorded, are designed to distinguish the smallest meaningfully distinctive units of language, and are thus broadly phonemic in the way in which they map the spoken mode – even though, given spelling-traditions, this mapping may reflect an earlier stage in the language's history.

Linguists have traditionally compiled a language's or variety's phonemic inventory by noting the existence of 'minimal pairs', that is, pairs of words in which a difference of a single sound in an identical phonetic environment indicates a difference of meaning. To distinguish allophones (i.e. varying realisations of phonemes) in orthography is in principle uneconomical and would be communicatively confusing. Efficient written communication therefore depends on a correlation between grapheme and phoneme. As a result, we can expect at least a tendency for allophonic variation not to be reflected in the written mode.

Yet to concentrate on phonological system at the expense of allophonic variation in a history of sounds can be misleading. To take a simple example: the major difference between the consonantal phonology of Middle English and that of Old English is the addition of a distinction between voiced and voiceless fricatives. In the case of /v/, /f/ this is frequently considered to be one of the few examples of French influence on the English phonological system. The addition of minimal pairs derived from French, such as *vine* : *fine*, to the English lexicon meant that [v] and [f], hitherto allophones, became phonemicised. The post-Conquest scribal distinction between ⟨v⟩ and ⟨f⟩ seems to result from this phonemicisation.

To state, therefore, that Old English had no distinction between /v/ and /f/, whereas Middle English did, is entirely fair – in phonemic terms. However, that is not to say that Old English did not distinguish between the sounds [v] and [f]. Almost all students of Old English agree that fricatives were voiced intervocalically and voiceless elsewhere during the historical Old English period. In Old English the distribution of [v], [f] was complementary, so that ⟨f⟩ in *fela* 'many' signified [f], but ⟨f⟩ in *yfel* 'evil' signified [v]. Moreover, some varieties of Old English, notably Southern ones, evidently had a much wider distribution of initial voiced fricatives than others; and some of these voiced sounds subsequently spread beyond their area of origin (cf. Present-Day English *vixen* beside the related male *fox*).[1]

It would seem, therefore, that the relationship between phonological system and allophonic variation has to be catered for in the practice of historical linguistics, even if the evidence for variation is uncertain. The relationship is – like all features of linguistic development – iterative: allophonic variation has the potential (although it need not) to lead to phonological change, and phonological system can (although it need not) constrain the range of possible allophonic variation.

PHONEMICISATION

In diachronic study, the relationship between allophone and phoneme can be seen very clearly in the process of phonemicisation. Phonemicisation may be defined as when two allophonic realisations of an original phoneme start to be used in situations where the choice of one or the other changes the meaning of the word; thus minimal pairs arise, such as /pʊt/ 'put' beside /pʌt/ 'putt' in some varieties of Present-Day English, reflecting a distinction which arose in Southern English in the seventeenth century; or the distinction between Present-Day English *house* (noun), with final /s/, and *house* (verb), with final /z/. The Old English forms for these words were *hūs* and *hūsian* respectively; the distribution of [s] and [z] was allophonic in Old English, in that [z] was used intervocalically whereas [s] was used finally. With the loss of the inflection on the verb during the

Middle English period, a new minimal pair existed and thus a new phonemic distinction arose, between /s/ and /z/.

As we might expect, the emergence of phonemes has an important impact on the evolution of alphabetic writing-systems; and we are fortunate in that, for much of the history of the English language, the forces of written standardisation did not obscure this process. To demonstrate the interplay between phonemicisation and writing-system an Early Old English example will be examined: the significance of *y*, and its representation in the runic script. The choice of such an early example is required because of later educational developments; as several scholars have pointed out, increasing conventionalisation of spelling since the late Middle Ages has brought about stability and conservatism in orthography, so that changes in phonological structure are no longer generally reflected in the written mode.

The appearance of *y* was for some time one of the major puzzles in the history of Anglo-Saxon orthography. The letter was adopted into the Roman alphabet from Greek *υ*, *Y upsilon*, a variant of *V* which has given the modern alphabetic *u* and *v*. In Roman practice, it was originally confined to Greek words imitated or reproduced in Latin, and it corresponded phonetically to [y], a front close rounded vowel. There is, further, some evidence in the Latin grammatical tradition that *y* is also the symbol for a diphthong [ui]. An awareness of this history of the letter is demonstrated by the eleventh-century Anglo-Saxon monastic writer Ælfric, who in his *Grammar* referred to *y* as *se grecisca y*, 'the Greek *y*'; the symbol is still referred to as *y-grec* in French. It seems likely that the early Anglo-Saxon orthographers were aware of the symbol as a marginal feature of Latin, and simply exploited it. In later Latin, those Greek words with [y] = *y* were reinterpreted as containing Latin [i], and thus *i*, *y* became alternative graphs – as they became in Middle English when, in most dialects, Old English *y* [y(ː)] was unrounded. In Middle English times, *y* was used instead of *i* especially in 'minim environments', that is where *i* appeared in a sequence preceded or followed by the letters *m*, *n* or *u*; in many varieties of medieval handwriting all these letters were written using the same minim-stroke, and there was thus scope for potential confusion which the use of *y* avoided.

In Old English, *y* is used (1) as the reflex in Late West Saxon of Early West Saxon *ie*, and (2) to reflect the outcome of a prehistoric Old English sound-change, the *i*-mutation of earlier *u*. The second of these usages, whose development can be reconstructed by logical means, will be discussed here.

The phonetic processes involved in *i*-mutation may be summarised thus: 'the mode of utterance of an accented vowel [is approximated] to that of an *i* or *i̯* [i.e. [j]] of the following syllable' (Campbell 1959: 72); in other words, to produce [y], an older close rounded *back* vowel [u] took on the *front* quality of the vowel in the following syllable. The [i, j] of the unstressed syllable was generally subsequently lost and does not appear in the written records of Old English, although its sometime presence can be detected, for example by comparison with the early Germanic language in which the mutation does not seem to have taken place, Gothic. The distinctive feature adopted was 'frontness' or palatality.[2]

The process of *i*-mutation is clearly demonstrated in the development of the Anglo-Saxon runic script, the *futhorc*. *I*-mutation is an innovation in prehistoric Old English, and the earlier West Germanic runic script, the *futhark*, did not have a rune for '*i*-mutated *u*'. The runemasters, therefore, faced by this new phenomenon, devised an ingenious expedient; they took the runes ᚾ and ᛁ, usually transliterated as 'u' and 'i' respectively, and blended them to produce ᚣ 'y'. That this represents the operation of *i*-mutation on older *u* is demonstrated by the inscription ᚹᚣᛚᛁᚠ 'wylif' (= Present-Day English 'she-wolf') on the Auzon (Franks) Casket (*c.* 700 AD). Old English *wylf* (fem.) corresponds to the masculine *wulf* (Proto-Germanic **wulfi-, *wulfa-*); the minimal pair in recorded Old English demonstrates the phonemicisation.[3]

ALLOPHONIC VARIATION

It will have been observed from the discussion so far that phonological changes in the spoken mode do map onto the written language when the latter is comparatively fluid, even if at some removes and even though the written mode needs careful philological analysis. It will also have been observed that *variation* in the allophonic realisation of phonemes is a necessary prerequisite – that is, it provides the *potential* – for the process of phonemicisation; and this observation correlates with the discussion of the mechanisms of change outlined in Chapter 3 above.

The production of allophonic variants, which may be metaphorically described as the small change of phonological evolution, can be widely observed in Present-Day English, and it is perhaps worth beginning this stage of the discussion by considering the sources and kinds of allophonic variation which can exist. These allophonic variants exist within the wide bounds of each phoneme's *variational space*, the important notion which was introduced in Chapter 3. Variation within the phonological space of an individual can be produced by such mechanical factors as follows:

1 *Assimilation phenomena*, whether between segments (e.g. Present-Day English [brɛtθ] *breadth*, where the original [d], indicated by the spelling ⟨d⟩, has taken on the voiceless quality of the neighbouring [θ]; cf. the related adjective *broad*) or at a distance (e.g. mutation or 'umlaut', as recorded in Present-Day Southern US English; cf. the difference in the quality of the stressed vowel in such pairs of words as 'jelly' with [ɛ] : 'cellar' with [ɛ̈], 'horrid' with [ɑ+] : 'horror' with [ɑ], recorded by Wells 1982: 533–534. The quality of the stressed vowel in

such words seems to be determined by the quality of the following unstressed vowel).

2 *Loss or addition of segments* (e.g. Present-Day Scots [fak] for fact, or Present-Day Southern US English diphthongisation ('breaking') in words like [lɪəp] *lip*; see Wells 1982: 535).

3 *Conflation of repeated sequences* (e.g. ['vɛtənrɪ] for *veterinary*).

4 *Dissimilation within phonological space*: a good example is found in the dialects of German in modern Switzerland. Samuels (1972: 31) notes that certain

> Swiss dialects possessing the three phonemes /ɑː/, /æː/ and /ɔː/ use only central allophones of /ɑː/, whereas those with only the two phonemes /ɑː/ and /æː/ have a greater allophonic range for /ɑː/ and typically show a more retracted vowel.

> In Present-Day English, it is noticeable that retraction of /ɑː/ is found in dialects where fronting of Middle English /a/ has occurred; retraction is not generally found in dialects where fronting of Middle English /a/ has not occurred, and which therefore retain original quantitative distinctions between /a/ and /aː/. A good example of the latter is Jamaican English (see Wells 1982: 575).

5 *Metatheses*, that is, reversal in the ordering of segments (e.g. Present-Day Southern English [aks], [wɔps] for *ask, wasp*), or *metanalyses*, where the boundaries between words are reassigned, such as Present-Day Standard English *an adder* for older (and still-dialectal) *nadder* (cf. the Present-Day German cognate *Natter*).

6 *Analogical formations introducing variable word-stress*, for instance ['kɔntrəˌvəsɪ] for [kən'trɔvəsɪ] *controversy*, on the model of [ˌkɔntrə'vəʃəl] *controversial*.

7 Variants may also be produced in conditions of *greater or lesser stress*. Thus a word like *yes* can be realised in speech as [jɛs] or [jə] depending on context. The effects of stress on segments have been experimentally proved: in vowels it has been shown that stress induces more close and fronted tongue-positions, for example stressed [dæʊn] *down*! beside less stressed [daʊn] *down* in Present-Day London English, while in consonants aspirated variants are produced, such as stressed [ghəʊ] *go!* beside less stressed [gəʊ] *go*. Similarly, the realisation of /iː/ in *meat* may vary between (say) [ɪi] and [iː] depending on the degree of stress assigned to the word.

8 Finally, phonetic realisations can change over time, as the individual grows. It is an observable physiological fact that a child's realisation of a particular sound differs in acoustic quality from that of an adult (see Lieberman 1984: 159).

Then there is *contact*-induced variation. It can, of course, happen on a microlinguistic scale; every individual's set of phonological realisations differs slightly, given the slight variation in size and/or shape of each human vocal tract, and thus any speaker will encounter a range of slight variation in everyday conversation. Processes of readjustment can follow as a result of monitoring. But this process also occurs on a macrolinguistic scale when one speech-community, through invasion, immigration or social aspiration, comes into contact with another; and it can be very subtle. Thus some Southern English people prototypically realise the ⟨a⟩ in *cat* with [æ], whereas other more Northerly people prototypically realise it as [a]. This kind of contact can introduce new elements into the variational space for an item within a community, and subsequent readjustments can result.

One such readjustment is *hypercorrection* or (perhaps more accurately) *hyperadaptation*, which has already been defined on pages 26–27 above. Faced with messy phonetic variation in their linguistic communities, users 'miss the target' in the way in which they interpret and reflect the phonetic outputs they encounter, in a situation of monitoring; pragmatic and socio-linguistic pressures are frequently present here. Thus an habitual '*h*-dropper' may, in certain circumstances, introduce an initial *h*- into all sorts of situations where initial *h*- never existed in the past (e.g. [haɪ] for *I*).

Such mechanical and contact-induced variation contributes to the pool of available variation in any speech-community, itself made up of usages inherited from earlier in the variety's history or borrowed from varieties with which the host variety has come into contact. These inherited and borrowed usages may be described as 'givens'; and it is argued here that the interaction between givens and the kinds of variation described above provides us with a good model of the variational space available at any stage in the history of English.

This range of variation represents the *potential* for linguistic change; the *triggering* (or *actuation*) and *implementation* of the change takes place when a number of linguistic processes interact to produce a systemic development. To demonstrate the workings of this interaction, two examples will be chosen: one is from Present-Day English, to do with the distribution of certain dental and fricative sounds in the Present-Day Liverpudlian accent, Scouse; the other example is the Great Vowel Shift of the fifteenth and sixteenth centuries.

TREES AND WAVES: A PRESENT-DAY ENGLISH EXAMPLE

The first example for discussion is a recent development which clearly demonstrates the close relationship of extra- to intralinguistic mechanisms in the triggering of sound-change, and which shows the emergence of a new phonological distribution. Incidentally, it also demonstrates nicely the way in which concentration on phonology at the expense of allophonic realisations can cause something significant to be missed about the way in which sound-change takes place.

The example chosen here is Scouse, a working-class variety of English spoken in Liverpool. The origins of this variety have been studied in detail by G. Knowles (1978: 1):

> Scouse is the dialect which developed in Liverpool in the nineteenth century, and has since spread to the surrounding dialects of Lancashire and Cheshire. Until the middle of the last century, Liverpool drew its population from the counties of the North-West of England; but after the potato famine of the 1840s, hundreds of thousands of Irishmen passed through its port, and many of them settled there. At the time of the 1861 census, 25 per cent of the city population were Irish immigrants. The resulting dialect is an interesting hybrid: on the phonological level it remains similar to the dialects of neighbouring Northern towns, but phonetically it has been heavily influenced by Anglo-Irish.

In Present-Day English, the blend of North-West English and Anglo-Irish culture manifests itself in Scouse pronunciation. On the one hand, Scouse shares important structural features with Northern England, notably in vocalism. Distinctions of the *foot*/*strut* and *trap*/*bath* type, characteristic of the Southern half of England, have not occurred in Scouse; thus *mud* : *good* (both with [ʊ]), *pass* : *gas* (both with [a]) are good rhymes in this variety (see Wells 1982: 371; cf. RP [fʊt, strʌt, træp, bɑθ]). The distinctions do, however, appear in Irish English (Wells 1982: 419), even if the phonetic realisations are rather different from Southern English usage.

The phonetic realisations of a number of phonemes demonstrate the clear impact of Southern Irish English on Scouse, however. Thus, for /θ, ð/, [t̪, d̪] appear; Knowles (1974: 323) found forms such as [t̪ɾiː] *three*, [t̪ɹuːt̪] *truth*, [mʊnt̪] *month*, [d̪at] *that* in the speech of many working-class Catholic Liverpudlians. Such forms are generally characteristic of Southern Irish English. In terms of phonemic structure, however, there is for the most part no difference between Scouse and more widespread Northern English usage, for minimal pairs such as *tin* : *thin* in both varieties attest to the existence of distinct phonemes. The difference is a phonetic one, and it seems to correlate with social class. In calling for a theory of 'sociolinguistic phonetics', Knowles has noted the importance of quite delicate phonetic distinctions in marking sociolinguistic differentiation.

There are indications, though, that contact with Irish English is beginning to affect the *phonological* structure of Scouse – in other words, allophonic variation is leading to a phonological development in the way described in general terms at the outset of this chapter. In some varieties of Scouse, [dat] *that* appears as a variable beside [d̪at]. The use of [dat] as opposed to [d̪at] is specifically a feature of urban varieties of Southern Irish English, for instance those used in Dublin. It may be presumed that this development is not unconnected with interaction with British English varieties, commonplace in the Irish capital. The English stereotype of Irish pronunciation, reflected in spellings such as *tink*, *tirty* for 'think, thirty', includes the use of /t, d/ for /θ, ð/. The reason is that [t̪, d̪] in British English accents are typically realisations of /t, d/ in particular conditioning environments, such as neighbouring /θ, ð/, for example *eighth*, *not that*, whereas in Irish English [t̪, d̪] are realisations of a distinct phoneme, /θ, ð/. In an urban environment of weak social ties, where Irish and British English accents will be monitored together, the adoption of the English stereotype by Dubliners marking their distinctive Irishness is to be expected.

The question of the appropriate phonemic symbol for the Irish dental phonemes corresponding to the English fricatives is worth some brief discussion. J.C. Wells puts the issue fairly as follows, and in so doing indicates that British and Irish English – just as Southern English and Scots – are part of the same linguistic continuum and thus liable to interact with each other:

> We could of course choose to symbolize the Irish English dental phonemes as /t̪/ and /d̪/ rather than as the phonetically inaccurate /θ/ and /ð/. But this would raise other difficulties, particularly when making a phonemic transcription of the many middle-class southern Irish who fluctuate between plosive and fricative realizations.
>
> (Wells 1982: 429)

The present-day Liverpudlian variety of English, it would seem, is a good example of at least three things relevant to the argument of this book. First, it shows how the variational characteristics of an individual variety relate closely to historical development. Second, it is a good example of the way in which, in the twentieth century, urban developments have become linguistic focal points for the surrounding countryside. Finally, it demonstrates the way in which a given variety emerges from a mixture of *inheritance* (i.e. from Northern ancestors) and *contact* (i.e. through interaction with Irish English).

A DESCRIPTION OF THE GREAT VOWEL SHIFT

It has just been argued that the triggering of a particular linguistic change was the result of the interplay between very small distinctions between varieties. In the remainder of this chapter, it will be suggested that the existence of such fine distinctions, with subsequent interaction between varieties, lies behind at least some of the most important large-scale sound-changes in the history of English, notably the Great Vowel Shift of the fifteenth and sixteenth centuries. This sound change, which was first christened 'Great' by O. Jespersen, was recently described as 'a revolution in the pronunciation of long vowels whose causes remain mysterious' (Pinker 1994: 250). The aim here is to present an account of the origins and development of the Shift which correlates with the model of change being developed in this book.

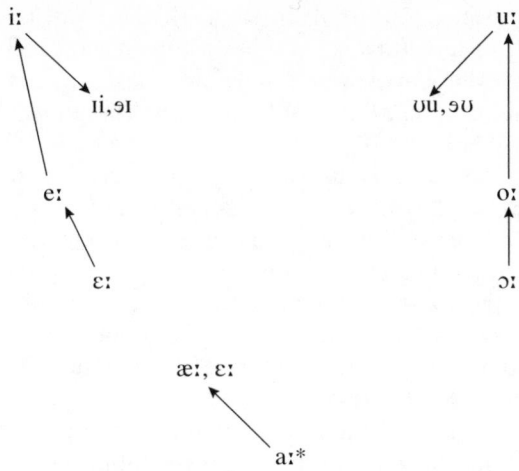

* the result of MEOSL, phonemicised through loss of final -*e*.

Figure 5.1 The Great Vowel Shift (traditional model, after Görlach 1991: 67)

It seems appropriate first of all, however, to give some account of the process of implementation of the change once triggered, since it is from the analysis of the patterns of implementation that the hypothesis as to the triggering of the Shift is derived. Figure 5.1 is a traditional diagrammatic representation of the process of the Shift (after Görlach 1991: 67). In brief: in the fifteenth and sixteenth centuries, the lexical distribution of the long-vowel phonemes of Late Middle English changed radically in an apparently ordered way. These vowels were raised or, if in close position already, diphthongised; examples in Southern English are /liːf/ > /ləɪf/ *life*, /huːs/ > /həʊs/ *house*, /deːd/ > /diːd/ *deed*, /goːd/ > /guːd/ *good*, /dɛːl/ > /deːl/ *deal*, /bɔːt/ > /boːt/ *boat*, /naːmə/ > /nɛːm/ *name*. The latter transcriptions given here, of course, represent the immediate outcome of the Shift-process; subsequent raisings, shortenings and diphthongisations during and since the Early Modern English period have modified these outputs.

Traditionally it has been argued that the triggering of the Shift demanded as a precondition two processes acting in combination: a tendency of the close vowels to produce diphthongal allophones, and a tendency of the mid- and open vowels to produce raised allophones. Both processes, whereby the *potential* for the triggering of change is set up, are entirely conceivable phonetically as the result of the selection of forceful- and relaxed-style variants within the variational space available for each phoneme; both phenomena have been observed in modern varieties of English.

In stage I, the phonemes /iː/ and /uː/ developed within their respective variational spaces a series of slurred relaxed realisations with preceding on-glides: [ɪi], [əɪ] and [ʊu], [əʊ]. In stage II, the mid-close vowels /eː/, /oː/ were raised, in forceful-style conditions, to /iː/, /uː/ respectively, and the [ɪi], [ʊu] type allophones were phonemicised; in turn, Middle English /ɛː/, /ɔː/ were raised to /eː/, /oː/, and Middle English /aː/ was raised to /ɛː/ (Wells 1982: 184–186).

At first sight, such an account of the Shift involves a major paradox, and a number of scholars have been reluctant to accept it (e.g. Stockwell and Minkova 1988a: 357). Why does it require in some parts of the process the selection of forceful-style variants and, in others, relaxed ones? The answer must be to do with functional monitoring, for if only forceful-style variants were always selected there would be a concentration of vowels in the close and mid-close area, reducing the potential for meaningful distinctions (Samuels 1972: 41–43).

Another characteristic of the Shift is that it appears to have operated more thoroughly in some parts of the English-speaking area than in others. In the North of England and in Scotland, for instance, the Shift seems to have operated on the front-vowel system inherited from Late Middle English, but to have largely failed in the back series; cf. the Present-Day Scots forms *coo*, *hoo*, *noo* [kuː, huː, nuː] 'cow', 'how', 'now', from Old English *cū*, *hū*, *nū*). The retention of undiphthongised close back vowels from the Middle English period is not restricted to Scots but is also found in Northern England (see Kolb 1966). The Shift, then, would seem to have operated to its fullest extent in the Southern half of England.

EVIDENCE FOR THE GREAT VOWEL SHIFT

The occurrence and dating of the Shift can be proved by an examination of the fate of loanwords into English. For instance, the stressed vowels in words such as *tureen*, *soup* in Present-Day English have not been subjected to diphthongisation because they were borrowed into English after the Shift ceased to operate, whereas words like *round*, *guile*, which entered English before *c*. 1400, have been so subjected. (cf. French *terrine*, *soupe*, *rond-/round-*, *guile*).

The development may be further illustrated by an early source of evidence: the late-fifteenth-century anonymous Welsh *Hymn to the Virgin*. The *Hymn to the Virgin* was composed, a little before 1500, as an attempt to apply Welsh orthography and metrical practice to an English text. The circumstances of its composition are peculiar; according to one version of its prologue, it was written because

> It happened once in Oxford that the Englishmen were scoffing at the Welsh and dispraising them greatly because of their lack of scholarship. ... [A Welshman responded by composing] this English ode in *Cynghanedd groes*, which an Englishman cannot compose.
>
> (trans. Dobson 1955: 112)

The importance of the Welsh *Hymn* is that it is the best early evidence for the diphthongisation of Middle English /iː, uː/ and the raising of Middle English /eː, oː/ to be had. Since the phonetic significance of the Welsh spelling used in the Welsh *Hymn* is known, it is possible to interpret forms such as the following as representing diphthongal or raised sounds, such as ⟨swn⟩ (with Welsh ⟨w⟩ /u(ː)/) 'soon' (Old English *sōna*); ⟨Kreist⟩ (with Welsh ⟨ei⟩ /əi/) 'Christ' (Old English *Crīst*); ⟨kwin⟩ (with Welsh ⟨i⟩ /i(ː)/) 'queen' (Old English *cwēn*); ⟨wythowt⟩ (with Welsh ⟨ow⟩ /əu/) 'without' (Old English *wiþūtan*).[4]

Other fifteenth-century evidence, such as sporadic rhyming practice in contemporary verse, or occasional spellings in private letters of the period, such as those of the Pastons and the Celys, is usually hard to interpret. However, for what it is worth, the evidence of the Welsh *Hymn* is supported by sporadic spellings in other fifteenth-century texts: *credyll* 'cradle' (Bokenham's *Poems*, *c.* 1443), *symed* 'seemed' (in letters written for Margaret Paston) (see further Wyld 1923: 21).

THE PROBLEM OF TRIGGERING

The evidence for the Shift's having taken place, therefore, is fairly clear, and the processes involved in its implementation seem to be phonetically straightforward. However, the problem of triggering remains: why did the change happen, why did it happen when and where it did, and why did it stop? What caused the selection of particular variables but not others in an apparently ordered sequence? In attempting to answer these questions, a number of different solutions will be put forward, for there seems at least a possibility that the circumstances (and perhaps even the date) of actuation varied diatopically. It will be demonstrated that an understanding of both extra- and intralinguistic contexts is essential if an understanding of the origins of the phenomenon is to be achieved.

EXTRALINGUISTIC CORRESPONDENCES I: THE RISE OF LONDON

In accounting for any historical event, the first objective is to assemble the correspondences between that event and others contemporary with it. The Great Vowel Shift seems to have begun in the South-East of England in the years after 1400, and there are two key extralinguistic developments which correspond with it: the development of an urban setting for the vernacular, and the appearance of class-based standardisation in speech.

It has long been known that the history of the English language correlates with geography. Even in Roman times, before the coming of the Anglo-Saxons, the province of Britannia was divided into a richer and more prosperous South and East, and a poorer and more barren North and West. This distinction derives from the geology of the countryside; most first-class land appears in an area to the south of a line running from the River Humber to the headwaters of the River Severn, whereas vast tracts of the West Country, Wales, the North of England and Scotland are characterised by much poorer land-quality than in more southerly and easterly counties. This distinction, of course, is a crude generalisation. There were, and are, obvious pockets of prosperity outside the South and East, such as Fife in Scotland, or the counties of Herefordshire and Worcestershire in the South-West Midlands; and agricultural developments, such as the clearing of fertile virgin land in Yorkshire associated with medieval monastic foundations, blur the North-West/South-East distinction. Nevertheless, such a distinction is accepted by geographers as a broadly true assessment of Britain's wealth in land. And wealth in land has been central to the nation's economic development; until the Industrial Revolution of the late eighteenth and nineteenth centuries, which brought about the rise of the great industrial cities of the North, Britain was an agricultural country with few urban centres.

The demographic implications of this geographical setting are plain. The population of the British Isles has always tended to be concentrated in the South and East; this area has traditionally attracted immigrants from the poorer parts of the country, and its societies may be characterised as consisting of rather weak social networks within a comparatively fluid class structure. In contrast, the North and West for much of the last two millennia has been an area of pioneering or wilderness societies, characterised by strong social ties over long distances – needed in a relatively hostile natural environment – and by long-sustained hierarchical loyalties.

It is, therefore, no coincidence that, until the Industrial Revolution of the late eighteenth and nineteenth centuries, the North and West of England was politically conservative, maintaining Anglo-Saxon and Norse traditions after the Norman Conquest, and supporting the Catholic Church against Henry VIII in the sixteenth century and king against parliament in the seventeenth. The South and East has been consistently more radical; it is in this area that we see the rise of a middle class towards the end of the Middle Ages and the creation, in London, of what was for many years the only English city comparable in size to European conurbations.

The rise in the size and importance of London is the most distinctive feature of late medieval society, and its rapid development seems to coincide in date with the triggering of the Great Vowel Shift. Towns in the Middle Ages provided trading opportunities, being centres for the markets and fairs which were essential for a developing economy; they also made possible the development of craft-skills. London was by far the most important of these concentrations, being the seat of government as well as the country's major trading port, and it attracted immigrants from further and further afield during the course of the period, especially as agrarian development increased the population beyond that which could

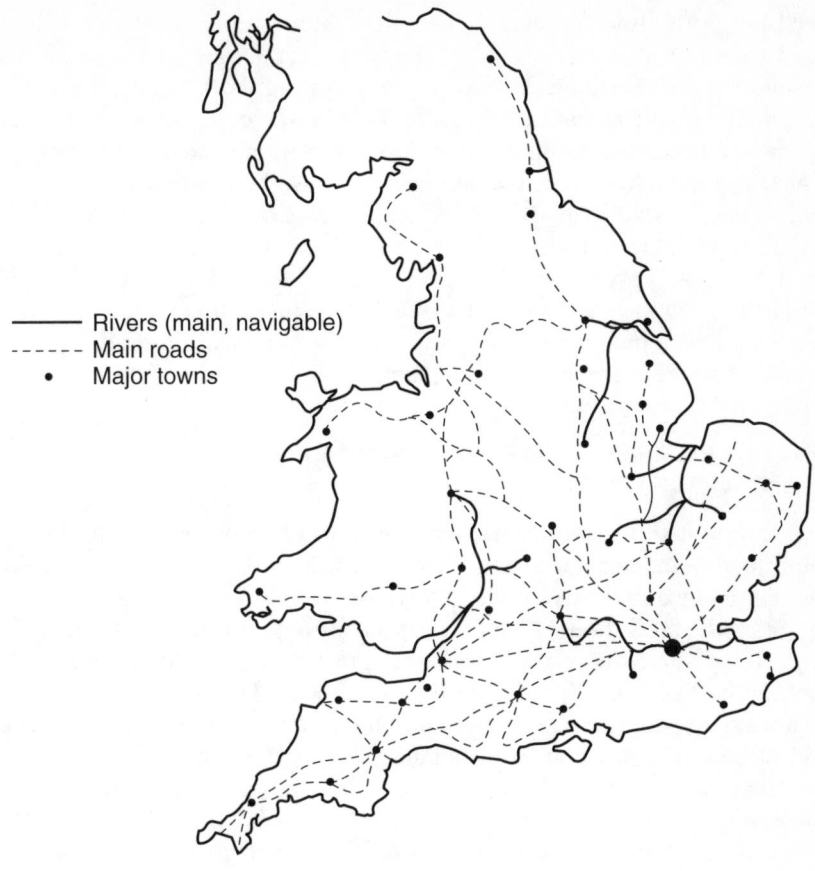

Figure 5.2 Main road and river systems, *c.* 1600 (after Falkus and Gillingham 1981: 179)

be supported by the land. Modern demographic research (recorded in e.g. Burnley 1983: 112–113) has reconstructed the pattern of immigration into the capital during the thirteenth and fourteenth centuries; this pattern has already been discussed in the previous chapter, in that the evolution of written language in London during the fourteenth and fifteenth centuries demonstrates the appearance within London usage of forms deriving from Midlands dialects. Figure 5.2 (after Falkus and Gillingham 1981: 179) shows how London was at the centre of contemporary road- and water-borne communication.

William the Conqueror's *Domesday Book* of 1086 reveals that the land, the basis of medieval economic and political power, was controlled by a relatively small class of landlords, consisting of the king, his magnates and leading churchmen and ecclesiastical institutions; and this structure persisted even after the Dissolution of the Monasteries by Henry VIII in the sixteenth century. However, there were fluctuations and signs of new developments. The slump in population following the Black Death in the fourteenth century meant a labour shortage and a consequent increase in prosperity for the remaining lower-class population, which could demand higher incomes. And the development of towns like London favoured the emergence of an urban middle class – a level of society which rose to prominence in the sixteenth and seventeenth centuries, asserting its power most formidably in the English Civil Wars of the 1640s. It might there-fore be expected, given the model of language in relation to society which has been developed in this book, that linguistic change during this period is likely to reflect dynamic social change.

EXTRALINGUISTIC CORRESPONDENCES II: STANDARDISATION

The second extralinguistic correspondence to the Shift is that it is during the fifteenth and sixteenth centuries that evidence begins to be found for the appearance of a standardised form of speech. Whereas the evidence for the standardisation of writing can be observed directly, through the analysis of surviving manuscripts and printed books, the evidence for the standardisation of speech can only be retrieved indirectly, through the analysis of contemporary commentary on the state of the spoken language, and through the procedures of linguistic reconstruction.

Before the sixteenth century, the evidence is very uncertain for stan-dardisation of speech. Often cited in this context is the attempt by the Londoner Geoffrey Chaucer to represent Northern speech in his charac-terisation of two students in *The Reeve's Tale* (see Tolkien 1934; also Smith 1995 and references there cited). However, although Chaucer may mock the Northernisms of these young men, his humour seems to be based upon the oddness of people from different parts of the country rather than from a sense of a standardised spoken language; the two Northerners in the poem seem, in any case, to be of a slightly higher social class than the Cambridgeshire miller whom they fool. Social class does not seem to have been distinguished by dialect or accent in the generations preceding Chaucer; rather, English-speakers who wished to mark their social distinc-tiveness during the fourteenth century seem to have adopted the expe-dient of studding their language with French-derived vocabulary.

During the fifteenth century, however, there is some evidence for the existence of prestigious models of speech in which the socially marked forms were not restricted to vocabulary. Perhaps the earliest example showing that spoken dialect (grammar and pronunciation) is socially significant is the use of a 'Southren tothe' by the comic sheepstealer Mak in the Wakefield (Yorkshire) *Second Shepherds' Play*, which dates from the early fifteenth century. Mak's affectation of Southern dialect

features of grammar, beside French-derived vocabulary, seems to correlate with the claim he makes that he is a 'yoman ... of the kyng' (Cawley
1958: 48).

It is true that, well into the sixteenth century, courtiers such as Sir
Thomas Wyatt could retain Kenticisms in their speech without, apparently,
any contemporary social stigmatisation; and, although his variety of speech
attracted contemporary comment, Sir Walter Raleigh seems to have
suffered no discrimination in his career on account of his Devon dialect.
Even so, from the sixteenth century the early writers on English pronunciation do begin to describe how the 'best' language is to be found at
'court'.

Probably the most famous contemporary comment on the evolution of
a spoken prestigious form of English is that made by George Puttenham
(*The Arte of English Poesie*, 1589). According to Puttenham, the accom-
plished poet should adopt the usage of 'the better brought vp sort':

> ye shall therfore take the vsuall speach of the Court, and that of London
> and the shires lying about London within lx. myles, and not much aboue.
> (cited Burnley 1992: 224–225)

Such descriptions have a sociolinguistic significance. If a prestigious
language-variety has emerged in a situation of social ferment – as we know
the period to have been marked by – then it may be presumed that there
were people seeking to achieve this prescriptive norm of English even if
it were not their original usage. The most obvious group to be identified
with such seekers are the emerging middle classes of the period; peasantry and aristocracy can be assumed to be comparatively secure in their
social position, and thus strongly tied to the society around them, whereas
the middle classes are notoriously a social group on the move, characterised by weak social ties.

Such weakly tied people were distinguished by contemporary writers
on language. A number of the orthoepists of the sixteenth and seventeenth centuries make similar comments to those made by Puttenham,
and, in doing so, they condemn those who practise 'dialectal' or 'affected'
speech. Perhaps the best-known group of folk thus stigmatised are those
known as the *Mopsae*, who are referred to by John Milton's teacher
Alexander Gil in his *Logonomia Anglica* (1619, 1621). What Gil meant
by the term is still a matter of scholarly controversy; but, if his statements
are taken at face value, the Mopsae would seem to be persons whose
social position has parallels in present-day society. The Mopsae were, in
the current jargon, 'upwardly mobile', the kind of people characterised
by sociolinguists as having weak ties to their social class and local area,
and thus prone to hypercorrect or overshoot when faced by linguistic
systems perceived by them as prestigious. In other words, they are people
who ape their social superiors while originating from lower strata
of society. The key point to note here is to do with the appearance of

perceived sociolinguistic hypercorrection in their language, which suggests that a 'higher' pronunciation was recognised by this date. Although Gil is vague about who they were – their name is simply a conventional adoption from classical pastoral, indicating country origins and femininity – they would seem most plausibly to be identified with the rising urban middle classes of the period; we shall be returning to them again towards the end of this chapter. Their significance at this point in our argument is to do with their appearance at this date; Gil, in fact, is the earliest of the orthoepists to assert clearly 'that all people who are well born and well educated use a common form of speech' (Dobson 1968: 142), and thus to identify a spoken form of 'Standard English'.

INTRALINGUISTIC CORRESPONDENCES I:
THE LOSS OF FINAL *-E*

In addition to correspondences with extralinguistic developments, the Great Vowel Shift corresponds in date and place with two intralinguistic phenomena: a grammatical change known as 'the loss of final *-e*', and the phonemicisation of a quantitative change known as Middle English Open Syllable Lengthening. It will be argued that there is a linkage between these phenomena and the origins of the Shift, and it is therefore necessary to examine each in turn.

It is a well-known phenomenon in the history of English that inflectional endings in Old English were subject to loss, syncretism and obscuration towards the end of the first millennium AD – all signs that inflections were less important for expressing relationships between and within phrases. This development, part of an ongoing process in the Germanic languages, will be pursued further in Chapter 7; however, it is relevant for the next stage of our argument that some discussion of the phenomenon is presented at this point.

In the fifteenth century inflectional endings other than those in use in Present-Day English were finally lost, the result being that 'the most significant prosodic change in the history of the language [took place] ... by which English became the most monosyllabic language in Europe' (Samuels 1972: 145). This change is known as 'the loss of final *-e*'.

There are already indications of the disappearance of final *-e* in unstressed, mostly closed-class words in Late Old Northumbrian texts of the eleventh century, where forms such as *hir, þær, þonn, son* appear beside *hire, þære, þonne, sona*; and, in Northern Middle English texts, final *-e* in stressed words disappears from at the latest the thirteenth century onwards. The obscuration of unstressed syllables is a feature of all the Late Old English dialects, but the dialectal distribution of the loss of *-e* suggests strongly that it was encouraged by contact with Old Norse. Large-scale contact between Old Norse and Old Anglian has traditionally been assumed to favour inflectional weakening and, ultimately, loss.

In the South and Midlands, final -*e* remained until the early fifteenth century, especially as an adjectival inflection. This is evidenced by (for example) the metrical usage of Chaucer, where final -*e* was used in adjectives as a marker of plurality and/or definiteness, thus:

the gode man 'the good man'
gode men 'good men'
but *god man* 'good man'

Particular pressure to retain such an -*e* would come about in poetic contexts, where rhythmical regularity would be an important requirement. (There would not be similar pressure to retain -*e* in polysyllabic adjectives, since they would not form part of a regular sequence of metrical feet.)

Final -*e*, although it performed a useful prosodic function in Chaucerian English, was eventually lost, however. The reason must be to do with language-contact; the evidence from the development of written incipient standardised language is that London English was becoming increasingly influenced by Central Midland dialects during the late fourteenth and early fifteenth centuries (see Chapter 4 above, *passim*), and these dialects, which had a distinct prosody, had ceased to use final -*e* long before. The complete loss of final -*e* in London English, therefore, may be seen as a belated and indirect effect of the Scandinavian invasions.

INTRALINGUISTIC CORRESPONDENCES II: MIDDLE ENGLISH OPEN SYLLABLE LENGTHENING

The obscuration of unstressed syllables in the history of English is relevant to the next stage of the argument, which is to do with quantitative change in the history of English.

In Old English, words could be distinguished in meaning by the quantity of the vowels they contain: thus Old English has minimal pairs of the type *god* 'God', *gōd* 'good'. However, this distinction began to be lost towards the end of the Old English period. The loss of this distinction demonstrates the interaction of two forces: articulatory change, and an isochronicity requirement which is an aspect of so-called phonological setting.

The second of these two concepts needs some explanation. It seems to be a feature of English throughout its history that there is a correlation between stress and the length of syllables. This is demonstrated by the way in which stresses occur at regular intervals in the spoken mode; such regularity lies behind the metrical norms of English poetry. Isochronicity, of course, can vary between languages. We perceive this variation, most obviously, in folk speaking a language not their own; thus Southern Europeans will often say something like 'Its-a-nice-a-day' when speaking English in order to maintain the isochronicity requirement of their own language. Such patterns are obviously maintained within speech-communities by the monitoring process outlined in Chapter 3 above; that they are extremely persistent phenomena is proved by the fact that non-native speakers of a foreign tongue, however otherwise fluent and accurate they may be, find it extraordinarily hard to overcome their native isochronicity requirements when attempting speech in another language.

Since this requirement has, amongst other things, implications for the practice of verse, it is from poetry that much of our information about quantitative distributions of Old English vowels is derived; for Old English scansion requires that stress should be placed upon long syllables – that is, a syllable whose end-rhyming element ('peak' and 'coda') consisted of either a long vowel followed by a consonant in the same syllable (e.g. *gōd* 'good'), or a short vowel followed by two consonants in the same syllable (e.g. *cild* 'child'). By a further process, known as *resolution*, stress may be placed on a cluster of two short syllables (e.g. *nama* 'name'). This last example shows that, very roughly, a short syllable was considered to be half the length of a long syllable, and that the rhyming element of a long syllable could consist of one of the following combinations: (where V = any vowel, VV = a long vowel or diphthong, C = any consonant) VCC, VVC or VCV.

Between the Late Old and Late Middle English periods, there seems to have been a series of changes in the quantities of English vowels: lengthening and shortening before certain consonant-groups in the Late Old English Period and, after *c.* 1200, Middle English Open Syllable Lengthening. For the purposes of the argument presented here, the most important was the last of these processes. (For a description and explanation of the Late Old English quantitative changes not discussed here, see Campbell 1959: 120–122, Hogg 1992a: 210–214.)

Middle English Open Syllable Lengthening is a process whereby originally short vowels were lengthened in the stressed open syllables of disyllabic words, for instance Old English *faran* > Middle English *fāren* [faːrən] 'go'. It seems to have been the result of a kind of compensatory lengthening, whereby the isochronicity principle referred to on page 95 above was maintained across two syllables. It would appear that forms such as *faran*, *nama*, which would count as 'resolved' elements in Old English verse, lost in metrical weight, possibly because the vowels in the unstressed syllables became even less stressed; such a process would produce a 'defective' rhyming element, which might be symbolised VCv.

It may be significant that the lengthening was earliest and furthest advanced in the North, where inflectional endings were obscured first as the result of contact between English and Scandinavian. The phenomenon certainly seems to correspond in date with other likely Scandinavian-influenced innovations such as the fronting of long back vowels. Both phenomena perhaps relate to the twelfth-century break-up of tight-knit communities which seems to have accompanied the spread of

Scandinavianised culture northwards and southwards from the original focal area of Viking settlement.

The process of lengthening seems to have taken place in two phases; an earlier phase in which *a*, *e*, *o* were lengthened, and a later phase in which lengthening of *i*, *u* took place. It has been argued that the lowering of *i*, *u* was delayed because closer vowels seem, phonetically, to resist lengthening (Jones 1989: 114). It is worth noting in this connection that, even in Present-Day English, vowels in the North tend to be realised phonetically as more open in quality than in the South (Wells 1982: 356); this fact might account for the reluctance of *i*, *u* to undergo lengthening in the ancestor of the Present-Day Southern English reference accent, Received Pronunciation (only a few examples showing lengthening of *i*, *u* exist in Received Pronunciation, e.g. 'evil' (Old English *yfel*), 'week' (Old English *wicu*); compare Present-Day Received Pronunciation 'written' (Old English *writen*)).

In support of this last point, it may be noted that there is some sixteenth- and seventeenth-century evidence that, in London, Middle English short *e*, *o*, the vowels which were subjected (in certain circumstances) to Open Syllable Lengthening but are otherwise comparatively stable in realisation in the history of English, were realised as a pair of intermediate vowels, half-way between mid-open and mid-close. Thus F. Cercignani (1981: 60) would interpret the evidence of the early phonetician Robert Robinson as implying that Middle English /ɛ/ could be realised at the beginning of the seventeenth century as [ɛ˖] in prestigious speech, a sound roughly comparable with its reflex in Present-Day English Received Pronunciation.

The evidence for the date of Middle English Open Syllable Lengthening is fairly firm. Important negative evidence in this regard is supplied by a poem called the *Ormulum* (MS Oxford, Bodleian Library, Junius 1). This text is a holograph cycle of metrical sermons written by a priest called Orm in Lincolnshire in the late twelfth century; the name of the poem, derived from that of its author, reflects a contemporary liking for titles such as *Speculum* etc. The literary interest of this exceedingly long work (20,000 lines survive, perhaps one-eighth of the planned collection) is slight; but its interest for the historical linguist is conversely great. Orm devised a special phonetic spelling for his sermons to indicate (amongst other things) quantitative distinctions; his use of rhythm suggests that the work was to be intoned, and the use of a special spelling would therefore be an aid to public performance. Because of this special orthography, Orm is an invaluable witness for contemporary English pronunciation. His spelling-practice was not generally imitated, although there are one or two parallels in some late-eleventh-century additions to two early-eleventh-century manuscripts of Ælfric's *Catholic Homilies* (MSS Oxford, Bodleian Library, Bodley 340 and 342; see Sisam 1953: 186–195 for an important discussion).

Most scholars consider that Middle English Open Syllable Lengthening had not happened in the language of Orm, who regularly uses a diacritic indicating a short vowel over vowels which might be presumed to undergo lengthening, for instance *tăkenn* 'take' vs. *takenn* 'token', 'and he avoids disyllabic words with original short vowels in an open syllable in the last foot of his verse, which is required to be a quantitative trochee' (Dobson 1962: 132). However, Middle English Open Syllable Lengthening certainly seems to have taken place by the mid-thirteenth century, being proved by rhymes in texts from that period. For instance, *On god ureisun of ure lefdi* in MS London, British Library, Cotton Nero A.xiv has *reade* 'red' (Old English *rēad*) : *iureden* 'injure' (Old English *gewerdan* with metathesis) 36–37, *ore* 'mercy' (Old English *ār*) : *uorloren* 'lost' (Old English *forloren*) 73–74. This latter text, although surviving in a West Midland manuscript, seems to be East Midland in origin. Middle English Open Syllable Lengthening seems to have begun in the North and spread South (Jordan 1974: 47–48).

It is perhaps worth noting that processes similar to Middle English Open Syllable Lengthening, with similar outputs, are recorded in Scandinavian and Low German (see Haugen 1976: 258–259). A distinction between 'weakened' and 'lost' unstressed vowels has been detected here (see Haugen 1976: 260); and, in the Scandinavian languages, the close and mid stressed vowels *e, i, o, u* seem to have developed more open realisations during the course of the thirteenth century, which realisations seem to have been a prerequisite for lengthening (Gordon 1957: 267). Given the similarities between Scandinavian and Anglian which predate the Viking invasions, it is possible that Old Anglian had lower realisations of the Old English short vowels than the Saxon dialects, which vowels were thus more predisposed to undergo lengthening. Further research, of a comparative nature, might be illuminating in this context.

Since it will be argued that the operation of Middle English Open Syllable Lengthening has a significance for the actuation of the Great Vowel Shift, a special notation (after Dobson 1962) is used from time to time in what follows to represent vowels subject to the process: *i-, u-, a-, e-, o-*. This philological notation has the virtue of avoiding a commitment to a specific phonemic or allophonic interpretation while making clear which vowels are being referred to.

DIALECTAL DIFFERENCES AND INTERACTION IN THE ORIGINS OF THE SHIFT

As in the investigation of any historical event, the origins of the Great Vowel Shift are to be found in the analysis of the correspondences described above. However, a caveat remains. One of the main difficulties faced by students of the Shift is the insistence by some authorities that it is a unitary phenomenon, that is, all manifestations of vowel shifting in varieties of English and Scots during the late Middle Ages are the result of the same triggering mechanism. Of course, this may not necessarily be the case; it is quite possible for two separate sound-changes to take place in different dialects but to appear – because very similar in their effects – to be the same phenomenon. Thus, in Old English, initial palatal consonants had a similar effect on following vowels in West Saxon and in Old Northumbrian, but the absence of a similar phenomenon in the intermediate Mercian dialects suggests that the two sound-changes, although similar in outcome, were triggered differently. (On the role of initial palatal consonants in sound-change in prehistoric Old English, see Campbell 1959: 64–71, Hogg 1992a: 106–121.)

Thus it is important in studying a major development, such as the Great Vowel Shift, to be aware that the triggers of the change may differ diatopically. Three regions of the country will be examined here, since they demonstrate the range of mechanisms that, it is suggested, was involved in the process: the North (i.e. the English- and Scots-speaking area to the north of a line running approximately between mid-Lincolnshire and the Wirral peninsula), London (with special reference to the class-dialects of the capital) and East Anglia (i.e. modern Norfolk and Suffolk).

THE NORTHERN SHIFT

(See Figures 5.3 and 5.4.) The process of the Shift in the Northern dialects has received, quite rightly, a good deal of attention from scholars (e.g. in Lass 1976). Although the processes involved in the Northern Shift are useful for our understanding of the process of triggering of the wider Shift, it is suggested here that the problem presented by these dialects is distinct from that manifested by more southerly varieties. In the North there was a superfluity of front vowels, brought about most probably through contact with Scandinavian. Thus Old English /iː, eː/ were joined in the front series by /øː/ derived from Old English *ō*, cf. Scots *guid* 'good' beside Southern Middle English *go(o)d*; and Old English *ā*, Old Norse *ā*, which seems to

iː	uː
øː, eː	oː (reflexes of MEOSL only)
ɛː	ɔː (reflexes of MEOSL only)
aː	

Figure 5.3 The Great Vowel Shift in the North (a): pre-Shift

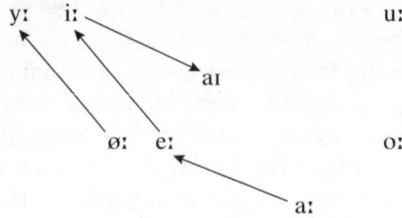

Figure 5.4 The Great Vowel Shift in the North (b): process of Shift

have been a back vowel, was fronted to /aː/, cf. Scots *hame* 'home' beside Southern Middle English *ho(o)m*. Subsequently, the Northern area developed a three-height long-vowel system, brought about by the raising of /ɛː, ɔː/ (see Dobson 1968: 612, 625, 674–675).

It is interesting that the Shift in the North operated in the front series but seems barely to have affected the long back vowels. Thus there must have been conditions that favoured shifting in the former but not in the latter. Part of the explanation may be to do with the comparatively crowded close and mid-close front-vowel system, which must have favoured the dissimilation of phonemes within the available variational space – a phenomenon recorded in a number of languages (see further Moulton 1962). There is a persistent tendency for rounded front vowels, such as /øː/, to unround in the history of English, since roundness, as a distinctive feature, seems to correlate in most dialects of English with back vowels. Thus some varieties of Present-Day Northern English have developed forms such as [gɪəs] 'goose' (Old English *gōs*) (Wells 1982: 359), as the reflex of Middle English [gøːs]; cf. also Present-Day Scots [fɪt] 'foot' (Old English *fōt*). For that reason /øː/, the peculiar Northern reflex of Old English *ō*, must have been liable to contribute, if sporadically, to this pressure.

The development of /aː/ in the North remains a little puzzling; in this region, *a-* had become identified with older /aː/ (derived from the fronting of Old English *ā*, Old Norse *á*), which seems to have undergone a raising to /ɛː/ (or even /eː/) earlier than in the South, especially in the environment of a following [s] (see Dobson 1968: 612, 625; Jordan 1974: 238). It is just possible that this change may have something to do with the Northern development whereby /ai/ merged with older /aː/; in certain parts of the North-West Midlands, Middle English /ai/ is realised as /ɛː/ and, in contact situations, it is possible that older /aː/ may have become associated with this development (see further Jordan 1974: 118, 135–136, 238). Whatever its origin – and further work is needed on this topic – the raising of /aː/ must have contributed to the pressures on the close front vowels which, it is suggested here, triggered the Northern Shift.

In the back vowels, the pressures for the Shift in the Northern dialects would have been much less strong, since original Old English *ō* had been fronted earlier and the system would have been considerably less crowded. This would account for the retention of Old English /uː/ in the North long after its phonemic diphthongisation in other dialects (Figure 5.3). It is even possible that /oː/ < Middle English /ɔː/ in the North is unconnected with the Shift. A Middle English [ɔː] would have appeared in the North probably only as the result of Middle English Open Syllable Lengthening, and there is some evidence that Northern dialects underwent early raising of this [ɔː] to [oː], predating the Shift (see Dobson 1968: 674–675). It can be argued plausibly, therefore, that the pre-Shift back vowels still remain, with slight modifications (notably, in some environments, quantitative), in Present-Day Northern English and Scots.

This Northern Shift may have been comparatively early – perhaps not very long after the merger of Middle English /ai/ with Middle English /aː/ in the late fourteenth century (see Jordan 1974: 135–136). There is some slight evidence that the diphthongisation of Middle English /iː/ proceeded more quickly in the North than elsewhere (see Jordan 1974: 237 and references there cited). However, the Northern Shift cannot have been the source for the similar process in the South, for at least two reasons: first, it took place in a part of the country comparatively isolated from the rest; and, second, it failed in the back series of Middle English long vowels, which were fully affected by the Shift in the South.

THE SOUTHERN AND MIDLANDS SHIFTS

The Shift was much more extensive in its effects in Southern and Midland Middle English; and here it is argued that the extralinguistic and intra-linguistic correspondences indicated on pages 89–98 above are crucial in accounting for the development.

The key process here is phonemicisation, as described on pages 80–81 above. In some dialect regions, new phonemes emerged in English as a result of Middle English Open Syllable Lengthening. These new phonemes, in many Southern and Midland areas, do not seem to have emerged until the loss of final -e. Until that time, a-, e-, o- would simply have been perceived as lengthened allophones of /a, ɛ, ɔ/ (= Old English a/æ, e, o), and court-poets like Chaucer and Gower, who represent the rhyming practice of an exalted social circle, distinguish between /eː/, /oː/, /ɛː/, /ɔː/ and e-, o- in their rhymes (see Dobson 1962: 134–135 and references there cited).

This habit contrasts with the practice of merging e-, o- with /ɛː/, /ɔː/ adopted in other Midland and Southern dialects, such as that represented by *On god ureisun of ure lefdi*, referred to on page 98 above. Since it seems to be the case, supported by Present-Day English and orthoepistical evidence, that Chaucer's short /ɛ, ɔ/ vowels had a slightly closer quality than those used further North, lengthened /ɛ, ɔ/ [ɛ⊥, ɔ⊥] would have been realised as [ɛː⊥, ɔː⊥] in the dialects descended from the poet's. The best-known evidence for such a distinction in Chaucer's own language is offered by the stanza from *Troilus and Criseyde* (Book V, lines 22ff.), in which *loore* 'teaching' and *more* 'more' have /ɔː/ (from Old English *ā*), and *forlore* 'lost entirely', *more* 'root' (Old English *moru*), *tofore* 'before' have *o-*:

> This Troilus, withouten reed or loore,
> As man that hath his joies ek forlore,
> Was waytyng on his lady evere more
> As she that was the sothfast crop and more
> Of al his lust or joies heretofore.
> But Troilus, now far-wel al thi joie,
> For shaltow nevere sen hire eft in Troie!
> (Benson 1988: 560)

With the loss of final *-e*, however, *a-*, *e-*, *o-* became phonemic in the dialect which descended from Chaucer's. There would thus have resulted two competing phonological systems in the London area:

System I /eː/, *e-* (now phonemic, presumably /ɛːˑ/), /ɛː/ – used by those people who may be roughly characterised as descendants of Chaucer (i.e. those from the high social circles which Chaucer represented); this variety, in which *e-* was a closer vowel than /ɛː/, may reasonably be supposed to have held prestige;

System II /eː/, /ɛː/, in which *e-* had merged with /ɛ/ – used by many Southern and Midland speakers other than those just characterised as descendants of Chaucer.

Parallel systems would have existed for the back vowels, that is, I: /oː/, *o-*, /ɔː/; II: /oː/, /ɔː/ (see Figure 5.5).

(For the next stage in the argument, reference should be made throughout to Figures 5.5 and 5.6.) When these two systems came into contact, as they would in early-fifteenth-century London, it would be

System I		System II	
iː > ɪi	uː > ʊu	iː > əɪ	uː > əʊ
eː > eːˑ	oː > oːˑ	eː > iː	oː > uː
ɛːˑ*	ɔːˑ*	ɛː > eː	ɔː > oː
ɛː	ɔː		aː* > ɛː, eː
aː* > æː			

Figure 5.5 Competing systems in early-fifteenth-century London (* MEOSL phonemes)

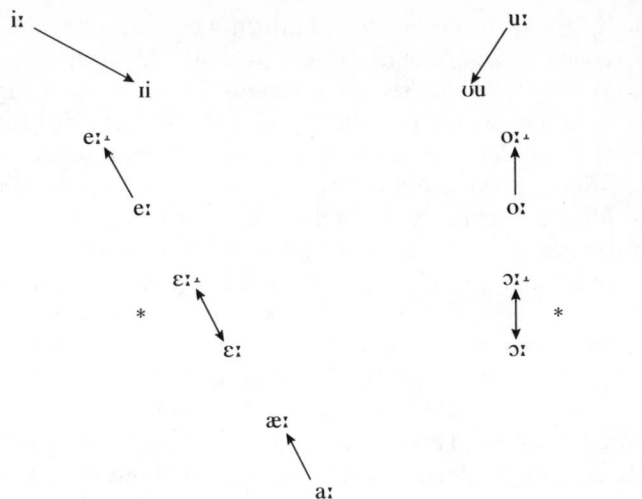

* subsequent merger of ME /ɛː, ɔː/ with ME *e-, o-* on /ɛː, ɔː/, through sociolinguistic distancing.

Figure 5.6 The Great Vowel Shift: Chaucer's descendants

apparent to System-II speakers that (prestigious) System-I speakers used /ɛːᴧ/ in many words where System II had /ɛː/. System-II speakers would have no means of determining which words should have /ɛːᴧ/ and which /ɛː/, since the grammatical marker, final *-e*, had been lost. Thus it would be entirely natural for those System-II speakers attempting to imitate System I to use [ɛːᴧ] – or, more probably, the next closer phoneme in their system, viz. /eː/ – in words in which System-I speakers would have /ɛː/, as well as in those in which System-I speakers had /ɛːᴧ/. A similar situation may be held to have occurred with regard to the back vowels. Such raisings may be considered to represent the beginning of the Shift.

The next problem is to do with the raising of /eː, oː/. Here there is good evidence that System-I speakers would have used raised variants of /eː, oː/, viz. [eːᴧ, oːᴧ]. That Middle English /eː, oː/ were realised in Early Modern English as 'rather lax' /iː, uː/, that is [ɪː, ʊː] or even [eːᴧ, oːᴧ], is proved by adoptions from, for example, Dutch (Dobson 1968: 617–618); a predisposing factor in this context might have been the especially tense [eːᴧ] favoured in contemporary French, which was sporadically realised as *i* in a few fourteenth-century English texts (Dobson 1968: 656). It may be that such uses were encouraged by the continuing habit of signalling social prestige by means of French-derived vocabulary.

System-I speakers, whose social milieu demanded at least an acquaintance with French-derived vocabulary if not grammar, ought to have been capable of realising such pronunciations; and R.B. Le Page has suggested (in Samuels 1972: 145–146) that there would be good reasons for the aristocracy of the late fourteenth and fifteenth centuries 'to adopt affected forms of speech as a means of "role-distancing" from the lower classes, from whom they had hitherto been differentiated by speaking French'. Such raised variants would have been 'marked', that is, stylistically salient, and thus especially liable to occur in forceful-style contexts. Furthermore, they would have been favoured, through functional monitoring, by the raising of Middle English /ɛː, ɔː/ referred to above.

System-II speakers, whose social standing did not involve as intimate a contact with French, would have perceived this raised sound /eː˔, oː˔/ as /iː, uː/, the next closer phoneme in their system. Such a choice would have been favoured by the tendency in their system to produce /eː, oː/ for Middle English /ɛː, ɔː/, which would have exerted upward pressure.

Finally, the diphthongal variants of Middle English /iː, uː/, which existed all the time in relaxed-style contexts, would have been favoured through functional monitoring and selected as 'core' realisations of their phonemes. If the argument above is accepted, it seems likely that this diphthongisation was less advanced amongst System-I speakers than amongst those who used System II, given that Middle English /eː, oː/ were realised as [eː˔, oː˔] in I but [iː, uː] in II.

HART'S *ORTHOGRAPHIE*

The main difficulty in seeing the raising of /ɛː, ɔː/ as the actuating factor for the Shift is that the evidence of the orthoepists, notably that of John Hart, has been held by most scholars to suggest that Middle English /ɛː, ɔː/ did not undergo raising until the end of the sixteenth century, whereas /eː, oː/ had been raised, and /iː, uː/ diphthongised, well before that date.

John Hart (d. 1574) was perhaps the most important English phonetician of the sixteenth century. He was the author of three works on spelling and pronunciation: *The opening of the unreasonable writing of our inglish toung* (1551), dedicated to Edward VI and surviving only in manuscript (MS London, British Library, Royal 17.C.vii); *An Orthographie*, a major work printed in 1569; and *A Methode or comfortable beginning for all vnlearned*, a small primer printed in 1570. Rather little is known of Hart's life, other than that he was from an early age a member of the College of Heralds, becoming Chester Herald in 1566 – an important court position, requiring him to act as a royal messenger as well as to be involved in the intricacies of ceremonial. From his writings on phonetic matters he seems, as might be expected, familiar with the court, and some of his recorded behaviour suggests that he thought himself the social equal of the noble military leaders with whom he had to deal. Despite ancestral roots in Devon, he writes as a Londoner (see Dobson 1968: 62–66).

John Hart's system (see Figure 5.7), as revealed in his *Orthographie*, may be taken to represent the speech of a socially sophisticated Londoner, well acquainted with the 'best' (i.e. most socially approved) contemporary

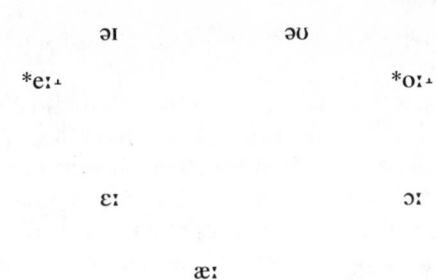

*perhaps more correctly /ɪːʊː/.

Figure 5.7 John Hart's system (1569)

speech through his contact with the court. We should therefore expect Hart to be fully conversant with the speech of the descendants of those who used System I. Yet he does not seem to exhibit a raising of Middle English /ɛː/, and this is apparently demonstrated by his identification of Middle English /ɛː/ with German *ä* and French *e* (see Dobson 1968: 620–621). It is therefore necessary to pursue the problem a little further.

The solution to this difficulty suggested here depends on sociolinguistic distancing. In conditions of interaction with System-II speakers, who would have been regarded as social climbers, it can reasonably be argued that System-I users would have tended to react against the use of /ɛːˑ/. There would be a tendency amongst the latter for a reactive hyperadaptation, in which /ɛː/ would be selected for the older raised phoneme /ɛːˑ/ derived through Middle English Open Syllable Lengthening and the loss of final -*e*. Since the grammatical marker had disappeared, System-I speakers – or, perhaps more correctly, the descendants of System-I speakers – would have no obvious means of distinguishing the correct use of the two vowels. Ultimately, of course, this usage disappeared, to be replaced by reflexes of System II – which, incidentally, is the usual system to be found in sixteenth-century rhyming and punning contexts (see Samuels 1972: 147, Dobson 1968: 400–401).

THE ESSEX CONNECTION

There remains the question of the raising of Middle English [aː]. Leith (1983: 148–149) holds that the Shift began with a raising of Middle English [aː], but this view cannot be accepted since the Shift in the South affected both front and back vowels; it seems clear that Middle English [aː] was a front vowel, and it cannot therefore have exerted pressure on the back series. The evidence, moreover, indicates that Middle English [aː] was not raised at the beginning of the Shift, although the circumstances of its raising, in the South at least, may have been sociolinguistically determined in a manner similar to that involved in the raising of Middle English /ɛː, ɔː/.

One possibility is that the determining factor in the South may have been to do with Essex dialect. In late-fourteenth-century London, poets such as Chaucer would have had a sound [aː] in native words only as a realisation of Middle English Open Syllable Lengthening *a-*, which would not yet be a separate phoneme because final *-e* remained; [aː] would therefore have been an allophone of /a/ (see Dobson 1962: 144–145; see also Cercignani 1981: 101). In Essex, however, whose dialect seems to have correlated with the 'old London' variety which ultimately gave rise to Cockney, *a-* would have become identified with /aː/, the special Essex reflex of Old English *ǣ* (see Jordan 1974: 81–83). When final *-e* was lost, it would have appeared to contemporaries that an Essex usage (viz. phonemic /aː/) had become more widespread; and an attempt would be made, by those seeking to distance themselves from the 'old Londoners', to use closer realisations available in forceful-style contexts, viz. [æː], for which the phonological space now existed given the raising of /ɛː/ to /ɛːⱶ/. Such realisations seem to have survived in fashionable use up to *c.* 1650 (see Dobson 1968: 594), only then being replaced in this register by [eː]-type forms when System-II usage became prestigious.

THE MOPSAE AND THE EASTERNERS

The discussion above throws light on two groups of people who have been felt by many scholars to have been important in the development of the Shift. Following the practice of Alexander Gil, these folk are usually called (a) the 'Mopsae' and (b) the 'Easterners'. As Dobson indicates, it is important not to confuse the two groups (1968: 147), even though their behaviour is in some ways similar.

Gil's 'Easterners' seem to be the inhabitants of East Anglia, and their evidence is of great importance for the later development of mid-vowels in the seventeenth and eighteenth centuries (see Samuels 1972: 146–153). However, their evidence is also important for the triggering of the Shift, for it would appear that many of the processes discussed above had taken place in East Anglia much earlier than in London, and this would seem at first sight to make less plausible the description of the actuation of the Shift offered above. The solution to the problem of the Eastern dialects presented here depends upon the interaction between varieties of contemporary English, one of which held greater prestige.

The key to the East Anglian problem is that there seems to have been a three-height system in pre-Shift East Anglia: /iː, uː, eː, oː, aː/ (see Figure 5.8). One reason for the emergence of this system was inheritance from the Old English period of Anglian *ē* for Saxon *ǣ*; another reason was to do with phonetic conditioning, notably raising in the environment of a following /d, t, n, s, l, r/ (see further Dobson 1968: 612).

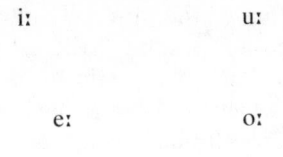

i: u:

e: o:

a:

Figure 5.8 The Great Vowel Shift in East Anglia: pre-Shift

Given the increase in trade and other contact between the East Midlands and London in the early and mid-fifteenth century, which was itself the result of the centripetal forces associated with urbanisation discussed earlier in this chapter, this provincial East Anglian system would have come into regular contact with the prestigious London System I, in which Middle English /aː/ was realised as [æː], Middle English /ɛː/ as [ɛː˔], Middle English /eː/ as [eː˔] (the 'French /eː/') and Middle English /iː/ was realised by diphthongal variants. In such circumstances, it is not surprising that hyperadapting tendencies took over. For East Anglians with their three-height system would tend to perceive System-I [æː] as /eː/; System-I 'French' [eː˔] would be perceived as /iː/. A similar situation would hold with regard to the back series of vowels. Since 'Middle English /eː/-words' and 'Middle English /ɛː/-words' had merged in this dialect before the Shift, both would have been involved in the raising to /iː/. This East Anglian system is the ancestor of that which became dominant in prestigious speech from the eighteenth century (see Samuels 1972: 147); it is already indicated by sporadic rhymes and spellings in the sixteenth century, for example *prych* in the *London Diary* (1550–1553) of the merchant Henry Machyn, and in rhymes such as *reach* : *beseech* which appear in the works of Henry Howard, Earl of Surrey, and Sir Thomas Wyatt.

The Mopsae, it is suggested here, are the descendants of those who used System II. By the early seventeenth century, the Mopsae would have had a system in which Middle English /iː, uː/ had diphthongised, Middle English /eː, oː/ had raised to /iː, uː/, and Middle English /ɛː, ɔː/ had become /eː, oː/. Moreover, it seems probable that System-II users had /aː/ rather than System-I /æː/; if the Mopsae had no /æː/, they would tend when attempting System-I usage to realise /æː/ as their next closer phoneme, /eː/ – although their realisations of /eː/ must have been fairly wide-ranging, given the phonological space available. This explanation would account for the most notorious habit of the Mopsae, the use of '*kēpn*, and almost *kīpn*' for 'capon' (see Dobson 1968: 145, 148). Gil plainly regarded as affected such raised pronunciations of a word which, for him, had /æː/, but, given his own phonetic script which reflected, in its essentials, the pronunciation used by Hart, he had no symbol for the Mopsae's /eː/. The speech of the Mopsae is that of the upwardly mobile, and it is therefore no coincidence that the pronunciations favoured by them became more widespread after the Civil Wars of the mid-seventeenth century and the rise to political power of a vigorously self-confident bourgeoisie.

The question remains as to why such pronunciations as those descended from System I should have taken on prestige at the end of the fourteenth and beginning of the fifteenth century. Part of the answer, as suggested by R.B. Le Page (in Samuels 1972: 145–146), may be to do with 'role-distancing' amongst the aristocracy. But, following Milroy (1992), it is argued here that the more likely innovators were the rising middle classes of the late fourteenth and early fifteenth centuries, immigrants into London like Dick Whittington, with comparatively weak ties to social class and local area. During the course of the late fourteenth and early fifteenth centuries, such immigrants originated from the East and Central Midlands – an area where System II was usual. These folk were the ancestors of Gil's Mopsae.

Such a solution to the problem of the origins of the Shift accounts for the comparative suddenness with which it took place; it also accounts for why the Shift's action ceased, since the trigger in the South and Midlands, the loss of final -*e*, could not recur. The output of Middle English Open Syllable Lengthening, the loss of final -*e*, and dialect contact in a setting of social change interacted to produce the development described at the outset of this chapter.[5]

SUBSEQUENT DEVELOPMENTS I: SEVENTEENTH CENTURY

It has been argued above that the origins of the Shift in London are to be found in the interaction of socially significant varieties. In the early seventeenth century, two varieties were in competition: the old System I, representing the speech of the descendants of Chaucer, and a rising System II, representing the pronunciations favoured by the Mopsae and their descendants. By *c.* 1650, these two systems had developed in the front series as follows:

I Middle English   /eː/ > /iː/, e.g. *meed*
/ɛː/ > /eː/, e.g. *mead*
/aː/, /ai/ > /ɛː/, e.g. *made, maid*
II Middle English   /eː/ > /iː/, e.g. *meed*
/ɛː/, /aː/, /ai/ > /eː/, e.g. *mead, made, maid*

The evidence for System I consists of that provided by the majority of writers on pronunciation during the period. Thus Middle English /eː/ is identified with Italian *i*; Middle English /ɛː/ is generally reflected as /eː/ by the orthoepists; and Middle English /aː/ (with which Middle English /ai/ had become identified) passed through a stage /æː/ to /ɛː/ by about 1650.

Possibly the best evidence for System I, and certainly the evidence of the best contemporary phonetician, is provided by the Hertfordshire schoolmaster Christopher Cooper (*Grammar*, 1685 (Latin), 1687 (English)). Cooper's aim in his handbook was practical: he wished to instruct foreigners and English schoolchildren in correct grammar, pronunciation and, above all, spelling. Although his information is occasionally inexact as the result of what has been called 'the typical seventeenth-century attempt at an unreal symmetry' (Dobson 1968: 291), he clearly has Middle English /eː/ reflected in /iː/, Middle English /ɛː/ in /eː/, and Middle English /aː/ in /ɛː/ (Dobson 1968: 286–291).

At the time when Cooper was writing, however, there is good evidence that his mode of pronunciation was already archaic. The system which rivalled it was System II, that of the Mopsae and their descendants, and it is demonstrated most clearly in contemporary rhyming and punning practice. The earliest such rhymes in verse appear in Spenser, writing at the end of the sixteenth century, for example *seates*: *states*; but Dobson describes this usage as based 'either on advanced London speech or on Northern pronunciation' (1968: 626). Such rhymes become much more common in the seventeenth century, as the Mopsae and their descendants became more socially significant, for the social developments of the seventeenth century – the Civil Wars, most notably – plainly had their impact in allowing an originally lower-class usage into a more prestigious environment.

Thus the following rhymes appear in the verse of seventeenth-century court poets: *speak* : *make* (Waller), *dream* : *shame* : *theme* (Dryden) etc. These rhymes demonstrate an identity of Middle English /ɛː/, /aː/ and /ai/, all of which have merged on /eː/, and show that such usage was current in the fairly prestigious milieu represented by these men. Edmund Waller (1606–1687) was educated at Eton and King's College Cambridge, was a Member of Parliament under both Charles I and Charles II, and was a member of the Royal Society from 1661; he fought on the Royalist side during the Civil Wars, being involved in a plot to seize London for the king in 1643. John Dryden (1631–1700) was a member of the lesser landed gentry, and his first major poem was the *Heroique Stanza's* on the death of Oliver Cromwell (1659); but he was to become Poet Laureate to the Stuarts and a prominent member of the intellectual establishment of his time.

System II is also found in the 'homophone lists' which start to appear from the middle of the seventeenth century. The most influential of these lists – in the sense that it was the most imitated and plundered – was that of Richard Hodges, who produced such lists in his *Special Help* (1643) and *Plainest Directions* (1649) and whose work continued to be plagiarised throughout the remainder of the seventeenth century. These lists show that rhymes such as the following were accepted in the society for which the lists were composed: *lead* : *layd*, *meads* : *maids*, *please* : *Plays*, *plead* : *Played*, *see* : *say* etc. (see Dobson 1968: 400). Such pronunciations obviously reflect those adopted by the Mopsae and their descendants.

SUBSEQUENT DEVELOPMENTS II: EIGHTEENTH CENTURY

Just as two systems are recorded in the seventeenth century – the 'proper' pronunciation in the writings of the orthoepists and phoneticians, and a 'vulgar' one in the homophone lists – so in the eighteenth century another dual system appears. One of these was the old System II. That System II survived in prestigious use into the eighteenth century is suggested by the rhymes of writers such as Swift (1667–1745) (e.g. *speak : awake*) and Pope (1688–1744) (e.g. *speak : take*), and even Cowper (1731–1800) (e.g. *survey : sea*) – although in these cases allowance must be made for the existence of conventional eye- (as opposed to ear-) rhyme. The other was the system which is the direct ancestor of Present-Day English Received Pronunciation: System III, in which Middle English /eː, ɛː/ appear with /iː/ (cf. Present-Day English *meed : mead*), and Middle English /aː, aɪ/ are reflected in /eː/ (cf. Present-Day English *made : maid*).

Although System III has just been termed 'new', it seems to have existed for some time in non-prestigious varieties, and has already been referred to. Its origins lie in East Anglia; it seems to be the result of continuing interaction of prestigious and non-prestigious varieties, whereby a non-London, especially East Anglian, three-height system came into contact with System I.

Part of the reason for the success of System III is, it would appear, functional in an intralinguistic sense: System III allowed fewer homophonic clashes than System II. However, this cannot be the whole story, for System II remains in a number of provincial, rural and traditional dialects (cf. e.g. 'stage-Irish', where *tea* is pronounced 'tay'; see Wells 1982: 194ff.).

This restriction suggests that System III's success in London is not solely due to intralinguistic functional reasons but also to extralinguistic social factors peculiar to the capital. System II and System III could only come into contact in a major urban centre, such as London; in more rural areas, the opportunity for the two systems to compete would have been much rarer and thus it would have been (and is) possible for the older System II to have been retained longer. The coexistence of System II and System III in one place, London, meant that it was possible for Londoners to choose between them.

CONCLUSIONS

If the argument presented here is accepted, its implications are major. First, it suggests that, at the beginning of the fifteenth century, notions of prestige have become associated, in London at least, with the spoken as well as the written modes of language, something which, hitherto, has always been treated by scholars with justifiable suspicion.

Second, it raises the question as to whether scholars should continue to refer to the Great Vowel Shift as a unitary phenomenon at all, a matter which has excited some controversy in recent years (see Lass 1988, Stockwell and Minkova 1988a and 1988b). Its actuation and implementation seem to differ in different parts of the country, and the processes involved are not to do with some massive, sudden 'sound-shift' – which excited no contemporary comment whatsoever – but rather with a series of minor individual choices which have interacted diachronically, diatopically and sociolinguistically, resulting in a set of phonological realignments. The view offered here is that the term 'Great Vowel Shift' remains a useful label for the phenomenon, but only in the same way as 'Industrial Revolution' is a helpful shorthand method of referring to how a series of minor technological advances ultimately brought about a major cultural change (see Lass 1988: 396).

Above all, it reminds us that the explanation of the triggering of a given linguistic change depends on an understanding of many interacting extra- and intralinguistic processes. A single explanation for the triggering of change is not enough; as in the physical or biological sciences, the multi-factorial causation of events needs to be an accepted part of the methodology of historical linguistics.

6 Change in the lexicon

VARIATIONAL SPACE AND THE LEXICON

In the last chapter, sound-change was investigated, and it was observed that change was the result of the complex interaction of a number of different mechanisms. In the following chapter, complex interaction will be observed with regard to lexicological change.

At first sight, the lexicon of a language seems a very simple category; it is to do with words, and for many lay people the history of a language is a history of individual words: their etymology, their meaning and their changing use. However, such a fragmented notion of linguistic historiography cannot be immediately defended against the charge of atomism and thus triviality. It is important, therefore, to establish a general theory of lexicology before proceeding to the particular concern of this chapter, which is to demonstrate how lexical change is bound up with intra- and extralinguistic developments elsewhere within the linguistic and social system.

Lexicology is the study of words and their structural relations, but it is worth noting that the concept 'word' is notoriously hard to define, and that the relationship between word and meaning raises a number of quite complex issues. Before discussing the diachronic development of words, it is therefore worth establishing some basic notions which will be useful in later discussion. A useful formal definition of the concept 'word' might be as follows: a grammatical unit which is marked within the clause by positional mobility, uninterruptability and internal stability (Lyons 1968: 202–204). Thus in the following sentence

(1) The papers reported the speech widely on their front pages

there are no fewer than fourteen *morphemes*, or minimal units of grammatical analysis, separated by a hyphen (-) in (1a) below:

(1a) The-paper-s-report-ed-the-speech-wide-ly-on-their-front-page-s

However, these morphemes cannot be placed in *any* order to produce acceptable English sentences; some permutations are acceptable, such as

(2) The-speech-was-wide-ly-report-ed-in-the-paper-s-on-their-front-page-s

but other combinations are not. Thus *speech, paper, page* etc. are potentially *mobile* or *free*, and can be employed in many positions, whereas *-s* and *-ed* in (1a) above are *immobile* or *bound* morphemes, that is, they must be attached to some other element to produce a 'block' within the sentence. Moreover, the ordering of elements within the block is *stable*, in the sense that *-s* and *-ed* have to follow, not precede, the element to which they are attached: thus *paper-s* and *report-ed* are acceptable, but not **s-paper* or **ed-report*. Finally, it is not acceptable to *interrupt* these blocks by interposing other elements, such as **paper-the-s*. These blocks may be termed *words*. Of course, there are items which are conventionally called *words* which do not fulfil all three criteria, for instance the article *the*, which may be interruptable (cf. *the page, the front page*) but is also stable and immobile, in the sense that it must always precede and accompany the noun which it modifies. Such items can be considered to be words since they fulfil one at least of the three criteria, but they are perhaps not as prototypical of the category as items which fulfil all three requirements (see further Taylor 1995: 173ff.).

The definition of *word* offered in the previous paragraph is, as has been stated, a formal one, in that it is to do with the grammatical role of the category in question and its structural characteristics. However, another, older definition is that words map onto concepts; and this leads us into the field of meaning-relations or *semantics*. Aristotle held that

> Words spoken are symbols or signs of affections or impressions of the soul; written words are the signs of words spoken. As writing, so also is speech not the same for all races of men. But the mental affections themselves, of which these words are primarily signs, are the same for the whole of mankind, as are also the objects of which those affections are representations or likenesses, images, copies.
>
> (*De interpretatione* (Ch. i), cited Waldron 1979: 16)

With some parts of this statement few modern linguists could agree, for example Aristotle's view, that for any one word in any one language we can invariably find an exact synonym in another, is simply wrong. We might note, for instance, the way in which English-speakers distinguish between *sheep* and *mutton*, whereas French-speakers use *mouton* for both living animal and the meat derived from it. However, most modern linguists would agree with the first part of the quotation, which is to do with the essential conventionality or *arbitrariness* of words; thus *table* may signify 'table' in English (and French), but the same concept is signified by a completely different word in Latin, *mensa*. Neither *table* nor *mensa* contains anything about its appearance or sound which causes it to be in form peculiarly appropriate to signify the real-world object to which it refers.

Left aside here are two phenomena which might at first sight seem to contradict the notion of the essential conventionality of word–concept relations: onomatopoeia and phonaesthesia. Onomatopoetic words may have arisen from an attempt at imitation of sounds but, as Waldron (1979: 17) points out, the fact that they vary so radically from language to language suggests that they are now, like other words, conventional: thus compare, as attempts to signify the cry of a cockerel, English *cockadoodledoo*, French *cocorico*, Danish *kykeliky*, German *kikeriki*. More interesting than this comparatively rare phenomenon are those cases of words in which the presence of a particular phonological component seems to correspond regularly – although not always – to a semantic component; for example, the element *gr-* shared by *grudge, gruff, grumble, gripe, grizzle, grumpy, grim, grunt* seems to signal a common element of rudeness and/or taciturnity in the meaning of these words. Such phonological components are known as *phonaesthemes*. However, the appearance of a particular phonaestheme in a language, such as *gr-*, does not deny the essential conventionality of words, for phonaesthemes seem to arise from the coincidental semantic proximity of words containing similar sounds, followed by a process of semantic 'attraction' of other words containing the same sounds; and this process does not work on all words containing the potential phonaestheme, cf. *grin, grip* beside the examples above. Another good example is the phonaestheme *sl-*; we might compare the semantics of *slippery, sludge, sly, sleaze* with *sleep* (see further Reay 1994 and references there cited).

Aristotle's main point in the passage quoted above, however, is central to the study of meaning, and was developed by Saussure and others. This point is to do with the relations between (1) the *signifiant* or 'signifier', the actual acoustic or written expression, (2) the *signifié* or 'signified', the mental concept, and (3) reality itself. K. Baldinger (1980: 6–7) gives a good example to demonstrate these notions:

> The acoustic image *table* only brings to mind a schematic representation of the thing. If I say, 'Tomorrow I'm going to buy a table', I do not know which table I shall buy. *Table* evokes the category. And if I say, 'Yesterday I bought a table', I know what the table is like in reality, but the person I am speaking to does not; he only has an idea of the category. ... This may seem very elementary and obvious, but it has far-reaching consequences for language and the science of language.

This description of *semantic relations*, as the notion is called (from Greek *semantikos* 'significant') is often expressed in diagrammatic form, the so-called *semiotic triangle* (see Figure 6.1, after Baldinger 1980: 3; cf. Ullmann 1962: 55 and references there cited).

The mapping word–concept, using the term *concept* as defined by Baldinger (i.e. 'idea of the category'), has not been uncritically accepted by linguists. Waldron (1979: 21–23) cites a number of objections of varying

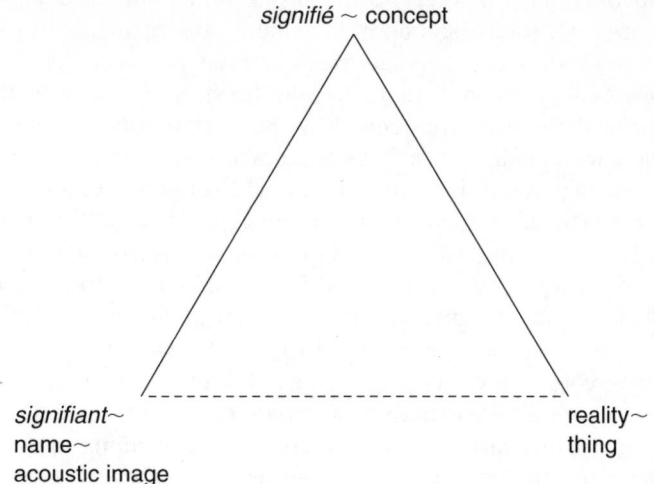

Figure 6.1 Ullmann's triangle

cogency, but he concludes that 'there is one powerful argument that men have not been entirely mistaken in supposing that it is possible to discuss meaning in conceptual terms and in relation to the individual word, namely its usefulness' (Waldron 1979: 23). Lexicography would be hard-pressed without the ability to map word onto definition; and children's language-learning would be impossible, for children build up their lexicons by isolating individual words and attaching them to individual concepts. It is for this reason that the word–concept mapping is pursued here.

Some scholars have attempted to express the conceptual meaning of a word contrastively, in binary (i.e. [+] or [–]) terms. Just as in some models of phonology it is possible to characterise a vowel-sound using formal labels such as [+FRONT], [–ROUND], so in the discussion of meaning some have tried to characterise individual words in a similar way – although it has to be accepted that the patterns of contrast suggested can be highly complex in comparison with those established in phonology, and the contrastive categories arrived at are extremely debatable. Thus, for instance, the word *woman* could be characterised as [+HUMAN], [+FEMALE], [+ADULT] in contrast to *man* ([+HUMAN], [-FEMALE], [+ADULT]) – although this characterisation, of course, depends on our deciding quite arbitrarily to define 'maleness' as simply the lack of 'femaleness'. More recently, such binary classifications have tended to be discarded in favour of 'prototype theory' (see further and most importantly Taylor 1995).

It is naïve, however, to deduce from such contrastive schemes that words map simply onto single conceptual meanings. The 'same' word can have different conceptual meanings in different collocations and contexts; thus a word such as *plane* is likely to mean one thing when accompanied by *airport*, *runway*, *pilot* but another when accompanied by *hammer*, *chainsaw*, *powerdrill* etc. This fact demonstrates not only that words can have more than one conceptual meaning (*polysemy*), but also the more general truth that words are defined by their relationship to other words. Thus, when we encounter an unfamiliar word we establish its meaning primarily through analysis of its context, and reference to a dictionary is something which takes place at a later stage (if at all). This context, of course, which is to do with the relationship of words to others, is the province of grammatical analysis, and it will be clear from the remainder of this chapter that the dividing-line between grammar and lexicon is a fuzzy one. This issue will be returned to at the beginning of Chapter 7.

Moreover, conceptual meanings are not the only meanings a word can possess; there are also associative or *connotative* meanings, to do with the associations a word carries. Thus the conceptual meaning of *beast* could be characterised in formalist, binary terms as [–HUMAN], [+ANIMATE], but the connotative meanings of *beast* include 'irrationality', 'brutality', 'amorality'. Often these connotations will be culturally and/or historically conditioned; thus a Victorian definition of the word *womanly* would carry with it associations of passivity, obedience, garrulousness, subordination etc. which many people would now find offensive.

Finally, words can develop 'non-literal' meanings which deviate markedly from those meanings deemed to be focal or conceptual. A good example of this kind of usage is a word like *pillar*, which could be defined conceptually as an architectural item (?[+DETACHED], [+SUPPORT]) but which has obviously been extended metaphorically in an expression such as

(3) She was a *pillar* of the community.

The importance of such metaphors in everyday use is such that it is frequently hard to realise that metaphor is being used at all; and as a figure of speech we tend to notice metaphor only when it is used in some extravagant or otherwise stylistically salient way (e.g. *Let's pour it into the cappucino machine and see whether it comes out frothy* for *Let's discuss an idea*). The work of (for example) Lakoff and Johnson (1980) has shown how endemic the phenomenon is in natural languages. The following is an example of one of Lakoff and Johnson's metaphorical groupings derived from common English usage: IDEAS ARE FOOD (1980: 46–47). Some of their citations are obviously more idiomatic in American English, and thus a little unusual to a British speaker or reader, but enough are held in common by the two varieties to make the point clear for non-Americans.

What he said *left a bad taste in my mouth*. All this paper has in it are *raw facts, half-baked ideas, and warmed-over theories*. There are too many facts here for me to *digest* them all. I just can't *swallow* that claim. That argument *smells fishy*. Let me *stew* over that for a while. Now there's a theory you can really *sink your teeth into*. We need to let that idea *percolate* for a while. That's *food for thought*. He's a *voracious* reader. We don't need to *spoon-feed* our students. He *devoured* the book. Let's let that idea *simmer on the back burner* for a while. This is the *meaty* part of the paper. Let that idea *jell* for a while. That idea has been *fermenting* for years.

Lakoff and Johnson, noting the all-pervading nature of metaphor, go on to make certain claims about human thought-processes; although I personally find their arguments very convincing, there is no need to pursue them here. The key fact to observe is that some metaphors are clearly part of the meaning of individual words. This fact is, of course, fully recognised by lexicographers; thus the word *star* is defined as follows by a leading British native-speaker desk-dictionary, extending from its literal astronomical meaning to a metaphorical use signalling human pre-eminence:

> any of those heavenly bodies visible by night that are really gaseous masses generating heat and light, whose places are relatively fixed . . .; more loosely, these and the planets, comets, meteors and even, less commonly, the sun, moon and earth; a planet as a supposed influence, hence . . . one's luck, or an astrologer's summary of planetary influences; an object or figure with pointed rays, most commonly five; an asterisk; a starfish; a radial meeting of ways; a star-shaped badge or emblem, denoting rank, honour or merit, used e.g. in grading of classification, as in *three-star general* . . . ; a white mark on an animal's forehead, esp. a horse's; a pre-eminent or exceptionally brilliant person; a leading performer, or one supposed to draw the public; a networking conformation in which the control point is linked individually to all workstations (*comput*).
>
> (*Chambers Dictionary* 1993: 1683)

It is to be expected that such developments as those described achieve different states in different varieties of the language. To demonstrate the kind of differentiation which can exist, the meanings of three forms in urban (Glaswegian) Scots will be examined in comparison with their Southern English equivalents: *ginger*, *refreshment* and *balloon*. The evidence for Glaswegian usage is derived from Munro (1985), a publication issued by the Glasgow District Libraries.

1 *Ginger*, an elliptical form of *ginger beer*, has developed a special conceptual meaning in Glaswegian Scots, viz. 'a general term for all varieties of fizzy soft drinks'. Munro cites an illustrative conversation: '"Gie's a boatle a ginger, missis", "What kinna ginger, son?", "Lemonade" ' (Munro 1985: 29). This usage seems to be unknown in Southern English.

2   *Refreshment* has developed a special connotation in Glaswegian Scots. Not only does it have the broader meaning found in Standard English ('the or an act of refreshing; the state of being refreshed; renewed strength or spirit; that which refreshes, such as food or rest; in (*pl*) drink or a light meal', *Chambers Dictionary* 1993: 1448), but it has become a euphemism for, specifically, an alcoholic drink: 'It's not unknown for Big George to take a wee refreshment of a Saturday night' (Munro 1985: 58).

3   *Balloon* is widely used metaphorically in Glaswegian English, meaning 'an empty boaster, a blowhard': 'Don't listen to that big balloon' (Munro 1985: 9). Again, there is no indication of this usage in Standard English.

SEMANTIC FIELDS

Words, then, map not just onto a single meaning, rather, they map onto a whole series of meanings, some conceptual, some connotative, some metaphorical. However, this is not the end of the matter. As was indicated briefly above, conceptual meanings are situated within a network of lexical relations, and the same goes for associative (i.e. connotative and metaphorical) usage.

That words are situated in a semantic network has long been accepted by scholars, although there has been debate about the precise nature of this structure. The key notion here seems to be that of the *semantic field*, which can be most easily demonstrated in 'reverse dictionaries' such as *Roget's Thesaurus*. Thus a word such as *star* forms a semantic field with other heavenly objects such as *galaxy*, *asteroid*, *planet*, *Black Hole*, *comet* etc., and – in theory at least – it can be given a distinctive conceptual definition in relation to them.

Some linguists have held that the vocabulary of a language is constituted of a mosaic of such semantic fields, in which the underlying conceptual level is covered completely without gaps and without any overlap between fields (see Waldron 1979: 100–101). However, it will be clear from the dictionary-definition cited on page 117 above that the noun *star* can also be found in other semantic fields, for example in one containing *medal*, *order*, *cross* etc., or in another containing *actor*, *cinema* etc., and so on. There is therefore lexical overlap between semantic fields. This property need not be confined to a distinction between literal and metaphorical usage, of course; thus the word *hot* can be used conceptually for [+SPICES] or for [+HEAT], for example *a hot curry*, *a hot drink*.

Moreover, elements *within* any one semantic field can overlap in meaning. Thus a word like *cut* overlaps for some of its conceptual and associative meanings with *slice*, but not all; thus one meaning of *cut* is 'ignore in a social situation', a meaning not shared with *slice*, and one of *slice*'s meanings not shared with *cut* is found in games such as golf – 'to hit (the ball) in such a manner that it flies or curves off the the right' (*Oxford English Dictionary*).

CHANGE IN VARIATIONAL SPACE

The notions established so far in this chapter are important when we move to the next stage of the argument, which is to do with the kinds of change which can take place within variational space. If, as was claimed in Part I above, the role of variational space is important for diachronic studies on every linguistic level, then it must be important for the lexicon.

It will be realised from the discussion so far that any word occupies semantic space, as specified by its conceptual, connotative and metaphoric meanings; it thus lies within a network of overlapping semantic fields. This space constitutes the variational space of the item's usage, that is, it constitutes the range of the variation without which linguistic change cannot take place. A diagram illustrating the notion of the variational space available to an individual word appears as Figure 6.2.

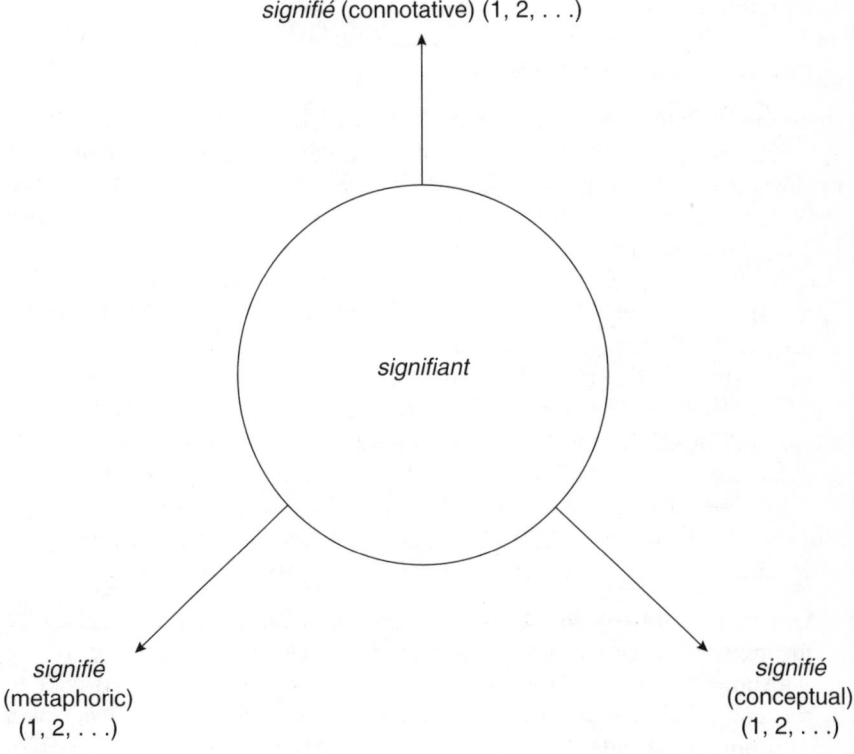

Figure 6.2 Signifiant and *signifié*: variational space

The focus of discussion so far has been synchronic, that is, concerned with the structure of vocabulary without reference to time or change. The next stage of discussion returns to the diachronic concerns of this book, in that it is to do with kinds of change. Various labels have been given to these processes, such as 'narrowing' and 'widening' (e.g. Old English *mete* 'food' > Present-Day English *meat*; Old English *bridd* 'young bird' < Present-Day English *bird*), or 'pejoration' and 'amelioration' (e.g. Old English *scitol* 'purgative' beside Present-Day English *shit*, or Old English *prættig* 'sly' beside Present-Day English *pretty*). It is possible to develop some broader terms for the process of change; R.A. Waldron thus distinguishes between *shift* ('modification of an existing linguistic category') and *transfer* ('change to a different category') (see Waldron 1979: 140). It is, however, perhaps not desirable to make a hard-and-fast division between these categories since words can undergo both processes at once. It is better to see them as poles on a cline, marked by the following stages (which need not, incidentally, be in the order listed):

1 The conceptual meaning of a word moves from one part of its variational space to another.
2 One (or more) conceptual or associative meanings of a word within its variational space is (or are) dropped.
3 A word develops a new conceptual or associative meaning and thus extends its variational space.

In the rest of this section, exemplification of these processes is offered, drawing examples from the history of the English lexicon. The sources of evidence in all cases are the *Oxford English Dictionary* (*OED*), which is the largest repository of historical material yet assembled for the English lexicon, and, for current modern usage, the *Chambers Dictionary* (1993) and the *BBC English Dictionary* (1992). The reasons for choosing the two latter authorities will be made clear as discussion proceeds. It will be observed in the discussion that the categories 1–3 above overlap.

To illustrate category 1, the history of the meaning of the noun *villain* will be examined. The word derives from Old French *ville* '(rural) settlement', and originally the term *villain* simply meant someone who lived in such a place, a peasant. One spelling of the word, *villein*, has been retained by historians of the medieval period with this original, technical sense. But the word nowadays spelt *villain* has undergone a quite radical change of meaning. The definition in the *OED* of *villain* is as follows:

> Originally a low-born base-minded rustic; a man of ignoble ideas or instincts; in later use an unprincipled or depraved scoundrel; a man naturally disposed to base or criminal actions, or deeply involved in the commission of disgraceful crimes. ... A bird (*esp.* a hawk) of a common or inferior character. *Obs.* ... A person or animal of a troublesome character in some respect.

The *Chambers Dictionary* (1993), a desk-dictionary which reflects a wide range of Present-Day English usage, gives the following definition:

> a violent, malevolent or unscrupulous evil-doer; the wicked enemy of the hero or heroine in a story or play; playfully, a wretch; a criminal (*slang*); (*orig*) a villein.

The word has plainly lost its older connotations to do with humble birth, and this is confirmed by the *BBC English Dictionary* (1992), which is designed for foreign learners of, and listeners to, the language and is thus careful to give current English usage of the kind such folk are likely to encounter on (for example) the BBC World Service:

> A person who deliberately harms other people or breaks the law is sometimes referred to as a *villain*. ... The *villain* in a particular situation is the person, group, or country that is held responsible for things going wrong. ... A *villain* in a play, film, or novel, is an important character who behaves badly and is responsible for many of the bad things that happen.

From this evidence the pattern involved in the history of this word is clear. The original conceptual meaning of *villain* might be expressed in formalist terms as something like [+HUMAN], [+BASE-BORN]; medieval views of society meant that connotations of 'evil-doing' were added to this core meaning. These connotations subsequently became part of the conceptual meaning of the word, and, after that, the original focal or conceptual meaning was dropped, to be later assigned to the related form *villein*. The originally associative meanings of *villain* have thus become the focal or conceptual meaning of the word.

The history of the meaning of *villain* could also, of course, be taken to illustrate category 2 above, in which one or more conceptual or associative meanings of a word within its variational space is dropped; the term *villain* does not in late-twentieth-century usage, as evidenced by the *BBC English Dictionary*, seem to carry with it the connotations of 'baseness of birth' which it had when it was first introduced to the language. However, the history of the verb *thrill* demonstrates the dropping of meaning more obviously, and will be investigated next.

During the history of the English language there seem to have been at least two verbs with the form *thrill*, with distinct etymologies; the link between these two is therefore more a matter of homophony than polysemy (see, for discussion of this distinction, Kay forthcoming). One survives only in some varieties, for instance Scots, as *thirl*; related to Old Norse *þræll* 'servant' with subsequent metathesis (i.e. internal exchange of phonetic segments), it has the present-day meaning of 'bind by ties of affection or duty' (see *Concise Scots Dictionary* 1985: 714). Important in its own dialectal area, this usage can be left aside for the purposes of the present discussion, other than to note that *thirl* has now completely replaced older *thrill* with the same meaning; the form *thrill* is in Scots retained for the same range of meanings as those found in Present-Day English.

The other, more common usage is in Present-Day English another metathesised form, this time derived from Old English *þyrlian* 'perforate, pierce, excavate'. *Chambers Dictionary* (1993) gives the following:

> [transitive] to affect with a strong glow or tingle of sense or emotion, now *esp* a feeling of excitement or extreme pleasure; to pierce (*archaic*) – [intransitive] to pass tinglingly; to quiver; to feel a sharp, shivering sensation; (of something sharp) to pierce or penetrate (with *through*) (*archaic*).

OED definitions are split between *thirl* (the older form) and *thrill*; I have conflated and modified some of the definitions for the reader's convenience. First and last dates of general occurrence, as recorded in *OED*, are also given.

1 To pierce, to run through or into (a body) as a sharp-pointed instrument does; to pierce (anything) with such an instrument; to bore a hole in or through; to perforate [*thirl* 1.; also *thrill* 1.] 1000–1661.
2 To pass right through, penetrate, traverse (anything). [*thirl* 2.] 1175–1560.
3 To make a hole in (the earth); to excavate [*thirl* 3.] 1000–1577.
4 *Coal mining.* To cut through (a wall of coal, etc.) [*thirl* 4.] 1686–1883.
5 To pierce, penetrate (as a sharp instrument) [*thirl* 5.] 1374–1600 (both recorded sixteenth-century uses are from Scottish authors).
6 To pass through or penetrate (*into* or *to* a place or thing) [*thirl* 6.; also *thrill* 2.] 1300–1565.
7 To cause (a lance, dart, or the like) to pass; to dart, hurl (a piercing weapon) [*thrill* 3.] 1609–1646.
8 To pierce, penetrate (as a sound, or an emotion) [*thrill* 4.] 1300–1642.
9 To affect or move with a sudden wave of emotion (*transitive*); to produce a thrill, as an emotion, or anything causing emotion (*intransitive*) [*thrill* 5.] 1590–1874.
10 To send forth or utter tremulously [*thrill* 6.b.] 1647–1868.
11 To move/cause to move tremulously or with vibration [*thrill* 6.a., c.] 1776–1878.

Of these definitions, only one survives in common usage as recorded in *BBC English Dictionary* (1992). In this authority the verb is defined in terms of the noun, thus:

> If something gives you a *thrill*, it gives you a sudden feeling of excitement or pleasure. .... If something *thrills* you, it gives you a thrill.

The process with regard to this word's change of meaning becomes clear once these various meanings are examined in chronological order. With the exception of the specialist meaning (4), the older meanings (1–7) die out by the middle of the seventeenth century. But during the Middle

English period a new meaning appears, meaning 8, which – through metaphor – introduces 'sound' and 'emotion' into the word's variational space. These metaphorical meanings become central (and thus conceptual) to the meaning of the word from the middle of the seventeenth century onwards and the older meanings disappear. Not only has the conceptual meaning of the word changed, but the older conceptual meanings have disappeared altogether from the word's variational space.

The extension of variational space to take on a new conceptual or associative meaning, category 3 above, like categories 1 and 2, is demonstrated by the history of *thrill*. However, it may be of interest to examine a more recent example of category 3, the extension in meaning undergone by the adjective *gay*. In the case of this word, conceptual meaning has changed in living memory. *Chambers Dictionary* (1993) gives the full range of current meanings:

> lively; bright, colourful; playful, merry; pleasure-loving, dissipated (as in *gay dog* a rake) (*archaic*); of loose life, whorish (*obs*); showy; spotted, speckled (*dialect*); in modern use, homosexual (orig *prison slang*); relating to or frequented by homosexuals (as *gay bar*). . . .

However, current usage as reflected in the *BBC English Dictionary* (1992) seems to be to regard the word as almost exclusively to do with homosexual orientation, whereas the wider range of meanings given in *Chambers Dictionary* is now regarded as obsolete:

> A person who is *gay* is homosexual. . . . *Gay* organizations and magazines are for homosexual people. . . . *Gay* also means lively and bright; an old-fashioned use.

OED records *gay* meaning 'homosexual' as a slang expression from 1935, but until the 1960s the quotations cited by *OED* tend to put the word in inverted commas, followed by an explanation; it is clear that the word had not entered common parlance. The association with homosexuality was obviously a secondary meaning for much of the mid-twentieth century since a related verb, *gayed up*, became current in the 1960s as a term of interior decoration without (as far as I am aware) any implication as to the sexual orientation of the designer or occupier of the building in question. However, the evidence of the *BBC English Dictionary* is that the conceptual meaning of this word is now essentially [+HUMAN], [+HOMOSEXUAL], and it seems likely that the older sense – still part of the word's variational space but now becoming obsolete – will eventually drop away entirely.

INTERNAL AND EXTERNAL SOURCES OF VARIATION

So far, the discussion has been concerned generally with description rather than explanation. Given the historiographical concerns of this book, however, it is now necessary to turn to the means by which the processes described are triggered and, once triggered, regulated. This investigation will take up the remainder of this chapter.

It will be recalled from Part I above that there are three interacting mechanisms of linguistic change: variation, contact and systemic regulation. The sources of variation in the lexicon fall into two categories: (1) those which derive from the internal resources of a given variety, and (2) those derived from contact between languages, or between varieties of the same language.

A form which demonstrates the way in which a language's internal resources contribute to the pool of available variation is the adverb *soon*, defined in the *BBC English Dictionary* as follows:

> If something is going to happen *soon*, it will happen after a short time. If something happened *soon* after a particular time or event, it happened a short time after it.

In Old English, the ancestor of this word, *sōna*, meant 'immediately', but in Present-Day English, as witnessed by the *BBC English Dictionary*, it now clearly means 'later on'. Only in the fossil expression *as soon as* does it retain its older sense in Present-Day English.

The process illustrated by the history of *soon* is interesting, because it demonstrates one of the reasons for the appearance of variant meanings within the variational space of a word: they are the natural result of universal human tendencies to expressive overstatement (exaggeration) and understatement. Metaphor, in this context, can be seen as a sub-category of the former. As M.L. Samuels has put it (1972: 53),

> In lexis, overstatement (exaggeration) could be regarded as corresponding to strong-stress phonological variation, and similarly understatement and euphemism would correspond to weak-stress phonological variation. The difference lies in the selection of discrete forms possessing 'stronger' or 'weaker' *semantic* (not phonetic) properties.

These stronger and weaker usages form part of the variational space of a word, and are thus available for later selection.

A minor, but possibly still important, internal source of variation is to do with phonaesthetic associations. Here a good example is the word *gruelling* 'punishing', 'exhausting'. Related to the noun *gruel*, a species of thin porridge, the history of this word demonstrates nicely the way in which phonaesthetic considerations have conditioned a semantic development.

Externally conditioned variation within a lexicon is rather more complex than that described in the last three paragraphs. In one sense, the impact of one language on another, or of one variety on another, is simple: items in one language are copied into another, and interact with those which are already there.

This is not the end of the matter, however, and it is worth making clear the range of types of borrowing which can be distinguished. A precondition for borrowing is that a role must be seen for the alien form in the receiving language. Sometimes this role is to do with the appearance in the receiving culture of a new concept or object with which the resources of the native language are unequipped to deal, for example *chocolate*, ultimately from Nahuatl/Aztec *chocolatl* (although probably immediately a borrowing from Spanish), or *bungalow*, from Gujerati *bangalo*, Hindustani *banglā* 'belonging to Bengal'. However, that languages can cope with such phenomena from their own internal resources through the processes of word-formation is proved by, for example, German *Fernseher* 'television' (*lit.* 'far-seer').

More important are occasions when a borrowed word and a synonymous or near-synonymous native word – which may or may not be related in etymology – become differentiated in meaning within the borrowing language. Two examples of such processes are:

1 The difference in meaning between Present-Day English *shirt*, *skirt*. In Old English, *scyrte* appears as a gloss for Latin *praetexta*, an outer garment (cf. Lewis and Short 1879: 1435). The Norse cognate of *scyrte* is *skyrta*, and originally the two words were synonyms. However, when the Norse word was borrowed it developed a meaning distinct from the English usage, and *shirt*, *skirt* have been differentiated in meaning ever since.
2 The difference in meaning between Present-Day English *ox*, *beef*. A similar process of differentiation can be seen with these words. The Old English word, *oxa*, was originally synonymous with Old French *boef* (cf. Latin *bōs*). The latter was borrowed into English as *beef*, but the meaning became narrowed as 'flesh of the ox'.

Both processes 1 and 2 display a differentiation of conceptual meaning; the pairs *shirt/skirt*, *ox/beef* form contrastive groups which could be expressed formalistically. But differentiation can also take place with regard to associative (connotational and metaphorical) meaning. One good example of this process is to do with register-distinctions between native vocabulary and French-derived loanwords; it is 'felt' by a speaker of Present-Day English that a French-derived word such as *commence* is somehow of a 'higher' register than *begin*, the latter form being directly descended from Old English.

L. Bloomfield's comment (1933: 394) is relevant to both internally and externally induced variation: 'where a speaker knows two rival forms, they differ in connotation, since he has heard them from different persons and under different circumstances'. As a result synonyms are never exact; the way in which the variational spaces available to words overlap with each other seems to be an established fact of the nature of the lexicon, and is the result of the varying nature of contacts between people. When these contacts take place between the users of different languages, the subsequent reorganisations seem to be particularly large.

The result of these two processes, externally and internally induced variation, is that any given language-state, whether individual or group, consists of a mixture of variant forms. These variants form a pool, rather like the pool of mutations in biological evolution, from which subsequent selection is made. And, just as in biological evolution, so in linguistic evolution there are factors which condition the kinds of choices which take place.

REGULATION OF SYSTEMS

In the previous section it was established that variation, representing the potential for linguistic change, could enter the lexical system through both internal and external routes. However, as was pointed out in Chapter 3, the systematic nature of language means that there are regulatory forces – the extra- and intralinguistic 'blind watchmakers' of linguistic evolution – which constrain the selection of variables. Outcomes which are traditionally held to be part of one level of language, in this case the lexicon, can be shown to be the result of dynamically interacting processes. To demonstrate these processes, the impact of two languages on English, Norse and French, will be examined.

The two languages which have left the strongest imprint on the lexicon of Present-Day English are Scandinavian (or Norse) and French, reflecting major invasions of the British Isles during the Middle Ages.

The Scandinavian-derived element in the English lexicon originates in a period of Viking expansion, roughly speaking the years between 750 and 1050 AD. A combination of factors, much discussed by scholars, brought about this historical development: Charlemagne's destruction of the Frisians, traditional seafaring rivals to the Scandinavians; apparent overpopulation in the Scandinavian homelands; the exile of war-chiefs and their supporters as a result of the appearance of centralising kings in Denmark and Norway.

Norse contacts with the Anglo-Saxons began with the Viking invasions of the eighth to eleventh centuries, which ended in England (though not in Scotland) with the battle of Stamford Bridge in 1066; but the influence of Scandinavian on English persisted long after that date. Scandinavian peoples spread and settled widely in Britain, particularly in the less-populated North in a great belt of land across Lancashire and Yorkshire (the focal area of settlement), in the far north of Scotland and in the Northern and Western Isles.

Recent scholarship has suggested that the impact of Norse culture on English has been, if anything, underestimated. Place-name evidence, for instance, shows that varieties of Scandinavian interacted in complex ways with English, and indeed Celtic, well outside the focal area of original settlement. Thus a place-name such as *Grimston*, common in many parts

of Northern England outside the focal area of Viking settlement, shows
a hybridisation of a Norse personal name (*Grímr*) with an Old English
generic place-name element (*tūn* 'settlement'). An even more complex
example of such processes is the place-name *Kirkcudbright* in South-West
Scotland, outside the focal area but within the area of secondary Norse
expansion. This form combines a Scandinavian generic element (*kirk*
'church') with an Old Northumbrian qualifying personal name (*cudbright*
'Cuthbert') within a Celtic element-ordering (generic + qualifier, as
opposed to the Germanic pattern of qualifier + generic). Such blends
suggest peaceful intermingling of peoples, contrasting with the habit of
order-replacement found when, in 638 AD, the Angles crossed the Tweed
into what is present-day Scotland and replaced Celtic *Din Eidyn* 'hill fort
of the sloping ridge' (generic + qualifier) with Germanic *Edinburgh*
'(Celtic *edin*) + fortress' (qualifier + generic).

Left out of account here is the problem of pre-Viking contacts between
Norse and Anglo-Saxon society, represented culturally in such Anglo-
Saxon artifacts as the Sutton Hoo ship-burial and the poem *Beowulf*. (For
a discussion of this problem, see Hines 1984.) It is worth remembering
that the Anglian homeland on the continent of Europe was in Angeln in
present-day Denmark, an area which abuts the zone of speakers of
varieties of North Germanic, and some at least of the similarities between
Anglian and Norse may date from this earlier contact.

The year 1066, of course, saw a more famous invasion: the beginning
of the Norman Conquest with the defeat of the Anglo-Saxon king Harold
at the battle of Hastings. In the next few centuries, England became part
of a 'Channel State' in which the prestigious *lingua franca* consisted of
varieties of French; and in the years after 1066 English gradually became
a debased vernacular, no longer used (as it had been in Anglo-Saxon
England) for such socially significant matters as the recording of royal
decisions through charters. Furthermore, the Conquest enabled England
to join in the rebirth of Latin learning on the continent known as the
'twelfth-century renaissance'. In the face of such competition in terms of
prestige, English became destandardised in the written mode, even though
it remained the first language of the vast majority of the population and
was soon adopted by its originally francophone conquerors; and English-
speakers developed the habit of studding their language with French-
derived vocabulary in order to signal their prestige.

Some scholars hold that the impact of Norse on English was much more
profound than that of French, largely because Norse seems to have
affected such features (sometimes and somehow deemed more 'basic') as
phonological structure or the pronominal system, whereas French seems
to have provided English with a good deal of its 'open' vocabulary (i.e.
vocabulary in the open word-classes, such as nouns, adjectives, adverbs,
verbs). Such a distinction would seem to privilege one level of language
over another; since a theme of this book is the interconnectedness of

linguistic levels, a decision as to the relative *importance* of the French and Norse impacts on English is avoided here. It is held rather that the impact of these two languages differed, even though the processes involved in their relative impacts subsequently interacted.

Three aspects of the interaction of the Norse and French languages with the English lexicon will be examined here. In each case, a formal change which may be assigned to the level of the lexicon is shown to be the result of extra- and intralinguistic interaction.

1 the impact of Norse on the English pronominal system;
2 the impact of French on semantic structure;
3 the interacting impact of Norse and French on English word-formation and on the creation of new vocabulary in English.

THE IMPACT OF NORSE ON THE ENGLISH PRONOMINAL SYSTEM

The history of the third-person pronouns, which has already been touched upon in Chapter 1 above, is well known.[1] As a reference-point, the pronominal system of Late West Saxon in comparison with that of Present-Day Standard English may be stated first (see Figure 6.3). There are a number of dialectal variants, the most important of which (for the later argument of this chapter) is the form *hīe* for the nominative singular feminine, found in the Mercian *Vespasian Psalter Gloss*.

It will be apparent from an examination of the Late West Saxon system that formal distinctiveness among the various pronouns was fairly minimal in comparison with Present-Day English. For instance, the nominative singular masculine and feminine and nominative plural forms are very similar in form; this indistinctiveness must have been exacerbated in reduced-stress situations, where pronouns are frequently to be found.

Now, a lack of distinctiveness in pronominal systems is not necessarily a dysfunctional element in the grammar of a language, and it is possible for languages to exist quite happily without formal distinctiveness of pronouns – or, for that matter, with any pronouns at all. Latin, for instance, seems to have used pronouns only emphatically, and Present-Day Finnish does not distinguish between male and female pronouns.

Figure 6.3 Third-person pronouns in Late West Saxon and Present-Day English

	Masculine	Singular Feminine	Neuter	Plural, all genders
Nominative	hē 'he'	hēo 'she'	hit 'it'	hīe, hī, hēo 'they'
Accusative	hine 'him'	hīe, hī 'her'	hit 'it'	hīe, hī, hēo 'them'
Genitive	his 'his'	hire 'her'	his 'its'	hira, heora 'their'
Dative	him 'him'	hire 'her'	him 'him'	him, heom 'them'

Nevertheless, the system changed. Once again, it is necessary to look for correspondences for an explanation of this development. Two will be selected here: contact with Norse, and the shift from grammatical to natural gender. These developments not only introduced a range of extra variation into the pronominal system; it is also argued here that they caused implementation of change.

FROM GRAMMATICAL TO NATURAL GENDER

In Old English, the relationships between and within noun phrases were expressed by the use of formal case and grammatical gender respectively. The inflectional endings and agreements which marked these categories were syntagmatic tracking devices, indicating the functions and dependencies which operated at the clausal and phrasal levels. Thus, in a simple sentence like *Se gōda hlāford bint þā yflan hlǣfdigan* 'The good lord binds the evil lady', determiners, adjectives and nouns are all inflectionally marked for agreement in terms of gender and case, the latter marking the function of noun phrases within the clause, the former relating elements within the phrase as well as acting as a discourse-marker when pronouns were used. Case and gender had an important function at a time when element-order of words and phrases was more fluid than in Present-Day English.

That this system was breaking down in the Late Old English period is well attested. Although the system has survived comparatively unchanged in Present-Day German, it died out in English during the Early Middle English period and is no longer a major feature of Present-Day English. The key pressure seems to be the steady obscuration of unstressed syllables which distinguished case, a part of the 'drift' of the language from synthesis to analysis. An hypothesis as to the origins of this drift, and some suggestions as to why it has proceeded further in English than in some other Germanic languages, will be offered in Chapter 7 below.[2]

The breakdown of the Old English system is well illustrated in the language of the *Peterborough Chronicle* (MS Oxford, Bodleian Library, Laud Misc. 636), a text referred to briefly in Chapter 4 above. The *Peterborough Chronicle* is a version of the *Anglo-Saxon Chronicle* copied at Peterborough in the first half of the twelfth century. Its original function was to replace an earlier text which had been burnt in a disastrous fire at the monastery where it was housed, and the annals up to the year 1121 were copied from another manuscript loaned for the purpose; in these entries (the Copied Annals) an attempt has been made to maintain the Late West Saxon standardised written language. After 1121, continuations were made to carry the record up to the year 1154, when entries ceased. These continuations fall into two scribal stints: the annals for 1122–1131 inclusive (the First Continuation), and those for 1132–1154 (the Final Continuation).

A comparison of the Copied Annals with the Continuations shows clearly that the old system of grammatical gender had disappeared in the East Midlands of England by the early twelfth century. Clark (1970) reports that, although the system survives in the Copied Annals 'with only rare lapses' (1970: lix), it has undergone 'almost complete effacement' in the Continuations. This effacement is indicated by the appearance of unhistorical usages, for example *seo kyning* 'the king', *se cwen* 'the queen', *þes cwenes canceler* 'the queen's chancellor' (cf. Late West Saxon *se cyning*, *sēo cwēn*, *þære cwēne *canceler*; *canceler* is a Norman-French loanword into English, and would therefore not have appeared in Late West Saxon). In all these examples, a 'wrong' form of the Old English definite article has been selected as a noun-modifier.

In other parts of the country, the system of grammatical gender seems to have lasted rather longer. In the West Midland 'AB-language' of *Ancrene Wisse* (MS Cambridge, Corpus Christi College 402 = A) and related texts in MS Oxford, Bodleian Library, Bodley 34 (= B), there are still fragmentary traces of grammatical gender congruence even though these manuscripts can be dated to the first quarter of the thirteenth century (d'Ardenne 1961: 229). And, even more thoroughly, grammatical gender survives in the major Middle Kentish text from the fourteenth century: the *Ayenbite of Inwyt* of Dan Michel of Canterbury, which survives in a unique holograph manuscript (MS London, British Library, Arundel 57), dated to 1340. Dan Michel may have been in his seventies when he wrote the Arundel manuscript, but – even if it is accepted as evidence for old-fashioned usage – it still represents a state of the language which dates from over a hundred years after the *Peterborough Chronicle*. It has been demonstrated that the *Ayenbite* sustains a high degree of traditional gender congruence (see Gradon 1979: 85–97).

It may be observed that the shift away from grammatical gender correlates with innovative developments in the third-person pronominal systems of these texts. Both *Ayenbite* and *Ancrene Wisse* (Corpus MS) are highly conservative in their third-person pronouns. The Continuations to the *Peterborough Chronicle*, however, are highly innovative. Not only does a new feminine nominative pronoun appear, *scæ*, but there are also interesting therapeutic reorganisations to remove other difficulties, such as the selection of *hire* and *he(o)m* as forms for the accusative feminine singular and accusative plural pronouns respectively (cf. the less distinctive *hīe* which occurs in the Late West Saxon paradigm in both positions).

VARIATION AND REGULATION IN THE PRONOMINAL SYSTEM

Ultimately, of course, the 'problem' of the third-person pronouns was solved by the adoption of even more phonetically distinctive variants; and here the role of Norse is crucial. Before the Conquest, standardisation kept most of the Scandinavian wordstock out of the Old English written record, and those few words of distinctly Scandinavian origin which are found appear late in the period, most commonly in the *Anglo-Saxon Chronicle* from the eleventh century. These early words, frequently assimilated to Old English phonological and morphological usage, belong to a fairly restricted set of domains, reflecting the chroniclers' political concerns and the military concerns of the invaders, for instance *griþ* 'truce', *hāsæta* 'oarsman', *nīðing* 'evil man', *ūtlaga* 'outlaw', *cnearr* 'ship', *seaht* 'peace' (cf. Old Icelandic *grið*, *hāsæti*, *nīðingr*, *ūtlaga*, *knorr*, *sātt*).

How far this pattern reflected the social relationship between Norse- and English-speakers before the eleventh and twelfth centuries is difficult to say; and the situation is complicated by the likelihood that speakers of the Anglian dialects of Old English may have had much more in common linguistically with Norse as a result of geographical proximity between their ancestors in the years before the Anglo-Saxons came to Britain. Certainly there were strong links between Anglian and Norse peoples. These links are reflected in a number of ways: the material remains found in the East Anglian Sutton Hoo ship-burial of the seventh century, for instance, show a number of connections between Norse and English cultural practice, and the poem *Beowulf*, which may well (despite the West Saxon dialect of the tenth-century manuscript in which it survives) have originated in the Anglian dialect area, is about events in ancient Denmark and Sweden. These parallels extend to language. The Old Northumbrian text of Cædmon's *Hymn*, surviving in a manuscript which predates the Viking invasions (MS Cambridge, University Library Kk 5.16, dated to about 737 AD), contains a prepositional form, *til*, which is also found in Norse (cf. West Saxon *tō*); and the Old Northumbrian gloss to the *Lindisfarne Gospels* (MS London, Cotton Nero D.iv), dating from the second half of the tenth century but representing the dialect of an area outside the focal zone of Scandinavian settlement, has the form *aron* 'are' (cf. Old Norse *eru*, West Saxon *sind(on)/bēoþ*).

It is certain, however, that, from the late eleventh and twelfth centuries, Scandinavian forms became much more widespread in writing, and this change must reflect (however belatedly) a development in the spoken mode. Scandinavian-derived words seem, unlike French vocabulary, to have been treated sociolinguistically as equivalent to items of English lexis, and thus available for use within the core vocabulary of the language.

It was of course from Norse that the new, phonetically distinctive third-person pronouns were derived. As might be expected, these pronouns appear first in the written record in texts localised or localisable in the areas with densest Scandinavian settlement, the Danelaw (the extent of which is indicated, for instance, by the evidence of place-names). However, the process was not one of simple transfer; the selection of variables followed complex and not always straightforward paths. Two sets of forms are relevant in this connection: (1) the third person plural pronouns, and (2) the third person feminine singular.

THE THIRD PERSON PRONOUNS

In the plural paradigm, the new Scandinavian-derived forms with initial *þ-* appear first in texts from the Danelaw, and slowly spread south. Thus the *Ormulum*, a Lincolnshire text of *c.* 1200 already referred to on page 97 above, has *þeȝȝ* 'they', *þeȝȝre* 'their'; the usual form for 'them' was *hemm*, but *þeȝȝm* appeared after a vowel to prevent elision. In the roughly contemporary 'AB-language' of Herefordshire these Norse-derived forms had not yet appeared. However, *they*-type forms evidently fulfilled a functional need and ultimately spread across the country. It is interesting that *they* advanced much more rapidly than *their, them*. The Ellesmere manuscript of Chaucer's *Canterbury Tales* (*c.* 1400) has *they* but *here, hem*, and in Present-Day English native-derived 'em' still appears as a spoken-language informal variant of 'them'. It is as if the crucial problem was to do with the nominative form, and that *their, them* were adopted, perhaps, by analogy. It is possible that this priority makes sense in discourse terms, since the theme of a text – the central piece of information which a text tries to put across – is usually focused upon the subject of the sentence or clause. However, there were pressures for the disambiguation of the oblique (i.e. 'non-nominative') forms of the third person plural pronoun; it is noticeable that the native 'em'-type, which has survived longest, was disambiguated even in the Ellesmere text by the choice of different vocalisms in *hem* 'them' and *him* 'him' etc. It is also interesting that *heom* 'them' is a comparatively late form in West Saxon at any rate, only found in texts dating from after *c.* 1000, and similarly disambiguating *heom* 'them' from *him* 'him'.

More controversial is the problem of 'she'. Many different theories have been put forward to account for this form. Most modern scholars hold that Present-Day English *she* derives from Old English *hēo, hīe*, although some still hold that a derivation is possible from the determiner *sēo* (which could be used pronominally in Old English). Few still hold that it is the result of some sandhi (word-boundary) articulation (an earlier view on the origin of the form offered in, for example, the *OED*). Arguments about the origins of the form are based essentially upon three observations of correspondences:

1 The form is found first in Middle English texts from the North and Midlands and then spreads South. The geographical patterning would seem to resemble that for the *þ-* forms for the plural third-person pronoun and a Norse connection would therefore seem to be likely on *a priori* grounds.
2 In Northern Middle English and in Older Scots, the form is *scho*. In the South, the usual adopted form is *sche, she*, giving the current Present-Day Standard English form.

3 In Middle English, border forms such as *ʒho, ʒeo* appear in the South-East Midland and South-West Midlands respectively; *ʒho* is recorded in the *Ormulum*, from Lincolnshire.

The evidence of the correspondences suggests strongly that the form derives from Norse and, if so, the process must have operated something as follows:

1 It seems that Norse-speakers had a series of 'rising' diphthongs (i.e. with stress on the second element), as opposed to the 'falling' diphthongs of Old English, which appear to have had stress on the first element; we might compare Old Norse *kjōsa* 'choose' with its Old English cognate *cēosan*. In such circumstances, and given the close relationships between English and Scandinavian in the North of England, a 'resyllabification' of Old English *hēo* to **hjō* would seem a fairly straightforward contact blend, whereby a Norse vowel-prosody was transferred to an English context. This was the opinion of E. Dieth (1955), who believed that the pronoun had been borrowed into the Norse of the area from Old English, subjected to resyllabification, and then, in the 'Anglo-Scandinavian' blend-dialect of the North, spread out amongst speakers of both Norse and Anglian ancestry. Such a dynamic picture of language-interaction fits well with what we know of the archaeology and history of the area.

2 The phonetic sequence [hj-] is comparatively rare in Present-Day English; it seems to be a marginal cluster in a few words not part of the core vocabulary of the language. That it has a persistent tendency to change to the much more common [ʃ] is exemplified by, for example, Present-Day Scots *Shug* [ʃʌg] etc. 'Hugh'. The place-names *Shap* (< *hēap*), *Shetland* (< *Hjaltland*) etc. also exemplify this tendency. There is no need to posit any outside connection to account for the development; it represents an accommodation of a marginal form to one much more commonly attested in the language, viz. [ʃ]. The resulting form, *scho*, is of course that attested in the North and North Midlands.

3 The movement to [ʃ] probably took place via the palatal fricative [ç]. The evidence of Orm's spelling-system may be relevant here; his *ʒho* seems to be an attempt to reproduce [çoː]. His graph-cluster *ʒh*, only used in this word, contrasts with *ʒ^h* , which he uses for [ɣ].

The existence of such an intermediate phase as that suggested by the evidence of the *Ormulum* would account for the existence in various Northern locations of another form for 'she', Middle English *ho* (cf. Present-Day English *oo* etc. recorded in, e.g. Lancashire). Recent work on historical phonotactics, notably by A. Lutz (e.g. Lutz 1992), has shown that initial fricatives have a tendency to disappear in the history of English. Forms with *oo-* would therefore be a residualism from an earlier stage in the history of the language before [ʃ-] emerged.[3]

THE IMPACT OF NORSE

If the argument above is accepted, it may be suggested that the shift from grammatical to natural gender could be related to the appearance of Norse-derived pronouns in the English lexicon. Some theorists would be faced with a difficulty here. Was it the appearance of the new, phonetically distinct variables which allowed the shift from grammatical to natural gender? Or did the loss of grammatical gender trigger the adoption of the new, phonetically distinct variables? These questions – of a 'which came first: chicken or egg?' kind – might seem at first sight unanswerable. However, in the context of the argument presented in this book, they are explicable. The relationship between the two developments can be seen as iterative: each encouraged each; since these processes were acting in combination, a larger-scale development took place. The triggering of the process was probably the general obscuration of unstressed inflectional syllables which was itself encouraged by interaction between Norse and English, referred to at various points above; this obscuration led to an inflectional deficit, and subsequent therapeutic reactions in various parts of the linguistic system. Such 'conspiracies' or 'snowballs' have already been referred to earlier in this book, in Chapters 4 and 5, and they will be encountered again in Chapter 7.

Which came first is, therefore, an ill-formed question. Rather, Norse-derived pronouns existed within the variational pool, but were selected therapeutically to deal with a situation which had become more urgent with the loss of the grammatical tracking device; as Norse-derived pronouns were selected, the remnants of the older system of grammatical gender became less necessary. The pronominal system, we might hold, became 'lexicalised', in the sense that the new tracking device within discourse was based upon lexical reference, that is, to sex; we know that *she* refers back to a female referent because the form *she* indicates *natural* sex. In the earlier state of the language, the choice of *hē* or *hēo* would have depended on the *grammatical* gender of the referent concerned.

The history of the pronominal system, therefore, may be taken to demonstrate the interaction of all the mechanisms outlined in Part I. Variants existed within a variational pool, the result of contact between languages brought about through extralinguistic developments. Selection of variables took place therapeutically to regulate a system into which disturbance had been introduced through earlier linguistic interactions.

THE IMPACT OF FRENCH ON THE SEMANTIC STRUCTURE OF ENGLISH

The general direction of French influence on English vocabulary is clear. Up until the thirteenth century, borrowings from French reflected in English texts are rather few. These words enter English through the medium of Norman French, which developed, in England, into Anglo-Norman; thus these early loans often display characteristics of the Norman French dialect rather than of Central French, for instance Present-Day English *war*, first recorded as *werre* in the *Peterborough Chronicle*, derives from Norman French *werre*; cf. Present-Day French *guerre*. The domains of language covered by these early loans are rather limited, and indicated by the following examples (taken from Serjeantson 1935: 105–120): *arblast, service, prison, countess, duke, rent, tenserie* 'protection money', *justice, mercy, standard, mastery, crown, obedience*.

From the beginning of the thirteenth century to the end of the Middle English period, however, French words enter the English language in large numbers. These loans are commonly from Central French, not Anglo-Norman; as contact with Normandy was lost, Central French became the prestigious variety of that language for English-speakers. The range of domains covered by these words is vast (see Serjeantson 1935: 121–156). This surge coincides with the shift by the higher social classes from French to English as their mother-tongue; and this at first sight may seem para-doxical. But it is explicable in terms of the social differentiation of language, for – given the status of French in England already discussed above – the use of French expressions is an obvious way of signalling higher social position, even if a more general use of French had fallen into disuse amongst the upper classes in England at this time.

As has been pointed out by a number of scholars, however, simply counting the number of French-derived words in a given English text is not sufficient for distinguishing social register. The connotations of French-derived vocabulary must have been constantly changing, and this may be illustrated by Chaucer's usage. For instance, in *The Parson's Tale* 869, we are told that the English word for Latin *fructus* is *fruyt*, while, in the prologue to *The Second Nun's Tale* 106, Chaucer tells us that for Greek *leos* ' "peple" in Englissh is to seye'. As J.D. Burnley has pointed out (1983: 135), both *fruyt* and *peple* are borrowed originally from French, but by Chaucer's time they had evidently lost any connotation of social status which they might have had earlier in the Middle English period (the equivalent Old English words are *wæstm* and *folc*). It is clear that much French vocabulary had become naturalised quite early on and, as with any introduction of new material into a linguistic system, reorgani-sation and systemic regulation is to be expected.

To demonstrate the reorganisation of the English lexicon subsequent to close interaction with French, two semantic fields will be examined: (1) words concerned with the notion 'benefit', and (2) words for the concepts 'mood, temper, spirit', 'mind' and 'memory'. Finally, (3) the role of French will be examined with regard to the taboo-development of the word *shit*.

For the following discussion, in particular for (1) and (2) which are taken from published and unpublished outlines respectively, I am extremely grateful to Profs M.L. Samuels and C.J. Kay, colleagues working on the

Historical Thesaurus of English. When this notional and historical classification of the English lexicon from Old English times to the present day is completed – probably by the end of the twentieth century – it will be possible to reconstruct the structural shifts in the organisation of the English lexicon in a much more thorough and more systematic way than has yet been attempted. A very small amount of data derived from this project has been utilised for the discussion here.

1 It has been discovered that there are three words at the core of the semantic field 'benefit' during the course of its history:

1 *fremu* + derivatives (from Old English), used from Old English times to 1340;
2 *prow* (from Old French *pru, prou*) used between *c.* 1290 and *c.* 1570;
3 *benefit* and related words (cf. Old French *bienfait, -fet*), used from 1393 to Present-Day English.

The chronological sequence of the overlap and replacement represented by these words demonstrates a pattern rather like that exemplified by the history of the meaning of *thrill* (see pages 121–123).

At first sight, it is hard to come to any conclusion as to why these changes might have occurred, and the temptation is simply to report the finding and then move on to other, more easily explained matters. But such an action would be to abjure historiography, which is concerned with the rational arguing of plausible hypotheses. As M.L. Samuels has asked:

> What is our attitude to be to these straightforward but gradual replacements? Do we profess ignorance, or call them simply random changes of fashion? Surely we ought at least to consider whether the forms were phonetically and phonaesthetically suited to carry their meaning? I am not speaking here of full homonymic clash with sudden dramatic consequences at verifiable dates. I refer rather to weaker pressures, present over long periods of time.
>
> (1987: 246)

Samuels goes on to argue that *freme* and *prow* died out because of pressures from words of similar form but with opposed and negative meanings. Thus, in the case of *freme*, there was the adjective *frem(e)d* which in Old English (as in Present-Day German) meant 'foreign' but underwent subsequent pejoration to 'unfriendly, wild, hostile' – almost antonymous to 'benefit'; while *prow* clashed with an earlier form of the same word, *prūd* 'proud' which had entered English in the Late Old English period and had undergone pejoration to its Present-Day English meaning 'arrogant, overweening, presumptuous'. *Benefit* had become available owing to subsequent contact with French, and was thus available for selection. The change is the result of accumulated opposed meanings, whereby a whole series of minor developments have brought about a major change in usage.

2 A more complex example of the kind of restructuring that can take place is offered by the words for the concepts 'mood, temper, spirit', 'mind' and 'memory': in Old English, *mōd*, *hyge*, *(ge)mynd* respectively. The definitions of these words in the standard Old English dictionary are as follows:

mōd:
1 'the inner man, the spiritual as opposed to the bodily part of man';
2 'with more especial reference to intellectual or mental qualities: mind';
3 'with reference to the passions, emotions etc.: soul, heart, spirit, mind, disposition, mood';
4 'a special quality of the soul, in a good sense: courage, high spirit';
5 'a special quality of the soul, in a bad sense: pride, arrogance'.

hyge:
'mind, heart, soul'.

(ge)mynd:
'mind, memory, memorial, memento, remembrance, commemoration'.

(cited from Bosworth–Toller 1898)

It is plain from the contexts in which it appears that Old English *mōd* was beginning to overlap with the variational space occupied by *hyge* towards the end of the Old English period, and it is noticeable, from an examination of the Toronto *Microfiche Concordance to Old English*, that *hyge* is, with a few exceptions, restricted to poetical (and archaic) rather than prosaic contexts (cf. *mōd* 1–3); this restriction suggests that the form was beginning to disappear, and it is not therefore surprising to find it rarely attested in *OED*, and there only commonly in the archaistic thirteenth-century poem, Laȝamon's *Brut*. *Mōd*, on the other hand, is found in many contexts, both in poetry and in prose. It is possible that the disappearance of *hyge* was encouraged by its identity with other common words such as the verb *hie* 'hasten' and the adjective *high*; this identity would have been steadily becoming more acute as the disambiguating features, nominal, verbal and adjectival inflections, were becoming obscured in distinctiveness or disappearing altogether.

With the disappearance of *hyge*, *mōd* was left occupying a wide variational space. It is therefore not surprising that *gemynd*, a word which in Old English overlapped with at least one of the senses of *mōd*, 'mind', eventually replaced *mōd* in that slot; certainly by the end of the Middle English period the appearance of *mōd* with the meaning 'mind' has become rare, and – according to the *Middle English Dictionary* – restricted to poetical and provincial texts.

Gemynd for a while was itself quite widely extended. In the fourteenth century, however, a new form, derived from Old French, appeared: *memorie* (Present-Day English *memory*). The availability of *memory*

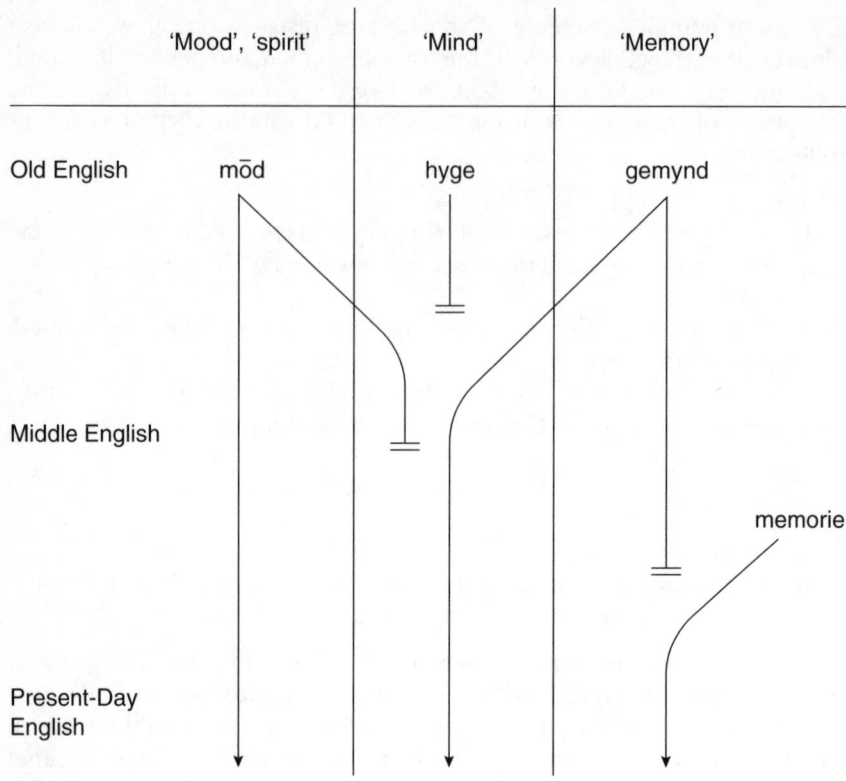

Figure 6.4 Restructuring the relationship between lexicon and semantics over time (after Samuels, priv. comm.)

overlapping with *gemynd* meant that *gemynd* could become transferred from the conceptual meaning 'memory' to the conceptual meaning 'mind'. *Mōd*, which did not overlap in meaning with *memorie*, reverted to its older conceptual meaning. By the middle of the fifteenth century, the modern pattern was established; the whole process of overlap and replacement described above may be given schematic form in Figure 6.4.

The history of the relationships between these words demonstrates a number of features, but they can be summed up as follows: intra- and extralinguistic forces interacted to produce a realignment of the lexicon. The pattern demonstrated by the 'mood'/'mind'/'memory' realignment is evidently one of therapeutic replacement in a situation of language-contact, where variables derived from various sources could be selected for functional reasons.

3 The final example to be analysed in this section is *shit* 'faeces', 'ordure' (noun), 'to excrete' (verb). In Present-Day English, the word is considered

rude; *Chambers Dictionary* (1993) classifies it as '(*vulg*)'. But this was not always the case; the evidence of *OED* and other authorities is that it could be used neutrally in Old and Middle English, in scientific or courtly contexts, for example *The adres shiteth preciouse stones* 'The snakes excrete precious stones' (in the romance *Kyng Alisaunder*, thirteenth century), *And bestes had þe schyt* (Trevisa, 1387). It is noticeable that the word begins to be restricted to vulgar use only when Latin- and French-derived near-synonyms start to be adopted, for instance *ordure* meaning 'dung', 'excrement' (first recorded in *OED* at the end of the fourteenth century), *excrement* and *excrete* (first recorded in *OED* during the sixteenth century). The process here is comparable to that which took place with *mutton* and *sheep*; differentiation of meaning (here of register) took place when the two words started to be used side by side.

THE INTERACTING IMPACT OF NORSE AND FRENCH ON ENGLISH WORD-FORMATION AND ON THE CREATION OF NEW VOCABULARY IN ENGLISH

Old English word-formation differs from that of Present-Day English in certain important ways, notably in its use of compounding. To a much greater extent than Present-Day English, Old English acquired new words in the same way as Modern German, either by compounding two words already in the language to cover a needed concept (e.g. *sciprāp* 'cable' derives from *scip* 'ship' and *rāp* 'rope') or by adding prefixes and suffixes. Of course, such habits of word-formation were not halted by contact with French – indeed, new methods of word-formation emerged, in which native and French-derived elements were blended – but it became more common for words simply to be borrowed rather than for the resources of the native language to be exploited.

The manner in which the Present-Day English pattern of vocabulary-creation emerged demonstrates a number of features relevant to the argument of this chapter. As an example the Old English verbs *brecan* 'break' and *forbrecan* 'destroy, break up' will be examined.

It is fairly obvious to the modern reader that Present-Day English *break* is directly descended from the Old English form. However, the related form *forbrecan* has not survived, and the failure of this derived form is illuminating for the history of English vocabulary. The Old English intensifying prefix *for-* has ceased to be productive; it appears in Present-Day English only in certain relict forms which have lost their original paradigmatic connections (thus Present-Day English *forlorn* is derived from Old English *forloren*, the past participle of an obsolete Old English verb *forlēosan* 'to lose utterly'). *Forbrecan* has been replaced, in Present-Day English, by two forms: (1) a comparatively colloquial phrasal verb *break up* (as in the expression *I'm gonna break up this joint*), and (2) by a French-derived loanword of comparatively formal register, *destroy*.

Such patterns are quite commonplace in Present-Day English. A large number of phrasal verbs can be paralleled semantically by non-phrasal verbs of greater formality. The origins of the phrasal construction seem to lie in interaction with Norse – certainly phrasal-verb constructions appear earliest in Norse, and seem to have spread into English from there – whereas the single-word, more formal equivalents to the phrasal verbs are derived from French or Latin. Examples are:

> come across – discover, take off – mimic, burn down – consume, butt in – interject, stand by – support, look after – superintend, see to – address, bring up – nurture, keep down – suppress, give up – surrender, talk into – persuade, drag into – entice, look forward to – anticipate, break through – penetrate, branch off – diverge, cross off – delete, pass around – circulate.

What seems to have happened here may be metaphorically described as another example of the snowball effect. Contact with Norse and later with French meant that borrowing, comparatively rare in Old English, became much more common in post-Old English and Middle English; and, as borrowing became more common, older methods of augmenting vocabulary by compounding became less used. New register-distinctions emerged, changing the structure of English vocabulary and its relationship with its semantic underpinning. Once again, extra- and intralinguistic processes have interacted to produce a further development.

As has already been pointed out, a number of the phenomena described above have had as much relevance for grammatical as for lexicological change. In the next chapter, the snowball effect on a much grander scale will be examined, in the shift of English from a (partially) synthetic to a (partially) analytic language.

7   Grammatical change

THE CATEGORY 'GRAMMAR'

Writing-system, phonology and even lexicology are fairly well defined categories of linguistic analysis. Grammar, however, is a more nebulous category, and this has left its mark in the confusion which sometimes marks its definition in the literature; for some scholars, grammar refers to the whole range of linguistic activity, with the exception of lexicography, for others, it has a narrower meaning. In this book, the term is used comparatively narrowly, to refer to *syntax* and *morphology*. Syntax is concerned with the way in which words combine to form clauses and sentences; morphology – referred to briefly at the beginning of Chapter 6 – is concerned with word-form. In other words, grammar is to do with such matters as element-order and inflectional variation.

It will be clear from the previous chapter that there is a fuzzy area between grammar and lexicology, and some areas traditionally considered the realm of grammar have been discussed in the previous chapter (e.g. some aspects of word-formation, the development of gender-systems with reference to pronoun-forms). This fuzziness should not be seen as too problematic; it is worth remembering that our categories of analysis are attempts to order complex things in as economical a way as possible, and it is therefore not surprising that these complex things do not always fit our necessarily clumsy attempts to force them into neat categories. Indeed, it is arguable that one of the characteristic faults of linguistics, especially as practised over the last thirty years or so, has been to try to force the complexities of linguistic behaviour into strictly formal categories which are unable to comprehend the diversity of natural languages.

The reason for the fuzziness of the division between grammar and lexis is that both are carriers of meaning, and it must be expected therefore that meaning is carried differently in different states of language. Such differences are clearly shown in diachronic study. For instance, the Present-Day English clause *I had loved*, consisting of subject-pronoun, verbal auxiliary and main verb, was expressed in Old English by the clause *ic lufode ær* (literally 'I loved formerly'), to be analysed as consisting of subject-pronoun, main verb and adverb. Both *I had loved* and *ic lufode ǣr* are attempts to express the 'same meaning', but one uses an auxiliary verb (traditionally seen as a category to do with grammar) and the other uses an adverb (traditionally seen as to do with lexis).

This interface is seen most characteristically in the process known as *grammaticalisation* (sometimes *grammaticisation*). In essence grammaticalisation is to do with the shift of an item from lexical to grammatical categories; its reverse, *lexicalisation*, was touched upon on page 134 above.

Once more, the history of the auxiliary verbs supplies a good example of the process, with the history of the form 'will'. The history of 'will' and its related verb 'shall' is of some interest for the study of the role of prescriptivity in the history of English. In Old English, *wille* etc. had a volitional sense 'want to', whereas *sceal* etc. meant 'must'. 'Shall' retains an obligatory sense in Early Modern English: thus the force of *Thou shalt not* in the Authorised Version of the Ten Commandments; and it retains this meaning in some, especially formal, varieties of Present-Day English (cf. *You SHALL go to the ball, Cinderella!*). However, the form is generally dying out in present-day varieties, either altogether (as in Present-Day Scots or in US usage) or retained only marginally through prescriptive or formalised use. In the eighteenth century, 'shall' was reinterpreted by the prescriptivists as the future auxiliary appropriate for government by first-person pronouns, and it is still taught as such (see Fowler 1965). Augustan grammarians such as Bishop Lowth put forward the interesting pragmatic argument that 'shall' is appropriate for first- but not second- or third-person use because to state obligation for the latter can be – to use a twentieth-century expression – a 'face-threatening' act. By the early twentieth century, these pragmatic arguments for usage seem to have been generally forgotten.

In an Old English clause, therefore, such as *Ic wille þone hlāford ofslēan* 'I want to kill the lord', *wille* is a lexical verb which implies *volition* as well as *futurity*. In Present-Day English, the reflex of the one-time lexical verb *wille* is an auxiliary signalling future tense, grammatically bound within the verb-phrase, and the semantic component *volition* is no longer salient. In other words, the verb has become grammaticalised. Thus *I will kill the lord* does not *necessarily* signal volition, and another Present-Day English verb, *want*, has to take its place if volition is to be signalled strongly. The key fact, of course, is that the Old English word *wille* 'want' necessarily has within its variational space the connotation of futurity, since 'to want' is to desire something not yet in one's possession; it is this connotation which has become the conceptual or focal meaning of the word. The word which has replaced 'will', 'want', had itself undergone a change of meaning, from 'lack' to 'desire'; this change has presumably itself been motivated in turn by the shift of the focal meaning of 'want'. The older meaning of 'want' survives only in a few fossil expressions, such as *found wanting*, and (of course) in biblical language, where Early Modern English usage has been retained (cf. Authorised Version, Psalm 23.1, 'The Lord is my shepherd; I shall not want').

GRAMMATICAL VARIATION

In the two previous chapters, it was observed how contact, systemic regulation and variation interact to produce phonological and lexicological change. In this chapter, the focus shifts to events which are traditionally assigned to the category of grammatical change; the aim of this chapter is to show how outcomes which are traditionally assigned to the category 'grammatical change' are the result of dynamically interacting intra- and extralinguistic processes.

At the level of phonology, it was observed that allophonic variation was the key to phonological change. Something similar can be distinguished at the level of grammar. One source of allophonic variation is, it was suggested in Chapter 5, to do with levels of emphasis: thus variants arise through emphatic or relaxed usage. In grammar, the equivalent sources of variation are similarly to do with formality or emphasis; thus, for instance, Classical Latin distinguished between *ego amo* 'I love' and *ad Romam ire* 'to go to Rome' (emphatic) and *amo*, *Romam ire* (relaxed). Over time, with the obscuration of unstressed syllables in the Romance languages, inflectional distinctions in the relaxed register became unclear, and the emphatic alternative, where the pronoun *ego* and the preposition *ad* were available to express the relationship between words, was preferred in all environments. Thus in Present-Day French the sole equivalent to *Romam ire* and *ad Romam ire* is *aller à Paris*.

Other sources of grammatical variation are the result of analogical and phonological pressures. The forces of analogy put pressure on inherited or borrowed forms which are perceived as irregular, for example strong as opposed to weak verbs. It is for this reason that, in Present-Day English, only the weak-verb paradigm is still productive, and many verbs which were historically strong have joined the weak set; for example, a recently coined verb such as *jive* has been assigned to the weak paradigm (past tense *jived* as opposed to **jove*), and the originally strong verb *help* (Old English *helpan* 'help', past participle *holpen*) is now weak (cf. the Present-Day English past participle *helped*). Phonological pressures in English have been to do with the reduction of stress on, and concomitant loss of distinctiveness of, inflectional endings; this development, as we shall see, has resulted in systemic pressure for grammatical change.

The interface between grammar and lexicon also introduces variation, in the development of periphrastic formations. A good example of this sort of thing is the appearance of the *do*-periphrasis at the end of the Middle English period, as an alternative mode of expression to signal causation or past tense. This example will be pursued further on pages 159–161 below.

Finally, as with phonological and lexicological change, there is an additional source of variation: contact with other languages. It is no coincidence that, in the history of English, inflectional innovation has been earliest advanced in the area of the country where English came into closest contact with varieties of Scandinavian. There is evidence that Scandinavian and English were, throughout the Anglo-Saxon period, to some extent mutually comprehensible; many lexical items occur in both Old English and Old Norse, since both are Germanic languages, and the pre-Viking connections between Old Anglian and Old Norse have already been touched upon in various places in the previous chapter. Norse certainly supplied English with a number of inflectional features which have since become standard, for instance the *-s* ending on third-person present-tense verbs. There are also syntactic loans, some of which, such as the phrasal-verb constructions, have entered the standard language, whereas others – such as the tendency to ellipsis of the definite article, represented by the much-parodied Northern usage *t'mill* 'the mill', which probably derives from interaction between native and Norse prosodic and grammatical patterns – have had a more restricted currency.

As we have come to expect from discussions in previous chapters, these innovative pressures do not act in isolation; they act in combination across the whole linguistic system, the dynamic interaction between them producing change. The importance of interaction in the history of grammar is underlined when innovations are compared in terms of success or failure, that is, how long they continue to be a living part of the language. In the remainder of this chapter, we shall first examine innovative failure and then innovative success. The chapter will then conclude with a history of the *do*-construction, an interesting innovation which at first 'succeeded' and then 'failed', the 'success' and 'failure' both being the result of inter-action with other parts of the linguistic system.

INNOVATIVE FAILURE I: INCIPIENT SYSTEMS OF NOMINAL INFLECTION

As was pointed out in Chapter 6, in Old English the relationships between and within noun-phrases were expressed by the use of formal case and grammatical gender respectively. That this system was breaking down in the Late Old English period is well attested. A good example of the kind of problem which was beginning to arise appears in the Old English poem *The Wanderer*, which survives in the Exeter Book (MS Exeter Cathedral 3501), a manuscript copied, probably at Exeter, where it still remains in the Cathedral Library, in the second half of the tenth century. In the standard edition of this poem (Dunning and Bliss 1969), line 102 reads *hrīð hrēosende hrūsan bindeð* 'a falling snowstorm binds the ground'. However, in the manuscript the line actually reads *hrið hreosende hruse bindeð*. Old English *hrūse* 'ground' is a weak feminine noun, and it is a reasonable editorial intervention to replace the 'mistaken' nominative form by the more 'correct' *-an*; such emendations are constantly (and quite legitimately, given the intended readership) made by editors of Old

Figure 7.1 Weak masculine and feminine declensions in Old English

| | Masculine | | Feminine | |
	Singular	Plural	Singular	Plural
Nominative	guma 'man'	guman	tunge 'tongue'	tungan
Accusative	guman	guman	tungan	tungan
Genitive	guman	gumena	tungan	tungena
Dative	guman	gumum	tungan	tungum

English texts. But the printed text misleads if it suggests to the linguist that *The Wanderer* was copied in a more normalised Old English than actually existed. As Dunning and Bliss (1969: 108 n. 23a) point out, such 'mistakes' may not be mistakes at all, but rather examples of the obscuration of inflectional distinctions in Late Old English, that is, the loss of distinctive case-markers.

That this levelling had been under way for some time in the development of the Germanic languages is illustrated by the history of the weak-noun declension. In Old English, the weak masculine and feminine declensions were as in Figure 7.1.

The Germanic ancestor of the *-an* ending which is so marked a feature of both these paradigms was much more confined in extent, however. The equivalent, and more archaic, Gothic paradigms, which demonstrate a much greater variety of endings, might be compared here (Figure 7.2). It will be observed that, in comparison with Gothic, the merging of case-distinctions ('syncretism') has been much more thorough in Old English.

The syncretism which marks Old English is, incidentally, shared by other contemporary Germanic languages, for instance Old Saxon has *tunga* (nom. sg.), *tungun* (acc., gen., dat. sg.), *tungun* (nom., acc. pl.), *tunguno* (gen. pl.), *tungun* (dat. pl.), with syncretism even of the dative plural. In both cases it is possible to speak of an obvious linguistic tendency towards the merging of case-endings.

During the transition from Old to Middle English, the original Old English noun-system underwent further analogical shifts. Old English had strong, weak and minor noun declensions, and by Present-Day English the strong system has become, almost everywhere, generalised; forms which in Old English were weak (e.g. *ēagan* 'eyes', *naman* 'names') or

Figure 7.2 Weak masculine and feminine declensions in Gothic

| | Masculine | | Feminine | |
	Singular	Plural	Singular	Plural
Nominative	guma	gumans	tuggō	tuggōns
Accusative	guman	gumans	tuggōn	tuggōns
Genitive	gumins	gumanē	tuggōns	tuggōnō
Dative	gumin	gumam	tuggōn	tuggōm

Figure 7.3 The Old English strong masculine declension

	Singular	Plural
Nominative	cyning 'king'	cyningas
Accusative	cyning	cyningas
Genitive	cyninges	cyninga
Dative	cyninge	cyningum

irregular (e.g. *bēc* 'books', *suna* 'sons') have conformed analogically to the strong paradigm. Only a few common relics remain in Present-Day English, for example *oxen, children, feet, mice*. The Old English strong masculine declension was as indicated in Figure 7.3.

Even in Old English there are indications of the reorganisation of this system. In the manuscript of the poem *Beowulf* (MS London, Cotton Vitellius A.xv), dating from the end of the tenth century, forms such as the tribal names *Heaþo-Rǣmes* (where the sense demands an accusative plural with *-as*, line 519) and *Heaðo-Scilfingas* (where the sense demands a genitive singular with *-es*, line 63) may be early examples of later developments, and the process may have been encouraged by a developing tendency towards syncretism (i.e. disappearance of formal distinctiveness) between dative and accusative which has been detected, for instance, in the process of revision of Ælfric's *Homilies*, composed around the year 1000. This process culminates during the Middle English period. Thus, for the Old English paradigm given in Figure 7.3, the usual Middle English pattern consists of *kyng* for nominative/accusative/dative singular, and *kynges* for the genitive singular and nominative/accusative/genitive/dative plural, from which pattern derives the common Present-Day English noun-paradigm.

There is, however, evidence that an alternative generalised system was being developed in the post-Old English period. In the 'AB-language' of *Ancrene Wisse* and related texts, it is possible to detect a paradigmatic pattern which differs from that described above. This variety of post-Old English was conservative, and attempted to maintain a distinction between weak and strong declensions, although there were some reassignments and a decay of irregular forms (thus AB-language has *bokes* 'books' for Old English *bēc*). The borrowing into English of French nouns, which in their native form were marked for plurality by *-es*, may ultimately have helped favour the choice of the Old English strong paradigm as the model for future developments. But, in AB-language, French loanwords were assigned to both paradigms, for example *patriarchen* (beside *patriarches*), *barren, trussen*, beside *ententes, beastes, leattres*. It appears that a semantic principle was at work:

> There was . . . a tendency to associate the plural *-es* with nouns denoting persons or classes of persons irrespective of the form of the nom. singular, and the plural *-en, -n* with nouns (denoting inanimate things)

ending in a vowel in the nom. singular, irrespective of the [Old English] plural or gender.

(d'Ardenne 1961: 207)

This principle was even extended to words of Old English origin; thus a form such as *wrecche* 'wretch' (derived from the Old English weak masculine noun *wrecca*) is assigned to the strong declension in AB-language, whereas, for example, *bruche* 'fragment' (cf. the Old English strong masculine noun *bryce*) is assigned to the weak declension in AB-language. An incipient restructuring of the system of declension, different from that which has survived in Present-Day English, seems to have been under way in this variety.

INNOVATIVE FAILURE II:
INCIPIENT RESTRUCTURING OF CASE-SYSTEMS

A similar incipient restructuring can be seen in the development of the Old English markers of grammatical case in the Late Old English and post-Old English periods. In Old English, grammatical case, as has been stated above, provided a useful syntagmatic tracking device, marking the functions of noun-phrases, and relating determiners and adjectives to nouns at a time when element-order was more fluid than in Present-Day English. However, although the system has survived in Modern German, it largely died out in English during the Early Middle English period and, with the exception of the genitive in 's' and the singular/plural distinction, is no longer a feature of Present-Day English.

The breakdown of the Old English system is well illustrated in the language of the *Peterborough Chronicle* Continuations (MS Oxford, Bodleian Library, Laud Misc. 636), a text which has been referred to on a number of occasions already. One especially controversial area of the language of the First Continuation has to do with the reflexes of the Old English determiners *sē*, *sēo*, *þæt* etc. (often referred to for convenience, if somewhat inaccurately, as the definite article), and also with the system of adjectival agreement.

In this portion of the *Peterborough Chronicle*, the Old English distinctions of grammatical gender have almost completely disappeared (see pages 128–130 above). However, there is evidence in the First Continuation that an attempt has been made to retain and reorganise the interphrasal tracking device, that is, the case-system. In the Anglian texts from the Late Old English period, there is evidence of an incipient restructuring of tracking-devices which, in Samuels's careful words, 'would have provided a remodelled paradigm for pre-modifiers' (1972: 156). The pattern is illustrated in Figure 7.4 with the Late West Saxon equivalents for the sake of comparison; the masculine accusative singular ending *-ne* appears in originally feminine and neuter contexts, the masculine/neuter

Figure 7.4 Incipient restructuring of the Old English determiner system (after Samuels 1972: 156; see further Jones 1988)

Late West Saxon system

	Masculine	*Singular* *Feminine*	*Neuter*	*Plural*
Accusative	þone	þā	þæt	þā
Genitive	þæs	þære	þæs	þāra
Dative	þǣm	þære	þǣm	þǣm

Incipient Early Middle English system

	Masculine	*Singular* *Feminine*	*Neuter*	*Plural*
Accusative	þone————————————————→			þā
Genitive	þæs————————→←————————— þæs			þāra
Dative	←————————— þære————————→			þǣm

genitive singular -*s* appears modifying historically feminine nouns, while the feminine dative singular -*re* is used to modify masculines and neuters.

Such patterns appear in the First Continuation of the *Peterborough Chronicle*, for instance *on þone mynstre* 'in the minster', *to þære mynstre* 'to the minster', where *mynster* is an historically neuter noun. The system has obvious advantages, not least because the selection of forms can be accounted for as being based on phonetic distinctiveness. A comparison of the incipient Early Middle English system with that of Late West Saxon suggests that selection of forms was based upon the singular/plural distinction; thus *þære* has been dropped as the feminine singular genitive because of overlap in form with the similar genitive plural *þāra*, whereas *þǣm* has disappeared in the masculine and neuter dative singular because of overlap with the dative plural form. Feminine *þā* was dropped in the accusative because of overlap with the plural form; the selection of *þone* rather than *þæt* seems most probably to be because *þæt* was beginning to perform a number of other useful functions, notably as a relative marker.

The system can be paralleled in the adjectives. Thus in the Northumbrian *Durham Ritual* of the early eleventh century we find masculine adjective endings applied to an originally feminine noun, for instance *ðerh allne woruld*, and this pattern is found as late as the thirteenth-century Caligula manuscript of Laȝamon's *Brut* (MS London, British Library, Cotton Caligula A.ix), where 'predictable variation within the same paradigm' (Samuels 1972: 156) is to be found in *hæfden muchelne care* 'had much sorrow' (object) beside *mid muchelere care* 'with much sorrow' (prepositional).

That this system was beginning to break down even in the First Continuation of the *Peterborough Chronicle* is, however, indicated by Clark (1970: lx–lxi), who lists a number of 'false' (i.e. unhistorical) case-forms which deviate from the incipient paradigm, for example:

þurh se Scotte kyng 'by the action of the king of Scots', Annal 1126 (with nom. *se* for the expected acc. sg.);

þone eorles sunu 'the earl's son', Annal 1127 (for gen. sg.; cf. Late West Saxon *þæs eorles sunu*, although it has been suggested that a different agreement pattern might have emerged);

þone abbotrice 'the abbacy', Annal 1127 (in subject position, and thus for nom. sg.; however, the expression *þone abbotrice* happens to be extremely common in object function in the annal for 1127, and its use here in subject position may be a simple slip).

As Clark points out, 'Statistically, false case-forms may be few; but their occurrence is none the less significant' (1970: lx). By the time of the Final Continuation, the determiner was invariably *þe*, whatever the historical case required, and Clark has suggested that the scribe of the First Continuation was attempting to maintain a system which was not part of his living language:

> If in his [i.e. the scribe of the First Continuation's] speech stressed [þeː][*sic*], unstressed [þə][*sic*], corresponded to West Saxon *se*, then he might have substituted *se* for his own form ... the orthography of the First Continuation suggests that the scribe, aware that by the standards of the *Schriftsprache* [i.e. the Late West Saxon standardised written language] his own usage was both provincial and new-fangled, was trying to palliate his own provincialism and modernity.
>
> (1970: lxi)

In other words, the scribe of the First Continuation occasionally hyper-corrected; his usage may be taken to represent a compromise between the (now extinct) incipient restructured system, the system that became widespread and appears in Present-Day English, and the West Saxon system found in the standardised written language.

INNOVATIVE FAILURE III: THE IMPERSONAL CONSTRUCTION

Old English had a number of impersonal verbs, that is, verbs without an expressed subject but with an accompanying pronoun in the accusative or dative case, for instance *mē þinceð* 'it seems to me', archaic *methinks*. The origin of such constructions has been much debated, and remains uncertain. Analysis shows that many fall into a fairly restricted range of semantic fields, and this might suggest one way in which they may have originated; a number of them, for instance, seem to be to do with physical and mental affections (cf. Wahlén 1925: 10, cited in Mitchell 1985: 429).

(I differ from B. Mitchell (1985: 427) by not including as impersonal those verbs governed by formal 'it', such as Old English *hit sniwð* 'it is snowing'. These usages seem to me to follow a different and distinct path in the history of English, witnessed by the fact that, unlike the impersonal verbs without any expressed subject, the construction is still used in Present-Day English, and has even taken over from what I would regard as 'true' impersonal constructions; cf. the Present-Day English translation offered for *me þinceð* in the previous paragraph.)

The interest of the impersonal construction lies in the process whereby it first became common but was subsequently replaced. The impersonal construction has been discussed by D. Lightfoot (1979: 229ff.); during the course of the Middle English and Early Modern English periods he detects a shift from impersonal to personal constructions, deriving from the 'rigidification' of Subject–Predicator word-order, as discussed on pages 156–157 below. The process seems to be one of analogy, whereby forms in the expected subject position ultimately conform to that position.

Following O. Jespersen, Lightfoot exemplifies the change as follows: *Þæm cyninge līcodon peran* → *The king liceden pears* → *The king liked pears* > *He liked pears*. As Lightfoot points out, 'If a language learner was confronted with the sentence "the king liked pears", there would be a tendency to analyse it as [Subject–Verb–Object]; this would conform to the canonical patterns of the language' (1979: 231). The example, however, is perhaps not a good one, because the Old English verb *līcian* means 'pleased', not 'liked', and the plural used here, *līcodon,* is not therefore a true impersonal verb, but rather a verb governed by a perfectly regular nominative subject, *peran.* Perhaps a better example would be *Þæm cyninge līcode wel þæt þū him þā bōc geaf* 'It pleased the king well that you gave him the book' – although, again, it could be argued that the subject of this sentence is simply the subordinated clause *þæt þū . . . geaf.*

Thus far, the process of change follows an analogous pattern we might expect. However, there is a problem with this straightforward description, which is that the number of impersonal verbs actually increased during the Middle English period. Millward (1989: 161) suggests that this increase is to do with language-contact, notably with French. If this is the case, then we are reminded that contact can interfere with patterns; that the change was not sustained, however, suggests that the contact-induced development did not cohere with other features of the language. It is an interesting fact that even in the Middle English period a 'dummy' subject *it* became frequent (e.g. *hit þe likede* 'it pleased you') beside more prototypically impersonal constructions such as *me thristed* 'I was thirsty'. By Early Modern English times, the form without *it* had largely disappeared; only *methinks* and *methought* appear commonly in, for instance, the works of Shakespeare, and, as Millward (1989: 240) points out, Shakespeare never uses **himthought, *usthinks, *youthinks* etc. It seems that, by Shakespeare's time, *methinks* was simply a fossil expression rather than a reflection of a still-productive usage.

NON-TELEOLOGICAL DIRECTIONALITY

There are at least two points worth making about the failure of the incipient innovations discussed:

1 They are evidence that linguistic innovation is non-teleological. If there were some ultimate goal for linguistic development, then such innovations as these would not have taken place. The appearance of these incipient systems shows that innovation can occur which may ultimately lead nowhere – rather like biological mutations which are not reproduced.

2 On the other hand, they are not evidence that linguistic change is non-directional; the distinction is an important one which has not always been understood clearly. These incipient restructurings did not succeed because there were other innovations – the fixing of element-order, for instance, or the generalisation of one system of nominal inflection – which were, it would appear, more in tune with the overall 'drift' of the language, that is, the ultimately successful system will be that which coheres best with developments of other neighbouring systems. Such 'success' in innovation will be pursued next.

INNOVATIVE SUCCESS I: 'MAY' AND 'MIGHT'

It is argued here that innovations can succeed when they cohere with other developments. The success of an innovatory pattern can be seen on a grand scale in the development of the auxiliary verb-system in the Middle English and Early Modern English periods, where lexis and grammar interacted in interesting and complex ways and – even more importantly – in the shift from synthesis to analysis. (In what follows, the forms 'may', 'might' etc. are used, for ease of reference, in preference to Old English *mæg*, *mihte* etc. and their various Middle English reflexes.)

Proto-Indo-European seems to have had no fewer than five formally expressed moods: indicative (for statements or questions of fact), subjunctive (expressing will), optative (wishes), imperative (commands) and injunctive (unreality). Germanic languages retained the indicative and parts of the imperative, but the subjunctive, injunctive and optative were merged to form a new category, known (in English) as the subjunctive mood, whose semantic range may be summed up as to do with hypothesis, potentiality and possibility.

In Old English, the subjunctive was formally distinct from the indicative: thus *hīe bundon* 'they bound' : *hīe bunden* 'they might have bound'. However, in Late Old English, the obscuration of unstressed syllables meant that this formal distinction was no longer made consistently, and -*an*, -*on*, -*en* are all used where the meaning of a passage would seem to require a subjunctive mood. In Present-Day English, only a few fossil formal subjunctives remain, such as *God save the king*, *If I were you* etc.);

the usual pattern is to express subjunctivity through the use of the auxiliary verbs *may* and *might*.

It seems fairly clear that the shift from Old to Present-Day English usage relates to the obscuration of unstressed syllables; since inflectional endings were no longer effective in signalling subjunctivity, other means had to be found for the purpose. It so happened that other Old English verb, *magan*, overlapped semantically with the subjunctive mood. The usual translation offered for Old English *magan* is 'can', 'could'. Present-Day English *can* includes a semantic component indicating possibility, potentiality, hypothesis etc., and this plainly overlaps with the range of meanings covered by the formal subjunctive. When the formal subjunctive became indistinguishable from the indicative, it is therefore not surprising that another verb, whose variational space overlapped with it, should have taken over its functions.

Subsequent to the grammaticalisation of *magan*, the semantic slot it had previously occupied was taken over by another verb which itself over-lapped with it: *cunnan* 'to be able', 'to know how to'. The shift in meaning of these verbs can therefore be seen as a 'chain-reaction', the result of an initial inflectional merger. The whole process, which might be termed the Modal Shift, is expressed in diagrammatic form in Figure 7.5. The poten-tiality for the Shift was only activated, and thus became a grammatical change, when the merger of inflectional endings had taken place.

The changes in the use of such verbs, in both 'modal' and 'premodal' usage, has been the subject of a study by D. Lightfoot (1979) which, although couched in generative terms, is in its essentials highly traditional and along the lines suggested here. Lightfoot shows that the development of 'may' and 'might' to their Present-Day English use was completed quite suddenly in the fifteenth and sixteenth centuries; such 'sudden'

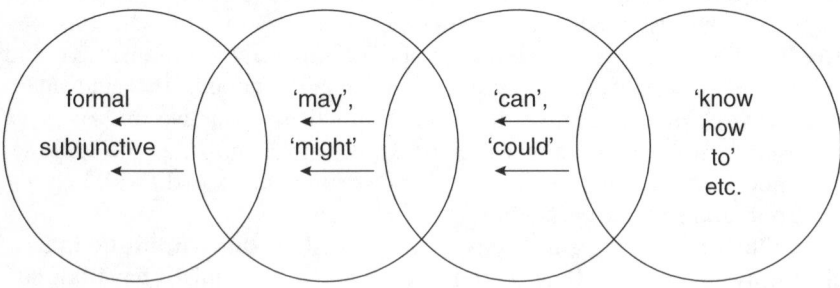

Figure 7.5 Changes in the formal expression of the subjunctive mood (simplified diagram)

completions of linguistic changes are fully explicable within the 'snowball' model which has been developed here. This shift must have been encouraged, moreover, by a formal factor; *magan* was no prototypical verb, being a member of the so-called 'preterite-present' verb-set. This difference suggests that, like other irregular verbs, *magan* was already on its way to becoming what it has ultimately become, viz. a grammatical auxiliary rather than a lexical verb; this, perhaps, is to be expected, given that *magan* at least in part overlapped semantically with a grammatical rather than another lexical item. (Lightfoot's work has recently been developed and augmented by A. Warner (1993).)

Hints of this shift in usage appear even in Late Old English; B. Mitchell notes 'the use of *magan* in the Northumbrian Gospels as an auxiliary in the translation of the Latin subjunctive, e.g. Matt (Li) 12.14, *huu hine mæhtes to lose gedoa*, Latin *quomodo eum perderent*' (1985: 423). It may be significant that this usage is recorded earliest in the North of England, where inflectional innovation is most advanced.

INNOVATIVE SUCCESS II: FROM SYNTHESIS TO ANALYSIS

It has been indicated already that 'failure' in grammatical change, like 'success', is to do with the way in which an innovation correlates with the larger contextual drift of the language. The major grammatical contextual drift during the history of English has been the steady shift from synthetic towards analytic structures, that is, from a language which marked relationships between words by special endings to one which used a comparatively fixed word-order and separable morphemes such as prepositions. It is time to see how and why this major development took place, and how it relates to the triggering of the specific phenomena described above.

Three related grammatical changes are relevant here:

1 the obscuration and loss of inflectional endings;
2 developments in the use of prepositions;
3 changes in element order.

Through an examination of the interaction of these three processes, it is possible to trace the shift in English from synthesis to analysis. Of course, the terms 'synthesis' and 'analysis' are relative, and are really the poles of a cline; Old English was much less 'synthetic' than are (for example) Present-Day Finnish or Present-Day Zulu, and Present-Day English is much less 'analytic' than, for example, the varieties of Present-Day Chinese. Nevertheless, there has been definite movement along this cline between Old and Present-Day English, and the three sets of changes here illustrate the processes involved.

1 The first of these phenomena, the obscuration and loss of inflectional endings, has already been touched upon at several points in earlier

discussion. It has been observed that obscuration of inflections is a characteristic of a number of the Germanic languages. This development probably originates in the shift to fixed stress which took place during the Proto-Germanic period, that is, soon after the birth of Christ. Before this shift took place, stress was mobile; after it, stress was fixed, usually on the initial syllable of a word. (The Germanic stress-shift is hard to date, probably because it was a gradual and sporadic process; it seems to have varied in its effects on the various Germanic dialects. See further Prokosch 1938: 118–120.)

The origins of this stress-shift are still a matter for scholarly debate; a recent plausible suggestion, which has caused some considerable excitement amongst historical linguists, is that it is a contact-phenomenon, the result of interaction between the Northern Indo-European languages (such as Celtic and Germanic) and what is known as Old European. Old European was a non-Indo-European language which had existed in the northern half of Europe since the last Ice Age 10,000 years or so ago. It was swept aside by the usage of the advancing Indo-European peoples, leaving traces only in a few place-names (notably of rivers) and in a few isolated pockets, represented in the twentieth century by Basque. Old European seems to have had initial stress, and the implication is that Germanic developed a new stress-pattern through what is known as 'substratum influence' (cf. the pronunciation of English by people from South Wales, who have retained Celtic intonation patterns even though they no longer otherwise speak a Celtic language; see further Vennemann 1994: 245–247, 271–272).

However it arose, the shift of stress away from inflectional endings made them vulnerable to what might be termed 'phonetic attrition'. It is therefore no surprise that inflectional syncretism results, as has been seen already in a comparison of the Old English and Old Saxon noun-paradigms with the older Gothic practice (see Figures 7.1 and 7.2 above). And, at later stages in the history of English, the loss of inflections must have been encouraged through interaction with Norse, whose inflectional system was distinct.

2 Most prepositions in Present-Day English derive ultimately from adverbs, and something of this origin is seen in the element-order of Old English. Thus *Hē cwæþ þæm mannum tō* and *He cwæþ tō þæm mannum* may both be translated into Present-Day English as 'He spoke to the men', but it is possible in Old English to parse *tō* as either an adverb or a preposition. The adverb *tō*, in Old English an 'extra', 'adjunct' element in the clause with a *lexical* function, has become in Present-Day English an essential *grammatical* word tied to a particular kind of phrase. The process is one of grammaticalisation, as defined on page 142 above. (For the derivation of prepositions from adverbs, see, for example *ODEE* sv. 'to'; the old adverbial use survives in fossil idiomatic expressions such as *to and fro*.)

By the time of recorded Old English, it is possible to establish a group of prepositions (which we will, arbitrarily, take to include the so-called postposition, as in *him tō* 'to him'); but it is still true to state that prepositions were not as essential to the meaning of the text as they are in Present-Day English. Important work by A. Dančev (all quotations from whom are taken from Mitchell 1985: 522–523) has shown three things:

(i) 'The more clear-cut a given pattern [in its formal distinctiveness], the higher the probability for the occurrence of prepositionless instances.' Thus, for instance, prepositions are less frequent with the dative plural *-um* than with the dative singular *-e*.

(ii) There is a relation between the meaning of the noun and the presence or absence of a preposition. Words referring to parts of the body, such as *cnēow*, *ēage*, *tōð*, and *tunge*, supply the bulk of prepositionless constructions.

(iii) There are 'recurrent collocations [i.e. formulae]', consisting of 'consciously archaic' and stereotypical constructions found in poetry and in the rhythmical prose writings of Archbishop Wulfstan, himself a poet.

There would seem therefore to be definite evidence, from the Old English written record, that prepositions retained the potential of being excluded in favour of more synthetic constructions. The point of pressure is indicated by Dančev's point (i), which suggests that a functional cause lay behind the selection of the prepositional rather than the prepositionless construction, while his points (ii) and (iii) indicate that prepositionless constructions were somewhat old-fashioned by the end of the Old English period.

Dančev's first point has a wider significance, since it suggests that the obscuration of inflections was the principal reason for the selection of prepositions; when the inflection remained distinct, then the preposition was less common. The older view, a strongly functionalist one, was that prepositional phrases had become formalised so that inflectional endings became redundant, and therefore disappeared. However, C. Clark points out that, in the language of the *Peterborough Chronicle* Continuations,

Contrary to the view that it was the previous existence of analytic machinery which brought about loss of inflexion, inflexional loss here seems to be more advanced than the procedures needed to replace it. Noun-inflexions [in the Continuations] are virtually reduced to the Modern-English level, whereas the analytic procedures destined to supply their place – fixed word-order, prepositional constructions – are only partially developed.

(1970: lxxiv)

3 The quotation from Clark's study leads us to the remaining grammatical development of relevance to the argument at this stage: the institution of a fixed word-order.

Although Old English word-order is certainly more flexible than that of Present-Day English, this is not to say that regular patterns had not emerged. The main element-order patterns in Old English may be roughly summarised as follows (where S = subject, P = predicator):

SP appears typically in main clauses (i.e., 'verb-second'; as in Present-Day English, the predicator immediately follows the subject of the clause): for example *Sum swīþe gelǣred munuc cōm sūþan ofer sǣ* 'A certain learned monk came from the south over (the) sea.'

S ... P appears typically in subordinate clauses (i.e., 'verb-final'; as in Present-Day German, the predicator appears at the end of the clause): for example *þe hit ǣr geseah* 'who had seen it' (*lit.* 'who it formerly saw').

PS appears typically in questions, and after initial adverbials, especially *Þā* 'Then' (i.e. 'verb-initial'; as in Present-Day German, the predicator precedes the subject): for example *Þā wearð se cyning Ōswold swīðe ælmes-georn* 'Then King Oswald became very charitable' (*lit.* 'Then became the King Oswald very charitable').

These patterns, however, are not strictly adhered to; rather, they are the unmarked patterns, deviation from which is a sign of stylistic salience ('fore-grounding'). Thus a skilled writer of prose such as Ælfric was able to adopt unusual word-orders for the purposes of literary effect, for example:

Sēo ylce rōd siððan ... þǣr stōd 'That same cross stood there afterwards' (*lit.* 'That same cross afterwards ... there stood') (main clause).

þæt fela þearfan sǣtan geond þā strǣt gehwanon cumene tō þæs cyninges ælmyssan 'that many needy sat throughout the street from all sides come for the king's alms' (subordinate clause).

Hwæt ðā Ōswold cyning his cymes fægnode 'Lo then, King Oswald rejoiced at his coming' (main clause with initial adverbial).

The traditional view is that Old English is at an intermediate stage where the S ... P element-order, characteristic of all clause-types in more archaic Indo-European languages (cf. e.g. Latin), is being steadily replaced by SP element-order:

> This verb final unmarked order was inherited from proto-Indo-European. A second order, also inherited from proto-Indo-European – verb initial – was a marked order in these early Germanic dialects, used in commands, conjoined clauses, and dramatic sentences. These two orders were evidently supplemented by a third order – verb second – which came on as a strong innovation.
>
> (Smith 1971: 291, cited Bean 1983: 45)

The older S ... P ordering as 'unmarked' and available in main clauses appears in the Gothic Bible (although here some influence from Greek

Figure 7.6 The Gallehus Horn inscription

·ᛗᛉ·ᚺ ᛚᛖᚹᚨᚷᚨᛋᛏᛁ�·ᚺᛟᛚᛏᛁᛉᚱᚤ·ᚺᛟᚱᚾᚨ·ᛏᚨᚹᛁᛞᛟᚱ·

'e k h l e w a g a s t i R h o l t i j a R h o r n a   t a w i ð o'

'I, HlewagastiR, the son of Holti, made the horn (*lit.* the horn made)'

is possible) and in the oldest Germanic runic inscriptions, for instance the famous fourth-century Gallehus horn inscription, transcribed and translit-erated in Figure 7.6. However, by the seventh century runic inscriptions cease to maintain this element-order; a good example from this date is the Early Old Northumbrian runic inscription on the Ruthwell Cross, traditionally interpreted as part of an early version of *The Dream of the Rood*: 'krist wæs on rodi' 'Christ was on the cross'. It would appear that the shift from S ... P to SP was well under way by this time.

Although Old English word-order, therefore, was still very flexible in comparison with Present-Day English, the key requirement for flexibility, the maintenance of an inflectional system to indicate the relationships between words, was, as was demonstrated on pages 153–154 above, itself under pressure. As Clark (1970: lxxi) puts it:

> sentence structure might *a priori* be expected to become less flexible: for, with subject-noun, object-noun, and indirect-object-noun (and on occasion adverbial noun as well) formally indistinguishable, they may have to take up, as they do in Modern English, set positions with relation to the verb.

Of the three available unmarked Old English word-orders, S ... P was unable to resolve this ambiguity when deviated from for stylistic effect. SP expressed a clear relationship between subject and verb, and it is undoubtedly for this reason that this structure was the one which succeeded. PS remained longer, but it had always been restricted to a particular set of environments and was not available as a general structural model.

The process, then, seems to have been a therapeutic one. Linguistic ambiguities appeared, and 'second-order' elements, such as emphatic prepositions and a fixed word-order based upon SP structure, took over. The final triggering was, presumably, the increased obscuration of inflectional distinctiveness which marks the shift from Old to Middle English and which was encouraged by the Scandinavian invasions. That ambiguities did exist is demonstrated once more by the *Peterborough Chronicle*. In the Final Continuation a number of ambiguities occur, where the old subordinate clause S ... P ordering is retained, as a result of lack of clear inflectional marking, for example:

for æuric rice man his castles makede, ðat ani god hefden (?'for every powerful man, who had any property, made castles for himself'), Annal 1137.

As Clark puts it, 'the evidence suggests that loss of the dative case, for
instance, takes place rather in spite of a lack of substitute procedures than
because its functions had already been usurped by them' (1970: lxxiv).

CONDITIONS DETERMINING 'SUCCESS' AND 'FAILURE': SUMMARY

Looking back over the three sets of changes described above, one
important point might be made: each system produces variation, but the
choice of one variable or another as ultimately 'successful' depends on
the relationship between systems. To repeat a theme of this book: *tout se
tient*, everything is connected to everything else. The relationship between
Old English and post-Old English developments in case and gender,
prepositional usage and element-order is one of interactive reinforcement.
Over time, a major set of changes in the grammatical structure of English
has been brought about; but these changes are the result of a series of
minor developments which have constantly interacted over a great number
of linguistic states. These minor developments are the result of variation,
deriving both from within the language and as the result of contact with
other languages. Case- and gender-endings become slightly obscured as a
result of changes in stress-patterns; adverbs become grammaticalised as
prepositions in 'marked' conditions and begin to be more commonly used
to avoid ambiguities arising from the obscuration of vowels in unstressed
syllables; marked word-order patterns are extended to resolve ambiguities;
in turn these developments encourage the further loss of inflectional
endings whereby case and gender are marked. These individual changes
have interacted to produce a major shift in the expression of relationships
between words.

   With hindsight, it is possible to see why some innovations failed,
such as the incipient restructuring of the noun-system to reflect the
animate–inanimate distinction in AB-language, the incipient restructuring
of the system of modifiers to express case without gender or the growth
of the impersonal construction. These innovations were unsuccessful
because they did not cohere with the other tendencies in the language
towards inflectional obscuration. These innovations were highly sophisticated, but had no future possibilities of development given the 'ecology'
of the system.

   This argument could be pursued further, because the 'success' of the
synthetic–analytic shift had implications for other parts of the linguistic
system, notably prosody. A 'typical' Old English phrase is trochaic,
consisting of a stressed lexical element and a less stressed inflection,
whereas a 'typical' Present-Day English phrase is iambic, consisting of a

less stressed modifying element (such as a determiner, a preposition or an auxiliary verb) and a stressed lexical element (such as a main verb or a noun). It is not surprising, therefore, that Old English poetry is based upon a trochaic metre with initial alliteration whereas later metres are iambic, with final rhyme. The interest of this example, of course, is that linguistic changes in one part of the system can have innumerable implications elsewhere in the system: *tout se tient*.

THE RISE AND FALL OF A CONSTRUCTION: THE *DO*-PERIPHRASIS

As a final demonstration of the themes of this chapter, a development which underwent *both* 'success' *and* 'failure' will be examined: the *do*-periphrasis. The construction expanded greatly in its range of usage during the Middle and Early Modern English periods, but underwent major reductions in the transition to Late Modern English. The history of this construction demonstrates not just the way in which dynamic interaction produces change, but also the non-teleological nature of change, for the earlier development was ultimately reversed.

'Do' was used as a lexical verb in Old English with causative sense, for example *Swā swā ðū dydest mīnne brōðor his gōd forlǽtan* 'Just so you caused my brother to abandon his goods', *Dōð þæt þæt folc sitte* 'Make the people sit' (cited Mitchell 1985: 266). However, its membership in Old English times of the anomalous group of verbs indicates that it was no longer a prototypical lexical verb and was therefore ripe for grammaticalisation. In the sixteenth and seventeenth centuries it underwent a marked widening of usage, and by the middle of the sixteenth century it could appear in five contexts:

1 negative direct questions: *Didst thou not heare a noyse?* (William Shakespeare, *Macbeth*, II.ii.16);
2 affirmative direct questions: *Did you send to him Sir?* (*Macbeth* III.iv.151);
3 negative declarative sentences: *You do not give the Cheere* (*Macbeth* III.iv.37);
4 negative imperatives: *Do not muse at me my most worthy Friends* (*Macbeth* III.iv.100);
5 affirmative declarative sentences: *the surfeted Groomes/Doe mock their charge with Snores* (*Macbeth* II.ii.5–6); *The chief both in antiquity and excellency were they that did imitate the inconceivable excellencies of God* (Philip Sidney, *Apology for Poetry*); *The bell doth toll for him* (John Donne, *Devotions upon Emergent Occasions*).

The first four of these usages are still current in Present-Day English, but the last of them has been obsolete since about 1700. It is with the failure of this last usage that we shall be concerned here.

Do + infinitive constructions in affirmative declarative sentences appear during this period in the following circumstances:

1 In some strong verbs, the vocalic distinction between present and preterite had disappeared because of sound-change, notably the merging and reorganisation of mid-vowels which accompanied and succeeded the Great Vowel Shift. Thus, for example, in Old English the verb *etan* 'eat' had a distinctive form of the preterite, *æt* (sg.), *æton* (pl.). However, by the fifteenth century, the short vowel of the infinitive and present tense had undergone lengthening, and in many dialects the mid-front vowels reflecting West Saxon *ē, æ* had merged. The result of this change was that there was no longer any sound-distinction between present and preterite forms of the verb. It is not therefore surprising that a new form appeared, *did eat*, which was used as an emphatic form beside the ancestor of Present-Day English *ate*; the *do*-construction was available as a variant through its use as a quasi-auxiliary causative, and it was therefore available for selection when the need arose. Example: *... and gave also unto her husband with her; and he did eat* (Authorised Version of the Bible, Genesis 3.vi).

2 In Present-Day English, a few weak verbs have become accepted as having invariable forms in both present and preterite tenses, for instance *cast*, *put*, *set*. For a time it was common for them to appear with auxiliary *did* to signal past tense. Example: *... and no man did put on him his ornaments* (Authorised Version of the Bible, Exodus 33.iv).

3 During the sixteenth century large numbers of polysyllabic loanwords entered English as a result of humanist interest in 'enriching' the vernacular through borrowing from Latin and Greek. This led to inflectional difficulties; when the loanword *illuminate* is inflected as *illumi-nateth* the resulting five-syllable form presents prosodic difficulties. It is not surprising, therefore, that the *do*-auxiliary was adopted for this group of words as well, for instance *doth illuminate*. (Lightfoot (1979: 118) has noticed this usage when he points out that it occurs 'particularly in learned writings'). Example: *I am the Lord that doth sanctify you* (Authorised Version of the Bible, Exodus 31. xiii)

4 The *do*-construction seems to have been used as a tracking device in contemporary written prose. Elizabethan prose-style, with its complex, latinate use of subordinate clauses, needed dummy-verbs to signal a return to the main clause after an interruption, and the *do*-construction was used for this purpose.

5 Finally, the use of the *do*-construction became so widespread that it was simply used analogously with a wide range of verbs, for example *... they did mock at her desolations* (Authorised Version of the Bible, Lamentations i.vii).

Changing stylistic conventions meant that case 4 ceased to be necessary, and 1 became less functionally desirable as new weak forms were developed and paradigmatic restructuring (e.g. Present-Day English *eat – ate*) took place. As regards 3, a competing system in the 3rd pres. sg., *-es*, derived ultimately from Scandinavian, was taking over, and this meant that *-ateth* was being replaced by *-ates*, a monosyllabic form more easily sustainable in English sentence-prosody. Case 2 does not seem to have been sufficiently frequent a usage to sustain the construction, and 5, as an analogous formation, was liable to disappear when the main body of usage had changed. In short, the innovation was not sustainable, and ultimately disappeared in most varieties of English, save in sporadic emphatic use (e.g. Present-Day English *I DO know*; Dr Johnson considered it 'a vitious mode of speech' (1755: 8)). The usage was retained, however, in questions and negatives, where it allowed the functionally advantageous use of a fixed word-order (i.e. subject preceding lexical verb; compare Present-Day English *Do you know ...?* with Early Modern English *Knowest thou ...?*), and this construction remains in Present-Day English.

A sixth usage is sporadically recorded by seventeenth-century grammarians. An example appears in the *Diary* of Samuel Pepys:

> In the morning I went up to Mr Crewe's, who did talk to me concerning things of state. From thence to my office, where nothing to do; but Mr Downing came and found me there all alone; and did mention to me his going back into Holland, and did ask me whether I would go or no.

In such passages, *did* for *-ed* may be simply for 'euphonic' purposes (cf. *talkt, askt*); but Prof. M.L. Samuels has pointed out to me that the verbs in the above passage fall into two semantic groups:

1 *did talk, did mention, did ask*: verbs without an obvious result, therefore 'imperfective';
2 *went, came, found*: verbs indicating completion, therefore 'perfective'.

In short, the *do*-construction seems to be developing as a means of marking aspectual distinctions. This method has not been sustained, and has been replaced by the longer and more widely established *be + -ing* construction. The innovation did not succeed, but it is of interest as another 'non-teleological mutation' of the kind discussed above, *passim*.

It is perhaps worth recording that periphrastic *do* in affirmative declarative sentences disappeared at different rates in different places, and that there are a few residualisms of this construction still in rural varieties, notably in the south-western counties of England (see further Ihalainen 1994: 225–226, and references there cited). A possible contributory factor to this retention is indicated by the pronunciation of *eat* as [ɛit], recorded in Devon and Cornwall in the *Linguistic Atlas of England*.

CONCLUSION

A number of conclusions can be drawn from the discussion above, but two are most important: (1) the sustainability of a grammatical construction in the history of a language depends crucially on its linguistic environment, and (2) any individual linguistic event or output depends on the dynamic interaction of a number of (metaphorically) conspiring or snowballing factors. In the next chapter, the interaction of varieties and languages will be examined on a macrolinguistic scale, through the history of some very diverse varieties derived from Old English: Scots and Scottish English, and Jamaican Creole and Jamaican English.

Part III

8   Two varieties in context

VARIETIES IN CONTEXT

In Part II, the theme of dynamic interaction has been explored through the examination of a set of particular linguistic outputs. The focus has been on individual events, and the aim has been to show how a particular event is the result of the interaction of intra- and extralinguistic processes working in combination.

The reader may be forgiven, however, for becoming impatient with the 'bittiness' of the discussion so far. To bring some coherence into the argument, the present chapter is designed to give an account of the emergence of the varieties of language in use in two communities: Scotland, and the London black community. The theme of this chapter is that whole varieties, not just individual linguistic 'events', are the result of complex processes of interaction.

The choice of the varieties discussed here is governed by a major consideration: English has become, in the twentieth century, a worldwide language, with more speakers than any other language (save possibly Chinese) has ever achieved. It therefore behoves anyone working in the field of historical study to avoid too anglocentric a focus, since English is no longer the property of just the English. For many years, the historical study of the language was taken to be a study of a steady development towards Standard English as used in the South of England. Since English is now the property of many people a long way from that part of the world, it seems worth while to make a conscious effort to overcome this focus, even though the expertise of the present writer means that the focus remains on the British Isles.

It is this orientation which has determined the choice of the two varieties given special attention in this chapter. In Scotland, the variety known as *Scots* has the longest attested history of any major language-variety derived from Old English outside the geographical boundaries of present-day England, and was the first non-English variety to begin developing a standardised form of the language. It therefore provides invaluable diachronic information distinct from the history of English varieties. Furthermore, Scots has had an especially intimate contact with English throughout its history, and it thus provides an excellent laboratory for the study of language-contact.

London Jamaican, unlike Scots, has not hitherto achieved the status of developing as a standardised language. However, like Scots, it has a lengthy history, going back to at least the eighteenth century, and the interest of this variety for historical linguists lies (amongst other things) in the fact that it has emerged through interaction with non-Indo-European languages. Its social setting, moreover, with origins in the slave-trade, supplies excellent exemplification for the working of sociolinguistic pressures in society.

Both Scots and London Jamaican are varieties which, in a sense, are under threat from normative pressures associated with the class-based state and its means of enforcement and socialisation: social structure and education. Yet, as will be shown here, both varieties have the validity which history confers. In the discussion which follows, each variety will be investigated as follows:

1 The present-day linguistic situation in each community will be described.
2 An outline history of the languages in use in both communities will be given.
3 A particular text will be subjected to analysis.
4 The process of divergence from other varieties will be discussed.

SCOTS AND ENGLISH IN PRESENT-DAY SCOTLAND

The community of speakers of Anglo-Saxon-derived languages in Scotland falls roughly into the following three groups:

1 Speakers of *Scots*, a variety derived from Old English but with a separate history since the late Middle Ages. Spoken Scots has become in general the preserve of the working classes, either rural or urban, and is still frequently subjected to correction in the classroom. Especially in urban usage, it is losing a good deal of its lexical (although not accentual or grammatical) distinctiveness as a result of exposure to UK-wide radio and television, and because of the greater range of social interaction which takes place in towns. Nevertheless, those signalling their identity with Scottish working-class culture continue to do so by using this variety. Scots can itself be subdivided into varieties, either geographically or socially distinguished.
2 Speakers of so-called *Scottish Standard English*. Scottish Standard English is frequently defined as 'Standard English with a Scottish accent', and this is a fair summary. It has a grammar and vocabulary almost (although not quite) the same as that used by educated speakers of Standard English in England, but it combines these characteristics with an essentially Scots pronunciation, albeit modified somewhat in

the direction of Received Pronunciation. This variety of English is aimed at by the Scottish middle classes and those aspiring to that status, although it seems to be part of the same linguistic continuum as Scots since many middle-class speakers in less formal situations use Scots items as opposed to those more characteristic of Scottish Standard English. However, the fact that it is modified in the direction of Southern English is also significant; evidently, middle-class people feel the centripetal pull of two different linguistic centres of gravity.

3 Finally, there is a variety which might best be termed *standardised Southern English*, consisting of the grammar and vocabulary of Standard English transmitted in an accent focused on Received Pronunciation, the prestigious, non-localised accent of England. This variety is spoken in particular by two groups of speakers living in Scotland: some English immigrants, and members of the Scottish aristocracy. The latter, who have traditionally been educated in an environment where this variety is spoken, have in general no wish to modify their language in the direction of Scots; their own social position is clear, they identify with it, and they feel no need to change their manner of speech to accommodate themselves to the wider society in which they live. More importantly, Scots regularly encounter (and thus monitor) standardised Southern English through audio-visual media such as radio and television – so much so that some occasionally confess to being disconcerted by encountering accents like their own in such situations.

Of these three groups of speakers, the second is perhaps the most interesting for students of linguistic change. Working-class and aristocratic Scots, relatively secure in their own social position, express that position through their choice of language. Linguists have noted for many years how prestige is associated with working-class and aristocratic varieties of language: so-called 'covert' usage in the case of working-class usage, 'overt' in the case of aristocratic. Choosing Scots or English is therefore in one sense a statement of social solidarity. However, middle-class Scots, like middle-class people elsewhere, poised between working-class and aristocratic groups, are comparatively weakly tied to the society around them.

Recent work, notably by James Milroy, has located the actuation of linguistic change among such weakly tied groups (Milroy 1992, *passim*). On the one hand, such people seek to imitate an overtly prestigious usage which reflects British rather than Scottish identity; on the other, they feel the pull of Scots. Although Scots may be essentially the usage of the present-day working class, it has also a distinct history; to use Scots, therefore, is to associate oneself with that history and to assert one's identity with it. It is therefore in a sense an assertion of nationality distinct from England to use a variety restricted to Scotland, and it is as a result not surprising that some advocates of the Scots language have tended towards nationalist aspirations in their political stance.

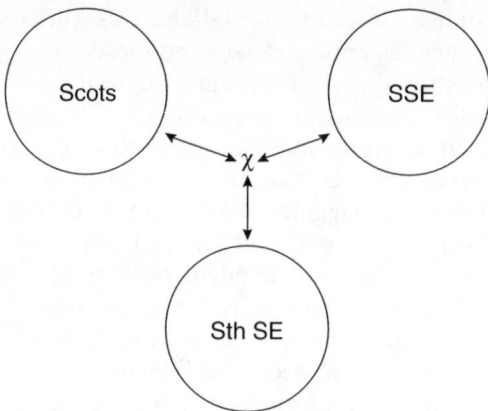

χ = given individual with weak social ties

Figure 8.1 The linguistic situation of an individual with weak social ties, living in Scotland (SSE = Standard Scottish English; Sth SE = Southern Standardised English)

Of course, the outline of Scottish class-structure given above will seem very crude to sociologists; and it is important to bear in mind that the relationship is not one of clear-cut division, but clinal; many, if not all, speakers shift from one group to another in different situations, and some – especially those whose social ties are weak – can drift fairly indiscriminately between varieties. This complex relationship is illustrated schematically by Figure 8.1, which shows how individual speakers are situated in relation to these three points of reference. Nevertheless, the description given above is perhaps enough to show that class and language have an intimate relationship, a relationship which will be returned to later in this chapter.

The key fact to note at this stage in our general argument, however, is that this social structure and its linguistic markers derive from the history of Scotland. English has overt prestige in Scotland because, since the seventeenth century, Scotland has been governed from England as a subordinate part of the United Kingdom. But Scots has covert prestige in Scotland, notably among the working classes, because Scottish workers have resisted perceived English oppression much more strongly than the Scottish upper classes. It is surely no coincidence that Scottish nationalism as a political movement runs most deeply among the Scottish working classes, and has a powerful radical (and specifically socialist) edge to it.

Scots as a variety of English can be discerned in the written record from the late fourteenth century onwards; before that date, the only evidence of any significance for this variety is to be found in place-names and in occasional glosses on Latin material. The extent of its divergence from Northern Middle English, however, does not seem to have been such that it was viewed by contemporaries as a language distinct from English. Fifteenth-century writers such as William Dunbar refer to Londoners such as Chaucer as using 'our' language, and the term *Inglis*, used to describe the non-Celtic language of the Lowlands of Scotland, was only joined (and not replaced) by *Scottis* in the late fifteenth century; until that date, the term *Scottis* was used to refer to Gaelic.

Like Middle English, written Older Scots was marked by dialect-variation, although a standardised norm of written Scots, comparable with that found in contemporary English, has been detected by modern scholars in fifteenth- and sixteenth-century texts. However, whereas standardised written English subsequently became the educationally enforced written norm, political and cultural events such as the Reformation (with the subsequent circulation of the English vernacular Bible), and the Unions of Crowns and of Parliaments, meant that standardised written Scots was replaced by Standard written English (see Chapter 4 above).

These political and cultural events meant that, during the late seventeenth and eighteenth centuries, written (as opposed to spoken) Scots became merely a curiosity, albeit sometimes a fashionable one, in (for instance) the poetry of Robert Burns. In the nineteenth century, however, a Scots prose tradition flourished in the developing popular press and in fiction generally (see Donaldson 1986, 1989), and in the twentieth century there was an attempt to create a prestigious written Scots, in the shape of *Lallans* (= 'Lowlands'), a synthetic mixture of Scots varieties, invented by the poet Hugh McDiarmid and others, and given normative form by a published style-sheet. However, the use of this so-called 'plastic' variety has not become common. A comparison is sometimes made between Lallans and Norwegian *Nynorsk*, which emerged in the nineteenth century in a similar way; interestingly, both varieties have developed strong political associations, especially radical ones. Unlike Lallans, Nynorsk has received a fair degree of state support, and has developed as an everyday language, spoken as well as written by persons with some social prestige. However, both Lallans and Nynorsk are marked by artificiality and, especially in the case of the former, restriction to a particular kind of literary usage, and their long-term prospects outside this register do not look good (despite McClure 1981; see also Oftedal 1981). Even in poetic use, Lallans seems now to be declining, to be replaced by an attempt to reflect working-class urban speech in writing (e.g. in the poetry of Tom Leonard, or in the novels of James Kelman).

SCOTS, ENGLISH AND SCOTTISH STANDARD ENGLISH IN THE POETRY OF ROBERT BURNS

In Chapter 4, there was some discussion of the 'failure' of standardisation of written Older Scots as a result of political events. There is some evidence, however, that a distinctively Scots linguistic identity was still being asserted as prestigious in the sixteenth and seventeenth centuries.

Alexander Hume's *Of the Orthographie and Congruite of the Britan Tongue* dates from about 1617, and it is therefore roughly contemporary with the writings of Alexander Gil (see Chapter 5 above, *passim*). Hume, a Scotsman a little older than Gil who had lived for some years in England, nevertheless felt confident enough about his native pronunciation (and spelling) to dispute the correctness of English in comparison with Scots (see Dobson 1968: 321). While in Bath, he tells us, he dined with an English doctor of divinity,

> to whom he advanced the argument that a labial symbol should not represent a guttural sound; that *w* was a labial symbol and the initial sound of *quho* 'who' a guttural; and that therefore the Scottish spelling *quho* was better than the English *who*. The doctor neatly and justly replied, 'The proposition I understand; the assumption is Scottish and the conclusion false.'

> (Dobson 1968: 321)

The interest of this anecdote is twofold: first, that the doctor had a conception of 'Standard English', as distinct from Scots, which he could assert; and, second, that Hume, despite spending several years in England as a schoolteacher, nevertheless believed written Scots could have prestige in terms of 'correctness'.

By the eighteenth century, however, things seem to have become more complex. The poetry of Robert Burns (1759–1796) may be taken to exemplify the interaction of varieties in eighteenth-century Scotland. One of his lesser-known poems, *The Brigs of Ayr*, although written largely in Scots, begins with the following English verse inscription to John Ballantine of Ayr:

> The simple Bard, rough at the rustic plough,
> Learning his tuneful trade from ev'ry bough;
> The chanting linnet, or the mellow thrush,
> Hailing the setting sun, sweet, in the green thorn bush;
> The soaring lark, the perching red-breast shrill,   5
> Or deep-ton'd plovers, grey, wild-whistling o'er the hill;
> Shall he, nurst in the Peasant's lowly shed,
> To hardy Independence bravely bred,
> By early Poverty to hardship steel'd,
> And train'd to arms in stern Misfortune's field,   10
> Shall he be guilty of their hireling crimes,
> The servile, mercenary Swiss* of rhymes?
> Or labour hard the panegyric close,
> With all the venal soul of dedicating Prose?
> No! though his artless strains he rudely sings,   15

And throws his hand uncouthly o'er the strings,
He glows with all the spirit of the Bard,
Fame, honest fame, his great, his dear reward.
Still, if some Patron's gen'rous care he trace,
Skill'd in the secret, to bestow with grace;   20
When B[allantine] befriends his humble name,
And hands the rustic stranger up to fame,
With heartfelt throes his grateful bosom swells,
The godlike bliss, to give, alone excels.
                    (Kinsley 1968: 226–227)

(*'Swiss soldiers were in the habit of hiring themselves to any country that chose to pay for their services' (Wallace 1990: 216).)

This extract, like most of Burns's poetry in Augustan English, has been neglected; we are taught to see such passages as conventional pieces of competent versification, and no more. As K. Wittig's survey of Scottish literature holds, 'Burns's own variety of literary neo-classical Augustan English . . . was diametrically opposed to his own genius, and it alone rings false' (1958: 203); and more recently A. Bold has stated that 'none of the English poems . . . is much more than a literary pastiche' (1991: 146). And yet analysis of this passage reveals a sophisticated handling of rhyme for which Wittig's comment or Bold's scorn does not prepare us, and which is of interest for our understanding of the contemporary relationship between Scots, Scottish English and English.

The poem is written in couplets, and two pairs of words here stand out as conventional eye- rather than proper ear-rhymes: *thrush : bush* (lines 3–4), and *Bard : reward* (lines 17–18). In the prestigious spoken language of eighteenth-century England, the first pair was pronounced much as in its present-day equivalent, Received Pronunciation; the two vowels were in Late Middle English probably pronounced as in Present-Day Northern English (i.e. [ʊ]), but a distinction between /ʊ/- and /ʌ/- phonemes emerged in Southern English dialects in the seventeenth century (Dobson 1968: 717). The latter pair of words in England probably, as in most varieties of Present-Day English, contained different stressed vowels in the late eighteenth century, since [w] had by that date caused rounding of vowel-segments immediately following in most words where the sequence occurred. It seems therefore fairly certain that the pairs *thrush : bush* and *Bard : reward* were eye-rhymes, and not good ear-rhymes, in prestigious English speech at the end of the eighteenth century.

The status of these two pairs as rhymes in eighteenth-century Scotland is less certain. The situation is complicated by there being in Scotland at that date, as now, three varieties of Anglo-Saxon-derived speech for the poet to reflect in writing: Scots, Scottish Standard English, and Standardised Southern English. The first, the traditional-dialect variety spoken in Southern, Central and North-Eastern Scotland, was (as now) essentially the preserve of the rural peasantry and the urban working classes; Burns's best-known poetry (e.g. *Holy Willie's Prayer*, most of *Tam O'Shanter*) was largely written to reflect this variety. It is distinctive at all levels of language: accent, grammar and vocabulary; and a distinctive orthography, derived from medieval practice, had sprung up to reflect it.

The second variety is in present-day Scotland generally spoken by the middle classes; as was indicated on page 166 above, it differs from Standardised Southern English by including a few lexical and grammatical items derived from Scots, but more especially by being spoken in a distinctively Scottish accent. There is evidence that something like it – a prestigious Scottish usage which differed from the contemporary Southern English prestigious norm especially in accent – was beginning to emerge, purged of so-called *vestigia ruris*, in Edinburgh and Glasgow during the eighteenth century. This variety was transmitted in the written mode in Augustan English, that is, in an orthography indistinguishable from that used in England to reflect contemporary prestigious English speech. It is thus certain that (as now) this precursor of Scottish Standard English was in close contact (if not in competition) with contemporary Standardised Southern English. In twentieth-century Scotland, this last variety, as was indicated on page 167 above, is in general the preserve of certain groups of English incomers, and of the English-educated Scottish aristocracy.

It has often been pointed out that even in *Tam O'Shanter*, one of his 'Scots' poems, Burns mixes Augustan English with Scots usage. In this poem, Burns seems to have distinguished between narrative description, written in Scots, and philosophical reflection, written in Augustan English; and this distinction is generally taken as reflecting Burns's assessment of the relative social significance of these varieties. The shifting usages of the poem may therefore be taken as exemplification of the points just made. The following passages might be compared:

lines 13–16:

This truth fand honest *Tam O'Shanter*
As he frae Ayr ae night did canter;
(Auld Ayr, wham ne'er a town surpasses
For honest men and bonny lasses)
                    (Kinsley 1968: 443)

lines 59–66:

But pleasures are like poppies spread,
You seize the flow'r, its bloom is shed;
Or like the snow falls in the river,
A moment white – then melts for ever;
Or like the borealis race
That flit ere you can point their place;

Or like the rainbow's lovely form
Evanishing amid the storm.
            (Kinsley 1968: 444–445)

In Scots, the rhyme-pair *bush* : *thrush* did not exist; the contemporary
Scots for the former was *buss* (pronounced [bʌs]), and, for *thrush*, either
mavie or *throstle*. *Bard* : *reward* were probably acceptable as ear-rhymes
in eighteenth-century Scots. The *Scottish National Dictionary* records the
pronunciations [berd] (beside [bard]) and [rə'weːrd]; but a following [rd]
is a frequent lengthening environment in many dialects of Present-Day
Scots, and the rule which predicts such lengthenings was already opera-
tional in Scots in Burns's time. However, in the incipient Scottish Standard
English of the eighteenth century the situation is rather less clear-cut. The
pair *Bard* : *reward* was probably not a good ear-rhyme in Scottish Standard
English at that time – the evidence is that polite speakers of contemporary Scottish Standard English produced a rounded vowel in the environment of a preceding [w] (Jones 1993: 231) – and the pair *bush* : *thrush*
was certainly not. Recent work by C. Jones (1991, 1993) suggests that the
two vowels in these latter words would have been realised as distinct
phonemes, even if the precise realisations were rather different from those
which generally obtain in Present-Day Scottish Standard English. Thus
Sylvester Douglas (*A Treatise on the Provincial Dialect of Scotland*, 1799)
distinguishes between a 'simple' and a 'smothered' pronunciation of the
grapheme ⟨u⟩, and this distinction is confirmed by Jones's analysis (1993)
of a recently discovered text written in a specially developed orthography,
Alexander Scot's *The Contrast*. The 'simple'/'smothered' distinction seems
to be phonemic between /u/ and /ɤ/; the reflex of the latter is /ʌ/ in
twentieth-century Scottish Standard English. Extrapolating from these
findings, it may be presumed that *bush* : *thrush* would not have made a
good ear-rhyme in eighteenth-century Scottish Standard English, just as
they fail to rhyme in its present-day equivalent.

Of course, the direct evidence for Burns's own pronunciation is very
slight. But the indirect witness of his poetry, combined with our knowledge
of his life-story and some contemporary references, suggests that, like many
people, he had the ability to 'codeswitch', that is, to shift from one register
or variety of language to another in accordance with the social situation of
his speech: in his case between Ayrshire Scots and 'polite' contemporary
Scottish Standard English. In this practice he would be exemplifying the
linguistic behaviour typical of a middle-class person with working-class
roots: a description which would accord well with his humble origins in an
Alloway cottage in Ayrshire, his subsequent lionisation in polite Edinburgh
society, and his later career in the public service as an exciseman. In
twentieth-century Scotland, the written reflection of differences between
Scottish Standard English and Standardised Southern English is minimal.
Similarly, Burns's written Augustan English could reflect either accent.

The introduction to *The Brigs of Ayr* is written not in Scots but in Augustan English, without any of the special spellings and other usages (notably of vocabulary) which Burns uses when signalling his use of Scots. So why is his use of conventional rhyme in this passage of interest?

In answering this question, it is useful to look again at the opening lines of the poem:

> The simple Bard, rough at the rustic plough,
> Learning his tuneful trade from ev'ry bough;
> The chanting linnet, or the mellow thrush,
> Hailing the setting sun, sweet, in the green thorn bush;
> The soaring lark, the perching red-breast shrill,   5
> Or deep-ton'd plovers, grey, wild-whistling o'er the hill;
> Shall he, nurst in the Peasant's lowly shed,
> To hardy Independence bravely bred,
> By early Poverty to hardship steel'd,
> And train'd to arms in stern Misfortune's field,   10
> Shall he be guilty of their hireling crimes,
> The servile, mercenary Swiss of rhymes?

As is invariably the case in the historical study of language, it is worth investigating the context of the linguistic forms in question. The body of *The Brigs of Ayr* is a debate poem between two river-bridges: the Auld Brig, which 'appear'd of ancient Pictish race' and the New Brig, which 'was buskit in a braw, new coat, / That he, at *Lon'on*, frae ane *Adams*, got' – an interesting contrast between Scottish tradition and an English-focused Enlightenment, even though both Brigs speak in Scots. (The reference to 'Adam' is to the celebrated architect Robert Adam (1728–1792), who, though born in Scotland, was buried in London's Westminster Abbey. The Auld Brig dates from the thirteenth century, and is still standing; the New Brig had to be pulled down after flood-damage in 1877, and was replaced.) The two Brigs proceed to debate their respective merits; their arguments can be roughly summed up as to do with tradition (the Auld Brig) and innovation (the New Brig). Their discussion ('clishmaclaver') becomes heated, and would, we are told, have resulted with 'bloody wars, if Sprites had blood to shed'; but they are interrupted by a fairy procession, which Burns uses as an opportunity to pass some elegant allegorical comments on various local worthies and personal friends. The prefatory epistle to Ballantine uses the modesty topos or *diminutio*, in which the poet states that, in his rural simplicity, fame is the only reward to inspire him and that the relationship between him and his patron is not venal but (a fine medieval touch, this) one of 'grace' – that is, a gift relationship of the kind approved of by premodern political economists.

That the passage is elaborately organised in terms of style does, of course, suggest that the claim of rural simplicity on the part of the Bard (Burns's persona) is to be treated with a degree of irony. Burns's pose was indeed noticed by contemporaries. For instance, Dr Robert Anderson, who met Burns in Edinburgh, wrote as follows:

> It was, I know, part of the machinery, as he called it, of his poetical character to pass for an illiterate ploughman who wrote from pure inspiration. When I pointed out some evident traces of poetical inspiration in his verses, privately, he readily acknowledged his obligations and even admitted the advantages he enjoyed in poetical composition from the *copia verborum*, the command of phraseology, which the knowledge and use of the English and Scottish dialects afforded him; but in company he did not suffer his pretensions to pure inspiration to be challenged, and it was seldom done where it might be supposed to affect the success of the subscription for his *Poems*.
>
> (Kinsley 1968: 1537–1538)

As A. Bold puts it,

> Burns *used* his humble birth to implant a sense of guilt in others who could expiate their sins by bestowing patronage on the unfortunate poet. ... There is, superficially, the sound of submission; on a deeper level, though, the authentic voice is authoritative.
>
> (1991: 154)

It is in this context that the rhyming practice of the passage is significant. The 'simple Bard' of line 1, the 'singer' of line 15 who 'throws his hand uncouthly o'er the strings', soon reveals himself as a conventional rhymester and rhetorician, happy to employ rhetorical devices such as alliteration, assonance and consonance within the verse-line, and quite complex metaphorical conceits (e.g. 'The servile, mercenary Swiss of rhymes'). To employ eye-rhymes appropriate to literary Augustan verse while asserting the oral setting of the traditional (and Scots-speaking) 'simple Bard' is a key to understanding the poem's effects.

These effects are perhaps most clearly demonstrated by the final set of rhymes analysed here: the sequence *rough*, *plough* and *bough* in

> The simple Bard, rough at the rustic plough,
> Learning his tuneful trade from ev'ry bough
> (lines 1–2)

The foregrounded word here is *rough*. That Burns considers the word important is signalled not only by alliteration (with *rustic*) but also by its appearing, within an overall metrical scheme of iambic pentameter, as the stressed element within a substituted trochaic foot.

Sylvester Douglas, in his 'Table of words improperly pronounced by the Scotch, showing their true English pronounciation [*sic*]', comments on the pronunciation of *rough* and (by implication) *bough*:

> ROUGH: This word is, to the ear, the same with *ruff*, and rhymes exactly with *stuff*, *muff*, *tough*. Perhaps it was formerly pronounced as *bough*.

Douglas goes on to back up this evidence with an amusing story:

> I knew a schoolmaster in Scotland who was fond of general rules, and thought because *tough* was pronounced like *stuff*, *ruff*, *huff*, that *bough* should be so pronounced likewise. He taught his schoolchildren to pronounce it in that manner. But this sounded so ridiculous, even in their ears, that they gave him the knick-name [*sic*] of *Buff*, which, if alive, he probably retains to this day.

> (Jones 1993: 176)

Rough, therefore, did not rhyme with *bough* in incipient eighteenth-century Scottish Standard English. However, an archaic variant form of 'rough' [rux] and a still-current form [bjux] 'bough' are recorded in the *Scottish National Dictionary* and in the *Concise Scots Dictionary*; both rhyme with the current Scots variant [pljux] 'plough'.

Thus a comparison of Douglas's evidence and that of Present-Day Scots dialects suggests that, as with *thrush : bush*, there would have been three sets of pronunciations for the words *rough*, *bough* and *plough* in eighteenth-century Scotland. In Scottish Standard English and Standardised Southern English the pronunciations must have been much as in their present-day reflexes, and the word *rough* would not have formed an ear-rhyme with *plough*, *bough*; however, in Scots pronunciation the rhymes would be acoustically accurate. If the Bard were truly simple, he could be expected to have *rough : bough : plough* as ear-rhymes; but, if the Bard were in reality a metropolitan sophisticate, the first in the sequence would be merely an eye-rhyme with the couplet. And, of course, the distinction correlates further with the oral/literary contrast between simple Bard and sophisticated littérateur.

A general conclusion which might be drawn from this discussion, and one sometimes ignored by literary scholars, is that an understanding of contemporary patterns of pronunciation enables a deeper appreciation of the relationship between form and function in the verse practice of poets in the past. The particular conclusions, relevant to the general argument of this chapter, are that Burns's employment of Scots and English was more delicately attuned than has been hitherto noticed to take account of contemporary concerns about the transition from oral to literate culture, and that his handling of Scottish Standard English (as opposed to Scots) deserves more study than has hitherto been devoted to it. There is, in fact, room for further work on Burns's rhymes in both his Scots and his English verse, in the light of our developing knowledge of contemporary eighteenth-century pronunciation; such a study would benefit from comparisons with the practice of Burns's most notable immediate predecessors, Allan Ramsay and Robert Fergusson.

NORSE IN SCOTLAND AND THE DIVERGENCE OF ENGLISH AND SCOTS

The previous section has been concerned with the ways in which English and Scots interact in the poetry of Robert Burns. In the next section, the divergence of Scots and English will be investigated, through the investigation of the impact of Norse on Present-Day Scots.

In the British Isles, the Viking period saw primary Scandinavian settlement concentrated in three areas:

1 in Ireland, coastal enclaves such as Dublin, Wexford, Limerick etc.;
2 in England, a swathe of settlement across Northern and Eastern England including the Danelaw and what was at one time the Viking kingdom of Jorvik;
3 in Scotland, settlement in the Northern and Western Isles (including Man), and in Caithness. These settlers established their own characteristic institutions, notably the *thing* or assembly found in other Scandinavian societies (cf. the Icelandic *Althing* and the Norwegian *Storting*). This custom has left its mark on the place-names of this area, such as *Tingwall* in Shetland and *Dingwall* at the head of the Cromarty Firth (and cf. *Tynwald* in the Isle of Man), *Dingieshowe* in Orkney, and *Thingswa* in Caithness (cf. Old Norse *þingvöllr* 'assembly-field', *þingshaugr* 'assembly-mound', *þingsvað* 'assembly-slope').

This comparatively simple picture, however, is complicated by later movement of peoples. In Northern England, tenth-century settlements of Norwegians in the west, many from the Irish enclaves, combined with the earlier Scandinavian settlements in the east to produce a phenomenon known as the Great Scandinavian Belt: a band of Scandinavian and semi-Scandinavian settlement which stretched between the Irish and North Seas. In Scotland there was secondary settlement in Galloway, and to a much less extent in the south-east, by peoples from the Irish enclaves and the Great Scandinavian Belt. This settlement took place probably from the early tenth century onwards, since the rarity of Norse-type pagan grave-goods in these regions suggests that the immigrants had adopted (in however partial a fashion) Christian habits. These folk were still sufficiently Scandinavianised to maintain the custom of the *thing* – thus the place-name *Tinwald* appears in Dumfriesshire – but they interacted with British, Gaelic and Anglian peoples to produce a situation of great ethnic complexity. (See Crawford 1987: 100, for the controversial matter of the *Gall-Gaedhil*, people of mixed Norse–Gaelic birth.)

Traditionally this complexity has been demonstrated by the existence of place-name types known as 'inversion compounds', whereby names of Germanic derivation are ordered according to the Celtic syntactic rule in which the generic element precedes the qualifier rather than the other way about, for example *Kirkcudbright*, where the Norse generic *kirk* 'church' is qualified by the name of an Anglo-Saxon saint ('Cuthbert') within a Celtic pattern of element-order. (Recent research suggests that such names reflect an even more complex ethnic history, for the *kirk*-names may have replaced earlier inversion-compounds with the cognate Old English generic element *cirice*; see again Crawford 1987: 100, and references there cited.) A slightly different kind of blend-form is *Corstorphine*, now a suburb of Edinburgh (Gaelic *crois* 'crossing' qualified by the Norse personal-name *Torfinn*).

The early presence of these Scandinavian and Scandinavianised peoples in Scotland seems, however, to have had little or no impact on the development of Scots, the linguistic variety derived ultimately from the Northumbrian dialect of Old English and which, in the eleventh century, was generally restricted to what is now South-East Scotland. Despite obvious English political influence at the court of Malcolm III, there is good evidence that Gaelic was the dominant and prestigious language of his kingdom, a situation which changed only with the accession of Malcolm's youngest son, David I (1124–1153), and of his immediate successors.

David had spent much of his youth in England and, by marriage, had become an English earl and therefore for part of his lands a vassal of the Anglo-Norman Henry I of England. Although David had definite claims of territorial independence in England, and sought on various occasions to rid himself of the vassalage he owed to the Norman rulers of England, he was deeply imbued with Norman culture; it is usually a mistake to endow medieval people with the culturally nationalist attitudes of later centuries. Thus David strove to 'improve' his kingdom along Norman lines, by introducing feudal institutions and notions such as fiefdoms and vassalage, and by installing Anglo-Normans – many from his own English estates – in important offices in church and state. It has been said that, 'under David I and his immediate successors, something very like a peaceful "Norman Conquest" of Scotland took place' (Dickinson 1977: 77). As the chronicler Walter of Coventry famously put it, 'the more recent kings of Scotland profess themselves to be rather Frenchmen' (cited in Dickinson 1977: 83).

In the train of these Anglo-Normans came English-speaking servants; English-speakers also settled in the royal and baronial fortified townships or 'burghs' which were established during this period. But the English spoken by these latter immigrants was not the ancestor of Present-Day Standardised Southern English, let alone the classical Late West Saxon familiar to students of Old English as the standardised written mode of late Anglo-Saxon England. It was a Northern English variety, the English of the Great Scandinavian Belt, so heavily affected by contact with Scandinavian that some controversialists have gone so far as to call it an English–Norse creole. It has been rightly argued that the contribution of this Scandinavianised Northern English to the development of Scots 'is probably even greater than that of the original Old [Northumbrian] English of south-eastern and southern Scotland' (*Concise Scots Dictionary* 1985: ix).

The student of Present-Day Scots can trace the impact of Scandinavian at all linguistic levels: phonology, grammar and lexicon. In phonology, for instance, the fronting of long back vowels (Old English *ā*, *ō*) seems to derive from contact between Norse and Northern English. In turn, this development may have given rise to the characteristic Present-Day Scots post-Great Vowel Shift system, wherein the long front vowel series has undergone the Shift but a long back vowel of Early Scots, *ū*, has been, with subsequent quantitative modifications in particular environments, retained; cf. the characteristic Scots spellings *hoose* 'house', *coo* 'cow', from Old English *hūs*, *cū*. In grammar, such a characteristic Scots feature as the present participle inflection in *-and*, *-an* [ən] most probably derives from Old Norse *-andi*.

Most noticeably, Scandinavian has had a profound impact on the Scots lexicon, contributing not only a wide range of words to the open word classes (i.e. nouns, adjectives, verbs, adverbs), but also to the closed word classes of 'grammatical' words – thus differing markedly in character from the other major source of loanwords into Scots, French. Examples of Scandinavian elements in the Present-Day Scots lexicon thus include not only such obvious forms as *bairn*, *brae*, *gate* ('road'), *graith*, *kirk*, *lass*, *flit* etc., but also prepositions such as *till* 'to' and *frae* 'from', and pronouns such as *thay* 'they', *scho* 'she'.

A slight difficulty here is that, since Norse and English are closely related languages, it is hard sometimes to decide whether a word in Scots is derived from Old English or Old Norse. For instance, the form *til*, usually considered to be a loanword into English from Old Norse, is recorded in prepositional use in an Old Northumbrian text which predates the Viking period; the Moore version of Cædmon's *Hymn*, which survives in a manuscript of Bede's (Latin) *Ecclesiastical History* dating from about 737 (MS Cambridge, University Library Kk. 5.16), includes the half-line *heben til hrofe*. However, this problem does not invalidate the main argument.

In stylistic terms, Norse-derived words, like those descended from Old English, contrast with French and Latin loans by being either neutral- or low-style. It is thus not surprising that fifteenth-century writers like William Dunbar use many Norse words in low-style verse such as the *Flyting of Dunbar and Kennedy* whereas, in his high-style court poetry such as *The Goldyn Targe* and *The Thrissil and the Rois*, French- and Latin-derived words are foregrounded. (Interestingly, there are French- and Latin-derived words which are distinctly Scots, and have not appeared in the lexicon of any variety of English south of the border, e.g. *disjune* 'breakfast', *dominie* 'teacher'. These words were borrowed independently into Scots, the result of cultural ties with Europe which were not shared with England.)

Figure 8.2 Linguistic features distinguishing Older Scots and Northern Middle English (after Jordan 1974: 18)

Scots	Northern English
is, ar	*es, er* (*is, ar*)
bigouth, couth 'began' (analogous to *cūþe* 'could')	*gan, can*
forʒet	*forget*
gif 'if'	*if*
qhou for *how* /huː/ 'how'	*how* /huː/
sik (*swylk, silk*, not *slīk*) 'such'	*swilk, slīk* (Old Norse *slīkr*)

The Scandinavian element in Present-Day Scots, then, is the ultimate, if indirect, result of events set in train in the time of David I. In the Older Scots period, the Scandinavian element, since further from its area of origin in the Great Scandinavian Belt, is rather less marked than that found in contemporary Northern English dialects. W. Heuser, many years ago (1908: 289), produced a useful table of some differences between Northern English and Scots in the Middle Ages, and noted that the Northern English forms are rather more markedly Scandinavian in appearance than their Scots equivalents for the same item. A modified form of this table, as revised in Jordan (1974: 18), is reproduced as Figure 8.2.

A conventionalised map of the late medieval distributions for three items, 'is', 'are' and 'such', appears as Figure 8.3; it is based upon the *Linguistic Atlas of Late Mediaeval English* (1986), and thus only covers the Early Scots period (between *c.* 1375 and *c.* 1450). It is perhaps sufficient to show the relationship between the two varieties, and confirms that the Scandinavian impact on Northern English, as reflected in the later medieval period, was stronger than on Scots. This state of affairs, after all, is to be expected; to use an image often adopted by proponents of linguistic diffusion, when the actuating stone of Scandinavian immigration was dropped into the pool of Late Old English, the implementing ripples found in late medieval Scotland were weaker than those in (say) the contemporary North Riding of Yorkshire.

It would, however, be a mistake to assume that the relationship between the Scandinavian elements in the lexicons of Scots and Northern English has survived unchanged to the present day. Languages, as was indicated in Part I, are dynamic open systems; the only languages which do not change are dead ones, such as Latin. Linguistic standardisation in England, focused on the south of that country, led frequently to the loss of distinctive forms in Northern England. And where the English standard form did not replace completely its provincial competitor, semantic and/or stylistic specialisation took place. These processes of loss and specialisation, because often to do with social standing, had their strongest impact on the forms derived from English and Norse; French- and Latin-derived

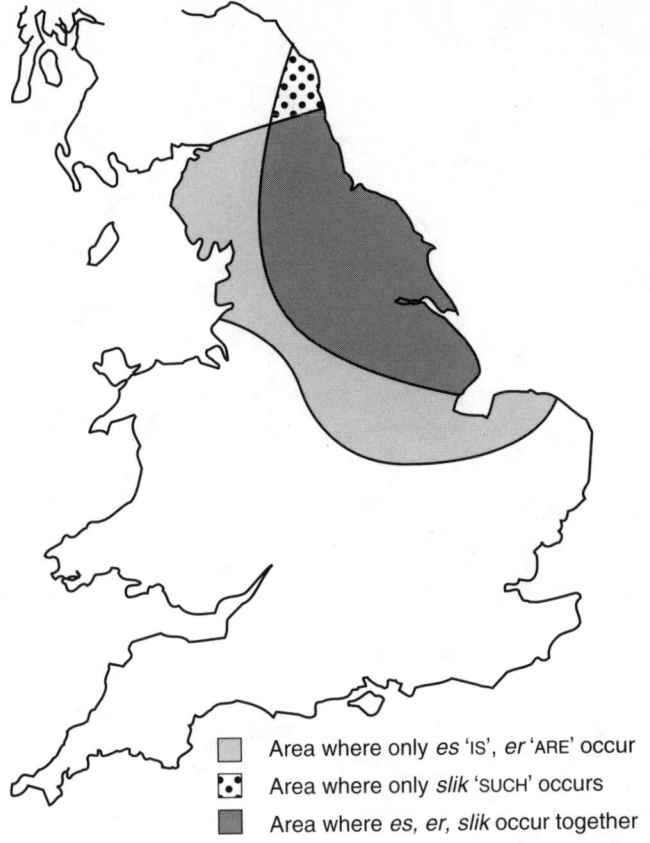

Area where only *es* 'IS', *er* 'ARE' occur
Area where only *slik* 'SUCH' occurs
Area where *es, er, slik* occur together

Figure 8.3 'IS', 'ARE', and 'SUCH' in later Middle English: schematised distribution of selected forms (cf. *LALME* 1986, Vol. I, dot maps 134, 121 and 72)

forms, because borrowed from the prestigious languages of medieval Europe, did not generally suffer from the same stigma. These processes were sometimes resisted in Scotland, where a focus of linguistic prestige distinct from Standardised Southern English has continued (albeit with many vicissitudes) to be sustained.

Examples of these processes are not hard to find. Figure 8.4, after McIntosh (1973), shows the distribution of *starn/stern*-type forms for the item 'star'; the form with *-n* derives from Old Norse *stjarna*. According to the *Oxford English Dictionary* (1989), the form was last recorded in an English text in the sixteenth century; the *English Dialect Dictionary* (1898) records it as sporadic in the speech of Northumberland and the North Country in general, but, according to the *Survey of English Dialects: the Dictionary and Grammar* (hence *Survey of English Dialects* (1994)) it

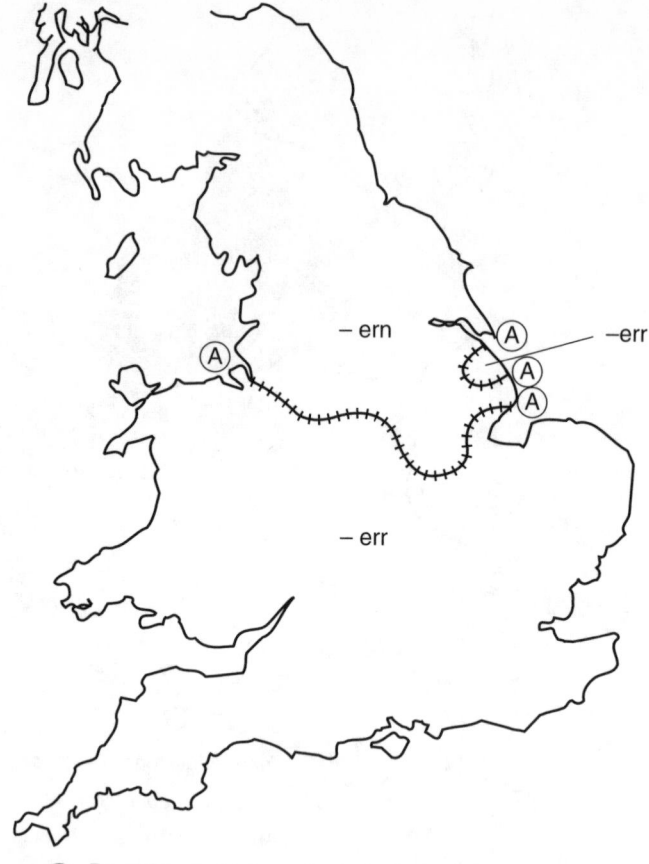

(A) ╂╂╂╂╂╂╂╂ (A) Boundary between *stern–* and *sterr–* types

Figure 8.4 'STAR' in later medieval English (after McIntosh 1973)

survives only as a sporadic form in Cumberland and Northumberland. However, the form is still recorded in the *Scottish National Dictionary* (1976), not just in Shetland and the North (where it may derive from primary Norse settlement) but also in Lanarkshire.

The English congeners of the Present-Day Scots word *thirl* (noun and verb) can be used to demonstrate specialisation. In Present-Day Scots the word has broadly two meanings: (1) 'pierce' (verb), 'aperture' (noun) (cf. Old English *þyrlian*, *þyrel*), and (2) 'bind, tie or oblige' (verb), 'bondsman, obligation' etc. (noun) (cf. Old English *þræl*, Old Norse *þræll*). Both these usages were once available in England, but the second has almost entirely disappeared there. Both usages are recorded in the *English Dialect Dictionary* (1898) in Northumberland, Cumberland and the North Country at the end of the nineteenth century, but the word has since undergone extreme specialisation, being used in Yorkshire, either on its own or in compound with *-hole*, to mean 'sheep-hole' (*Survey of English Dialects* (1994)), and figuratively, in Standardised Southern English, in the metathesised form *thrill*. The second meaning of the Present-Day Scots word seems to have disappeared in England. (*Survey of English Dialects* (1994) records a separate usage, the adjective *thirly* 'hungry', now found in Cornwall only; *English Dialect Dictionary* (1898) records the form in Somerset and Devon as well. This usage is interesting, but its development seems unrelated to that found in the rest of the country.)

All these examples may seem to demonstrate the uncertainty of the processes involved in linguistic change; each form, it would appear, needs microlinguistic investigation. They would thus seem to exemplify nicely the classic dictum of linguistic geography, 'every word has its own history'.

Linguistic historiography is trivial, however, if it cannot draw general patterns from evidence. Adequate linguistic historiography – like historiography in general – is practised through the observation of correspondences between phenomena, and there are some interesting correspondences to do with the survival of Norse words in the Scots lexicon. Two examples will be examined here: *kirk* and *thole*. The changing distribution of *kirk* is illustrated by Figure 8.5, a schematisation of maps found in McIntosh (1973, based upon the work of the Middle English Dialect Survey) and Wakelin (1972, based upon the material gathered for the Survey of English Dialects). In Middle English times, the form *kirk* 'church' was widespread south of the border. Although it survived south of the border into the beginning of the twentieth century – the *English Dialect Dictionary* (1898) records the word in counties as far south as Lincoln – M. Wakelin (1972) showed that it has been largely replaced in England by Southern and official *church*. In Scotland, despite its official replacement by *church* at the Westminster Assembly of 1648, *kirk* has remained as the distinctive Scots word for this item. The boundary between *kirk* and *church* now roughly corresponds to the political and geographical boundary between the two countries.

It seems certain that the word *kirk* is now distinctively Scottish, despite its appearance sporadically south of the border. Wakelin has suggested a number of reasons for the sporadic survival of *kirk* in the far north of England. Most plausibly, he quotes H. Orton (private communication), who pointed out to him 'the fact that Presbyterianism is very strong in Northumberland, but not in Durham, and suggests that Scottish influence disseminated by the Scottish ministers might help to account for the *kirk* forms in Northumberland' (1972: 87).

A similar picture can be drawn for the distribution of the word *thole* 'suffer'. Although the etymology of this word, recorded as common in the *Scottish National Dictionary* (1976) but no longer found in England, is generally considered uncertain – it may be from Old Norse *þola* or from Old English *þolian* – the general pattern of its distribution in the *English Dialect Dictionary* (1898) suggests that its presence in Scots derives at least in part from its use in the Great Scandinavian Belt. The latter

(A) ┼┼┼┼┼┼┼ (A) Southernmost extent of *kirk* type in Middle English

(B) ┼┼┼┼┼┼┼ (B) Southernmost extent of *kirk* type in Present-Day English
(c.1950)

Figure 8.5 Geographical recession of *kirk* 'CHURCH' over time

authority records *thole* in Northumberland, Cumberland, Westmorland, Yorkshire, Lancashire, Staffordshire and Derbyshire, and this correspondence to a great extent with the area of primary Norse settlement strongly suggests that the Norse etymology for the word should be given primacy. As with *kirk*, the southernmost limit of its distribution now corresponds roughly to the political and geographical border between present-day England and Scotland (see Figure 8.6, after Glauser 1974: 98–101). (The form is not recorded in *Survey of English Dialects* (1994). Unfortunately, the *Middle English Dictionary* (1952–) has not yet reached *thole*, so the distribution of this form in Middle English texts cannot yet be pursued.)

These two forms are not the only ones which have receded towards the political border over time. The border between Scotland and England has been shown by scholars to correspond to a remarkable bundle of lexical isoglosses, of which the most marked are the recessive ones. As Glauser

Ⓐ ╟┼┼┼┼┼┼┼┼╢ Ⓐ Rough indication of boundary between *bide* and *thole*

Figure 8.6 Responses from informants to the query 'Sometimes toothache may get so bad that you think you can hardly . . .' (after Glauser 1974: 99)

puts it, 'With the recession [of dialect words towards the political border] continuing, the dividing effect of the geographical Border can be expected to increase' (1974: 284).

In the light of the political history of Scotland and England, this development becomes explicable in historiographical terms. As has already been pointed out, Northern English was affected by a Southern-focused standardisation which had less effect on Scots. To adopt once again the terminology of diffusion, a second wave of influence, this time originating in the south of England, overlapped in part with the earlier wave originating in the areas settled by the Scandinavians. The process is represented in diagrammatic form in Figure 8.7.

It would seem therefore that the bundling of isoglosses along the political border between the two countries is a gradual process, corresponding

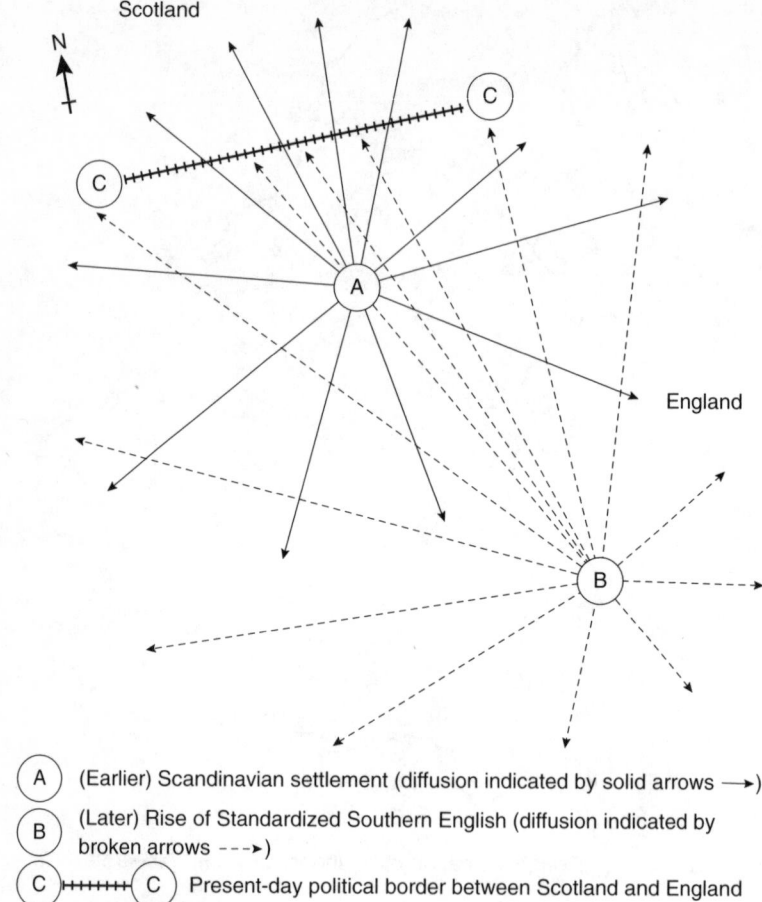

Scotland

N

C

C

A

England

B

○ A ○ (Earlier) Scandinavian settlement (diffusion indicated by solid arrows ⟶)

○ B ○ (Later) Rise of Standardized Southern English (diffusion indicated by broken arrows ---►)

○ C ⊢++++++⊣ ○ C   Present-day political border between Scotland and England

Figure 8.7 Schematic representation of two processes of linguistic diffusion (after Smith 1994b)

to the gradual differentiation of English and Scots. A question frequently arousing scholarly controversy is to do with the status of these two varieties as separate languages. It would appear that the dialect continuum between English and Scots has become increasingly disrupted as isoglosses build up at the political border – the kind of process which lies behind the differentiation of cognate languages stemming from a common ancestor. Whether this process has resulted or will ever result in a true separation of English and Scots into distinct languages in the same way that (for instance) French and Spanish have diverged from their Latin ancestor is hard to say, for there are powerful political and cultural forces working against it (reflected, for instance, in McClure 1988). But the potential for such a development is undoubtedly there.

BLACK ENGLISH: ITS ORIGINS AND HISTORY

The remainder of this chapter will be concerned with the rise and diffusion of a 'new English': the British derivative of Jamaican English, London Jamaican. The history of this variety demonstrates the way in which a given language-state is the result of the complex and continual interaction of intra- and extralinguistic processes.

More work has been done on Black English in the United States than in Britain, so it is perhaps appropriate to start with a contrast. A typology of the varieties of English used by black speakers in the United States is given by J. Rodby (1992). Following Labov, Rodby distinguishes two poles of a speech-continuum:

1 speakers of Standard Black English, 'used by educated black speakers in public and formal situations. It contains phonological variation from standard forms, but the same Standard English syntax';
2 speakers of Black English Vernacular, 'used by children growing up in the Black community and by adults in the most intimate in-group settings' (quoted from Labov 1983: 33).

In England, a situation of greater complexity than that reported by Rodby has been distinguished. Recent work by M. Sebba (notably Sebba 1993) has identified four parameters governing the linguistic usage of black speakers living in London:

1 Standard British English, with a grammar and lexis indistinguishable from that in prestigious dialects of English. This usage can be accompanied by a developed British (as opposed to African) accent, focused on Received Pronunciation.
2 Standard Jamaican English. In grammatical and lexical terms this variety is largely indistinguishable from Standard British English, but there are accentual distinctions. This usage is comparable with Scottish Standard English.
3 London English, notably the working-class usage of the metropolis, which is distinguished from Standard British English in grammar and vocabulary, and has a distinctive accent.
4 Jamaican Creole, the 'low-status' variety originating in the pidgin English of the West African slave-trade. A pidgin variety is the native language of no-one but is used, for communicative purposes, among disparate peoples; such a variety develops into a creole when it becomes the native language of a particular group. Typically, a pidgin derives its lexis from a high-prestige language, its *lexifier*: the lexifier of Jamaican Creole is English, although the nature of that English differs quite markedly from Standard English, much of it being regional, nautical or vulgar in origin; cf. *krabit* 'cruel' in Miskito Coast Creole (Scots *crabbit* 'ill-tempered'), and *piss* 'urine', which has no vulgar connotation

in Creole (Holm 1994: 356–357). However, equally typically, a pidgin derives its grammar and phonological structure from the native languages of those who have adopted it.

There is an obvious parallel in both the Black American and Black London situations with the variation between Scottish Standard English, standardised Southern English and Scots. The usage of an individual speaker can move between the reference points distinguished depending on such factors as the social setting of linguistic interaction.

The American version of Creole, Black English Vernacular, may be described as the 'first clearly discernible and reportable dialect of American English' (Dillard 1992: 60), presumably in the sense that it is the first distinguished in the written records. Its origins lie in the African slave-trade of the seventeenth and eighteenth centuries, in the creolisation of a pidgin variety. Similarly, Jamaican Creole derives from the pidgins which arose during the period of the slave-trade.

The present population of Jamaica is largely descended from slaves brought there by European colonists in the seventeenth and eighteenth centuries, the original Arawak inhabitants of the island having died out by the end of Spanish rule in 1655. One of the mechanisms by which the slave-trade was practised was linguistic:

> The means used by those who trade in Guinea, to keep the Negroes quiet, is to choose them from severall parts of ye Country, of different languages; so that they find they cannot act joyntly, when they are not in a Capacity of consulting one an other, and this they can not doe, in soe farr as they understand not one an other.
>
> (Simson, *Voyage to the Straits of Magellan & S. Seas* (1689), quoted in Dillard 1992: 61)

Since there was no language held in common, the slaves adopted the pidgin usage spoken from the early 1600s by slave-traders, in preference to their various native tongues. Once speakers of this pidgin had children, and these children learnt the pidgin as their own native language, creolisation took place.

During the late 1950s and the early 1960s, there was considerable migration from the West Indies to Britain, notably to London. There had in fact been a black community in London for several centuries, but the numbers had been rather few, and there is little evidence of their speech-habits. The generation, however, which arrived in Britain in the 1950s and 1960s has had children and grandchildren, and forms with them a substantial part of the community, with distinctive and proud cultural traditions. It is generally recognised, however, that there remains an element of racism in British society, from which this community suffers and which has led to feelings of social insecurity and cultural rejection. Since language reflects social situation, it is not surprising that the usages of this community reflect the complex reactions of a people whose place in society is still not wholly secure.

AFRICAN AND ENGLISH

The main question which seems to underlie recent debate on Black English Vernacular/Jamaican Creole is stated by Wells (1982: 554–555): 'do its special characteristics derive from the popular local dialects of England or from an African-language substratum?' This question remains currently under discussion, but it seems to be generally agreed that there are structures in Black English Vernacular/Jamaican Creole which derive from usages in African languages.

Many examples of 'substrate-influence' could be chosen, especially in the field of pronunciation (see Holm 1994, Wells 1973), but one example of usage current in Black English Vernacular/London Jamaican Creole, as evidenced in the speech of Harlem in New York and in that of black Londoners, has attracted particular attention: the use of the *copula verb*. Copula verbs are those verbs which connect a subject to a subject complement. The most common of these is the verb *to be*; thus the word *is* in the sentences *The boy is foolish*, *The boy is a fool* etc. is a copula verb. Other common copulas are *become, seem, appear*.

The formal omission of a copula is frequent in a number of languages, for instance Present-Day Russian што это [ˌʃtɔ ˈɛtə] 'What is it?' is literally 'What it?', and such an omission also occurs in Black English Vernacular and in the speech of some black Londoners. This usage was already recorded in the eighteenth century, when Alexander Hamilton, a Baltimore doctor journeying through New England and the Middle Atlantic colonies of British North America in 1744, recorded in his *Itinerarium* a frequent use of a 'zero-copula', for example *You a black bitch*. By the time of W. Labov's classic study of 1972, the grammar of the copula in Black English Vernacular had become a rich source of discussion for sociolinguists and others interested in the evolution of language. Labov found that the main rule for copula omission was as follows:

> wherever [Standard English] can contract, [Black English Vernacular] can delete *is* and *are*, and vice versa; wherever [Standard English] cannot contract, [Black English Vernacular] cannot delete *is* and *are*, and vice versa.
>
> (Labov 1972: 73)

Given the focus of interest on the verb *to be* in American speech, it is not surprising that the usage has also been investigated in Black varieties of British English. M. Sebba (1993: 151) identifies the following categories of use for this verb in Standard and London English:

1 As an auxiliary verb: I am writing, etc.
2 As an equative verb: I am a teacher, she is the doctor etc.
3 As a locative verb: We are in London, I want to be here, etc.
4 As a copular verb with an adjective: This book is old, I am tired now, they were fat, etc.

Each of these usages appears differently in Jamaican Creole, as follows:

[1] Auxiliary verbs are not used to form tenses or aspects of the verb in Jamaican, but the translation of [Standard English] sentences like these would require the [Jamaican Creole] particle *a*: *Mi a rait* ['I am writing'] etc.

[2] The [Jamaican Creole] equative verb is also *a* which 'regularly connects two nominals' ..: *im a di tiicha, im a di dakta* ['I am a teacher', 's/he is the doctor'].

[3] [Jamaican Creole] has a separate locative verb *de*: *Wi de a London, mi waant de ya* ['We are in London, I want to be here'].

[4] With true adjectives in [Jamaican Creole], no copula is required. This can be explained by saying that in [Jamaican Creole] grammar, adjectives are a special class of verbs: they take the same preverbal tense/aspect marking particles as verbs. *disya buk uold, mi taiad nou, dem bin fat* ['This book is old', 'I am tired now', 'they were fat'].

The last of these usages can be directly paralleled in African languages, where the verb-form would be subsumed in the adjective (see further Alleyne 1980). The example of the copula verb construction in Jamaican Creole is therefore a good demonstration of how a particular language-state is the result of interaction between languages, brought about through contact.

ENGLISH AND JAMAICAN CREOLE IN CARIBBEAN VERSE

One of the most interesting cultural developments among London black youth since the 1970s has been to do with the assertion of the value of creole culture. This cultural assertiveness is no doubt a reaction to the racism of British culture as a whole, but it is also a positive statement of certain traditional values. M. Sebba (1993: 6) has identified three characteristic expressions of this culture: Rastafarianism, reggae and 'toasting'. All three phenomena are marked by distinctive linguistic usages. Rastafarianism, which may be crudely defined as a religious movement stressing the African roots of Jamaican society, asserted the value of Jamaican Creole as something not to be ashamed of, and reggae music, which is generally connected with Rastafarian attitudes, was also associated with Creole – although, as Sebba points out (1993: 8), 'Bob Marley, a Rastafarian reggae musician idolised by millions of all races, sang many of his lyrics in something much closer to Jamaican-accented Standard English than broad Jamaican Creole.'

'Toasting' is a phenomenon which has appeared in a number of black communities, possibly a carry-over from traditional African oral culture. Toasting is the public recitation of verse; in Britain it has become a feature of youth culture, expressed in discos and dance-halls. It has also found expression in related developments, such as 'dubbing', the composition of poems to accompany music. It is characterised by an assertive use of Creole combined with a high degree of linguistic creativity.

Of course, many poets with roots in the Caribbean have resisted easy pigeonholing. A good example is John Agard, whose poem *Stereotype* (1985) is a demonstration of such resistance. The 'point' of the poem lies in its final stanza, when the poet abandons his use of markedly Creole forms:

I'm a fullblooded
West Indian stereotype
See me straw hat?
Watch it good

I'm a fullblooded   5
West Indian stereotype
You ask
if I got riddum
in me blood
You going ask!   10
Man just beat de drum
and don't forget
to pour de rum ...

Yes I'm a fullblooded   55
West Indian stereotype
that's why I
graduated from Oxford University
with a degree
in anthropology   60

There are more complex linguistic responses to institutional racism than Agard's irony. One of the best-known Caribbean poets active in recent years is Linton Kwesi Johnson, and Johnson's poem *Youtman* exemplifies one way in which creole culture is expressed.

youtman,
today is your day say di time is now.
site? ovastan. youtman.
check out di shape yu haffe faam;
mind who yu harm.   5

youdauta,
you are di queen of di day an di nite is your mite.
site? overstan. youdauta.
check out di tide before yu jump in di watah;
den swim, yea sing, sing youdauta.   10

youtrebel,
yu know bout di flame yu livin fire.
yu know, youtrebel, yu livin fire.
guide di flame fram di wheat to di tares;
watch dem burn an flee free   15

fram yu kulcha,
tek in di love say tek in di love.
dont lay in di way dat will cause decay,
an folly is di way of di fool.
site? youtman? scene. move on.   20
            (quoted from Brown 1992: 25)

(*youtman* 1 'youths, young men'; *site?* 3 'you see it?'; *ovastan* 3 (= 'over-stand'), emphatic form of 'understand'; *haffe faam* 4 'have formed'; *yout-dauta* 6 'young black women'; *mite* 7 'might', 'realm of power'; *scene* 20 'good').

Youtman, an address to Caribbean youth written in a language which is designed to exclude those not accustomed to its conventions of wordplay (cf., e.g. the meaning of *overstan*, a characteristically Rastafarian usage), is nevertheless a poem which merges Caribbean Creole usage with something else: the traditional language of the Authorised Version of the Bible. Thus 'fram di wheat to di tares' is an obvious reference to Matthew 13, while line 19 is a clear echo of various passages in the Book of Proverbs, for instance 'The wisdom of the prudent is to understand his way: but the folly of the fool is deceit' (14.8). The resulting mixture is a complex and sophisticated one, and is markedly divergent from Standard English usage.

JAMAICAN CREOLE IN BRITAIN

It has been argued by some linguists that Jamaican Creole is a language separate from English; and it is certainly true that the process of divergence from English represented in Creole has gone at least as far as that achieved by, say, Scots; Scots, for instance, has nothing comparable to the 'copula-deletion' practised by Creole users, the result, it would appear, of interaction between English and African languages. Until quite recently, Jamaicans themselves would not have held this belief; J.C. Wells reported in 1973 that 'Jamaicans consider themselves speakers of English, and are offended when ignorant English people inquire what their mother tongue might be' (1973: 3).

It may be that the assertion of Jamaican Creole culture, as demonstrated in (for instance) the poetry of Linton Kwesi Johnson, will lead users of Creole to assert their linguistic distinctiveness as a political act, much as some Scottish people assert that Scots is a language separate from English as a political statement of nationhood. Emphasis in education on 'language awareness' – encouraged in Britain by the Kingman Report (1988) – has been part of an attempt to encourage a relaxed attitude to linguistic variation, in which various codes are appropriate for various situations. But M. Sebba cites a Caribbean child in 1981 writing as follows:

> I feel that there is nothing wrong in speaking Creole as there is nothing wrong in speaking Cockney, but I feel that when you go for an interview or you are speaking to someone important you should try and speak as close as possible to Standard English.
>
> (Sebba 1993: 144)

It is hard to surpass this statement in its perceptiveness of social realities.

9   Conclusion

It will, it is hoped, have become clear from the preceding chapters that an argument about the nature of linguistic change in the history of English has been developed. Change, it has been argued, is the result of the complex interaction of extralinguistic and intralinguistic developments, and any resulting change itself interacts with further developments to produce yet more change. The conception is therefore a *dynamic* one, to use a term which has become popular with linguists (e.g. Bailey 1973, Sebba 1993). Although it is not possible, given the limitations of the evidence, to offer absolute proof as to the motivation of a particular linguistic innovation, or to predict the precise development of linguistic phenomena, nevertheless a rationally arguable historical explanation can be offered for the kinds of changes which languages can undergo, and a broad prediction can be made about the kinds of change which are liable to happen. This seems a reasonable goal for any historical enquiry which seeks to go beyond the simple chronicle.

Nevertheless, some historical linguists have worried over the years about the epistemological status of offering explanations for linguistic change; and this concern has led from time to time to such statements as the following:

> there is no more reason for languages to change than there is for automobiles to add fins one year and remove them the next, for jackets to have three buttons one year and two the next.
>
> (Postal 1968: 283)

It will be clear from the argument that has been developed in the preceding chapters of this book that this belief in the inexplicable nature of linguistic change is not accepted here, although there would appear to be two possible reasons why one might be tempted to avoid the question 'why'. One is plain modesty; the other has a philosophical basis.

In his book on evolutionary biology, *The Blind Watchmaker* (1986), R. Dawkins describes a conversation he had with a 'distinguished modern philosopher, a well-known atheist':

I said that I could not imagine being an atheist at any time before 1859, when Darwin's *Origin of Species* was published. 'What about Hume?', replied the philosopher. 'How did Hume explain the organised complexity of the living world?', I asked. 'He didn't', said the philosopher. 'Why does it need any special explanation?'

(1986: 5)

Dawkins disagreed; he *knew* that a special explanation was needed, and he suspected 'that in his heart of hearts my philosopher companion knew it too' (1986: 6). David Hume, one of the masters of the eighteenth-century Scottish Enlightenment, aimed to disprove the 'argument from design' for the existence of God; that argument held that God's existence could be deduced from observing His earthly activity. Hume offered no alternative. As Dawkins puts it, 'I can't help feeling that such a position, though logically sound, would have left one feeling pretty unsatisfied' (1986: 6).

The historical linguist who refuses to explain seems to me rather like Hume in Dawkins's characterisation. The belief expressed in this book has been that plausible explanations for language change can be offered as a result of historical insight. These explanations are rationally arguable, in the sense that they seek to present better solutions to problems; but they are empirical also, in that they seek support from observed factual correspondences.

Such a multifarious conception of language change, moreover, seems to correspond to the most recent paradigm in both the natural and human sciences: 'chaos-theory'. Chaos-theory is really about order, about the way in which order results from complex interaction. The best-known popular example of this process – the butterfly stamping in the forest causing a storm a thousand miles away – is really about how a tiny innovation can make a difference, by interacting with other innovations to produce a snowball effect. If language is a metastable system deployed by interacting innovative and conservative language-users, it does not, in a chaotic world, require or imply some divine plan or overall grand design. Rather, living languages are the result of what Dawkins has called a 'blind watchmaker' effect, whereby order comes out of chaos.

Such an approach is hardly revolutionary, and – as throughout this book – no claims of special newness are made here. Chaos-theory is obviously a contemporary 'paradigm', using the term in the sense coined by T. Kuhn (1970): a way of thinking about the world which has become generally accepted by scientists. But Kuhn, as he pointed out in the epilogue to the second edition of *The Structure of Scientific Revolutions*, has been fundamentally misinterpreted as someone who thinks of science as simply a series of changes in fashion, where one paradigm is, relatively speaking, no better than any other. As M.A.K. Halliday has put it (1987: 152), 'We have to learn to build on our predecessors and move forward, instead of constantly staying behind where they were in order to trample them underfoot.' It is for that reason that this book has repeatedly drawn on both philological and linguistic traditions of writing about the history of English; both approaches have valuable things to contribute to our greater understanding of human language and its history, and it is in integrating these approaches that our understanding of the history of languages will progress.

It may be objected by some that such a survey, because it is the product of historiography, lacks scientific rigour. Such comments seem to the present author to be the product of a division between the humanities and the natural sciences which needs to be overcome; linguists, it has sometimes seemed, have had a sneaking inferiority-complex about their craft, and therefore have felt the need to turn it into their own conception of more 'mature' science. In this context, it seems significant that modern physicists, for example, are now taking history into account in their theoretical orientation. The biologist E.O. Wilson called some time ago for 'a deeper and more courageous examination of human nature that combines the findings of biology with those of the social sciences' (1978: 195), and this call finds an echo in the work of other scientists:

> A new type of order has appeared. We can speak of a new coherence, of a mechanism of 'communication' among molecules. But this type of communication can arise only in far-from-equilibrium conditions. ... What seems certain is that these far-from-equilibrium phenomena illustrate an essential and unexpected property of matter: physics may henceforth describe structures as adapted to outside conditions. ... To use somewhat anthropomorphic language: in equilibrium matter is 'blind', but in far-from-equilibrium conditions it begins to be able to perceive, to 'take into account', in its way of functioning, differences in the external world. ... The analogy with social phenomena, even with history, is inescapable.
>
> (Prigogine and Stengers 1984: 13–14)

To quote Halliday again, 'From now on, the human sciences have to assume at least an equal responsibility in establishing the foundations of knowledge. Their coat-tailing days are over' (1987: 152). In this situation, historiography has a crucial role; and it would be foolish for those working in the humanities to dispose of historiography just when the scientists are taking it on board.

Notes

2 ON EVIDENCE

1 There are of course languages, such as Chinese or Japanese, whose scripts include or are made up from non-alphabetic elements. A good example of non-alphabetic script in present-day use is the Japanese *kanji*, itself based on Chinese pictographic script, which represents concepts rather than sounds. Such practices, of course, are also found in English, although to a much more restricted extent; the conceptual symbol '5' might be compared with its alphabetic equivalent 'five'. Perhaps also relevant in this context are the pre-Columbian Mesoamerican glypts or carved inscriptions representing deities, people and places; such forms are found throughout Mexico, but map onto distinct languages, being allotted a different phonic significance depending on the native speech of the reader (see Davies 1982: 15). Classical Chinese pictograms perform a similar function (see Needham 1971: *passim*).

2 It may be significant as to the marginal phonemic status of /θ, ð/ that both sounds are represented by ⟨th⟩ in Present-Day English orthography. See further Aitchison 1991: 29–30.

3 It should be noted that recent very important work by P. Kitson (see 1993 and references there cited) is currently causing a reappraisal of the limitations of the evidence for Old English dialects, and further research in this area is eagerly awaited by scholars. My comments on page 19 above on the limitations of statistical method should not be taken as a general hostility to statistics in historical linguistics; see Benskin 1994 for an important discussion.

3 LINGUISTIC EVOLUTION

1 For the notion 'prototype' applied to linguistic study, see most notably Taylor 1995, who bases his approach on the work of cognitive psychologists, particularly that of E. Rosch. Psychologists have found that any given notion normally has a core or centre of reference which is generally accepted in a given community of speech-users, and a periphery of reference which is less clearly perceived as belonging to the field. Thus, for Western Europeans, the notion *vegetable* has at its core such items as *potato, onion, turnip* etc., whereas *tomato* and *garlic* are more peripheral. It could therefore be argued that *potato* etc. are more prototypically vegetables than *tomato* etc. That this is not a universal notion can be proved experimentally by the different sets of prototypical vegetables found in non-Western European cultures. A colleague reports that an Egyptian student in her class – who was, incidentally, an excellent non-native speaker of English who had no difficulty in expressing

himself fluently and intelligently in the language – chose *garlic* as a much more prototypical vegetable than any others. The parallel between such phenomena and the notions of variational space described above is an interesting one.

2   'Borrowing' is the usual term adopted to describe the process where speakers take on a usage characteristic of another contemporary variety or language. It is, of course, metaphorical; but the metaphor is not a good one, because the 'donor' language or variety generally retains the usage which it has 'lent'. However – although a number of scholars have tried – it is difficult to think of a better short-hand descriptive term for the process.

5 TRANSMISSION II: SOUND-CHANGE

1   The above represents a simplified account of a somewhat tricky problem. The single occurrence of the form *hliuade* 'towered' (3 pret. sg.) in the late-tenth-century manuscript of the Old English epic poem *Beowulf*, beside more regular *hlifian*, *hlifade*, is an early sign of uncertainty about the phonemic status of the [f]/[v] distinction.

2   A full description of the processes involved in *i*-mutation is not the province of this book, but it is perhaps appropriate to describe it more fully in a note. In brief: when /i/ or /j/ stood in the following syllable, all stressed back vowels, both long and short, were fronted, thus: *a > æ* (although this *a* had in most cases become *æ* before the period of *i*-mutation, the result of an earlier sound-change), *o > oe*, *u > y*. In the same situation, open front vowels were raised, thus *æ > e*; it is also possible that *e > i*. All diphthongs, both long and short, became *ie*; subsequently, *oe* unrounded to become *e*. Examples are Old English *reccan* (Proto-Germanic **rakjan*), Old English *gylden* (Proto-Germanic **guldin*), and Old English *ieldra*, *fieht*, *smīecþ* , *nīehsta* (cf. Old English *eald*, *feohtan*, *smēocan*, *nēah*). See further Campbell 1959: 71–85; Hogg 1992a: 121–138.

3   The scheme of transliteration adopted in this paragraph is that laid down in Dickins 1932, a scheme which is widely used, for example in Page 1973, which is still the standard account of the English runic inscriptions. It has limitations, in the sense that it makes no definite claims as to the phonemic interpretation of the runes, rather offering an adoption of typically equivalent spellings in the Old English version of the Latin alphabet; but this is arguably a good thing, since to offer a transliteration based upon, say, the International Phonetic Alphabet is to jump from transliteration to interpretation (and thus, strictly speaking, to offer a transcription rather than a transliteration). I owe this point to Dr P.V. Stiles. However, see King 1994 and references there cited for an important alternative view and a useful conspectus of literature on this subject.

4   Recent work by M. Black on copies of the letters of the Wycliffite heretic William Swinderby appears to supply evidence for the Shift comparable with that supplied by the Welsh *Hymn*, but from earlier in the fifteenth century; I am grateful to Ms Black for discussing this with me. See Black forthcoming for an account.

5   Dr B. Glauser has raised with me a couple of interesting objections with regard to the hypothesis presented here. First, he notes that the number of words in which Middle English Open Syllable Lengthening takes place in the mid-vowels is rather small. My answer to this is that the *number* of words may be small, but the *occurrence* of those words in the history of English is rather frequent; for instance, these words include verbs belonging to Classes IV and V of the Old English strong-verb system, words used commonly enough to

have sustained even into Present-Day English times an 'irregular' system of conjugation. A more serious objection is to do with systems outside the South of England; in parts of the North, for instance, a distinction has been sustained between vowels derived from Middle English Open Syllable Lengthening and older mid-open vowels which were long at an earlier stage. My answer to this objection is that such areas were quite able to sustain an older system *because the conditions of social interaction which induced hyperadaptation did not exist.* After all, older pronunciations can be sustained at various places in the English-speaking world, if the conditions of social interaction allow; cf., for instance, the Irish English pronunciation of *meat* beside *meet*, a usage which has died out in many other places within the English-speaking community. A system distinguishing reflexes of Old English *ēa, ǣ* and vowels affected by Middle English Open Syllable Lengthening would be quite stable until the process of interaction took place. I would therefore argue that the survival of such distinctions in certain North Midland dialects illustrates that the potential for change can exist, but that change itself need not occur until some triggering actuates it.

6 CHANGE IN THE LEXICON

1 I have assigned the discussion of the pronominal system to this chapter because the competition between pronominal systems seems to me to have a bearing on the lexicological arguments put forward above. It is of course arguable that this discussion of the pronouns should have been assigned to the chapter on grammar. My view is that the boundary between grammar and lexicon is fuzzy, and any division is arbitrary; but since one of the themes of this book is to do with the interaction of levels of language, any mistaken assignation of category is perhaps not too serious. Readers will, of course, decide for themselves on this matter.

2 The often-quoted example of calling a ship 'she' may be ignored here; this seems obviously metaphorical rather than any true relic of grammatical gender. Similarly, the alternation *blond* : *blonde* – only observed in the written language in English – derives from the status of these words as French loans.

3 A potentially difficult problem is raised by the hypothesis put forward on page 133 above, given conventional views on the pronunciation of the Old English diphthongs: where does the [oː] come from in Northern Middle English and Older Scots *scho*? It is possible that the resyllabification took place while the unstressed part of the diphthong, conventionally transcribed by scholars as [ə], still had a rounded quality. Moreover, although the above account explains the occurrence of the form *scho*, difficulties remain in explaining the more southerly form *sche*. One problem is to do with *-e* for *-o*; another is presented by the early occurrence of *scæ* in the *Peterborough Chronicle* Continuations for the years 1140–1141. Although there are Norse words in this text (e.g. *carlmen, oc, tacen*), some well-founded doubts have been expressed as to how such a form could have spread south so comparatively early, given that the more northerly and later Orm used the (apparently) intermediate form *ȝho* (see Britton 1991). Here it may not be necessary to take Norse developments into account. It may be that the older theory of derivation from the Old English definite article is relevant – although the lack of any evidence for a [ʃ-]-type pronunciation of the article itself would militate against this explanation. Alternatively, the form in the Midland *Vespasian Psalter Gloss* is *hīe*, and this could in principle undergo resyllabification to produce **hjē*, followed by a shift of **hj-* to *sch-* comparable to that described on page 133. However, the trigger

of the resyllabification, if not the result of interaction with Norse, needs to be addressed. One possible argument might run as follows: as Campbell points out (1959: 98 n. 2), *īe* in non-West-Saxon dialects seems to have been disyllabic (see, e.g. the metre of the second line of the Old Northumbrian *Bede's Death Song*, where *sīe* fills a lift and a dip). Thus it might be argued that *hīe* in the *Vespasian Psalter Gloss* was a disyllabic word, presumably realised as ['hijə], where [j] would seem a necessary intersyllabic glide. It does not seem phonetically implausible that, in weak-stress situations, this *hīe* could be realised with syncopation as [hjə] – and thus liable for the further change to [ʃ-]. A restressed [ʃeː] would then emerge in the same way that Present-Day English *I* derives from Middle English [iː], a restressed form of the reduced-stress variant *i* derived from Old English *ic*.

Suggestions for further reading

The following is a list of book-length resources and studies relevant to the argument of this book. No claims of fullness are made here; this list simply represents some works the present author has found useful. All books mentioned contain their own suggestions for further reading, including discussions of earlier controversies. Full bibliographical details appear in the list of References. Those suitable for beginners are marked *; those of special importance or usefulness are marked +. A major limitation is that this list of suggestions for further reading is restricted to works written in or translated into English; thus, for instance, K. Luick's extremely important (although incomplete) *Historische Grammatik der englischen Sprache* (1964) has not been included.

BIBLIOGRAPHIES

Fisiak, J., *A Bibliography of Writings for the History of the English Language* (1987).
Tajima, M., *Old and Middle English Language Studies: a Classified Bibliography* (1988).

ENCYCLOPEDIA

+Asher, R. and Simpson, J.M.Y. (eds), *The Encyclopedia of Language and Linguistics* (10 vols) (1994) (An extraordinarily useful, major survey of the whole field of linguistic study, with many bibliographies and suggestions for further reading.)

DICTIONARIES ETC.

BBC English Dictionary (1992).
Chambers Dictionary (1993).
Concise Scots Dictionary (1985).
English Dialect Dictionary (1898).
Middle English Dictionary (1952–).
Oxford Dictionary of English Etymology (1966).
Oxford English Dictionary (2nd edn, 1989).

Roget's Thesaurus (1962 edn).
Survey of English Dialects: the Dictionary and Grammar (1994).
A Microfiche Concordance to Old English (materials for a new *Dictionary of Old English*) (1980).
Roberts, J. and Kay, C. with Grundy, L., *A Thesaurus of Old English* (1995).

USEFUL COLLECTIONS OF TEXTS

Bennett, J.A.W. and Smithers, G.V. (eds), *Early Middle English Verse and Prose* (1974 edn).
Benson, L. (gen. ed.), *The Riverside Chaucer* (1988).
Burnley, J.D. (ed.), *The History of the English Language: a Source-Book* (1992).
*Burrow, J. and Turville-Petre, T. (eds), *A Book of Middle English* (1992).
Chambers, R.W. and Daunt, M. (eds), *A Book of London English 1384–1425* (1931).
Davies, C., *English Pronunciation from the Fifteenth to the Eighteenth Century* (1934).
Davis, N. (ed.), *Paston Letters and Papers of the Fifteenth Century*, Vol. I (1971), Vol. II (1976).
+Görlach, M., *An Introduction to Early Modern English* (1991) (includes an excellent Appendix of illustrative texts, with bibliographical references).
Hoad, T., rev., *Sweet's Second Anglo-Saxon Reader* (1978).
*Mitchell, B. and Robinson, F., *A Guide to Old English* (1995 edn).
Whitelock, D. (ed.), *Sweet's Anglo-Saxon Reader* (1971 edn).

The machine-readable historical *Helsinki Corpus of English Texts: Diachronic and Dialectal*, general editor M. Rissanen, is an invaluable resource, soon to be supplemented by the *Helsinki Corpus of Older Scots*, general editor A. Meurmann-Solin.

GENERAL READING

The new +*Cambridge History of the English Language* (general editor R. Hogg, in progress 1992–) includes many major essays, with important bibliographies, on matters relevant to the arguments of this book. The volumes published so far, edited by Hogg (1992b), Blake (1992) and Burchfield (1994) appear in the list of References. I have also included below some standard introductions to grammar (Leech *et al.* 1982), phonetics (Gimson 1989), phonology (Lass 1984), semantics and lexicology (Waldron 1979), sociolinguistics (Hudson 1980), dialectology (Chambers and Trudgill 1980), pragmatics (Leech 1983), general linguistics (Simpson 1979) and historical linguistics (Lehmann 1992), all of which themselves make suggestions for further reading. The collections of texts edited by Bennett and Smithers, Burrow and Turville-Petre, Görlach and Mitchell and Robinson, all cited above, all contain valuable introductory material. Other book-length studies or collections of papers include the following.

*Aitchison, J., *Language Change: Progress or Decay?* (1991 edn) (An important study of the principles of language change, written in an accessible manner.)
*Barber, C.L., *The English Language: an Historical Introduction* (1993) (An updated and considerably rewritten version of the author's *The Story of Language* 1964. An exceptionally clear and useful single-volume account – perhaps the best now available for the beginning student.)
*Baugh, A.C. and Cable, T., *A History of the English Language* (1993 edn) (Probably the most widely used single-volume history. The book contains a mass of useful material, but is perhaps a little weak in theoretical orientation. Good

on such matters as the 'external history' of the language – an area comparatively neglected in the *Cambridge History*.)

+Bloomfield, L., *Language* (1933) (A classic account by one of the founding fathers of American linguistics. Still valuable.)

*Brunner, K. (trans. G. Johnston), *An Outline of Middle English Grammar* (1970) (A handy single-volume survey of Middle English sounds and morphology; nothing on syntax, however.)

*Burnley, J.D., *A Guide to Chaucer's Language* (1983) (An account of Chaucerian usage which makes a valuable supplement to Sandved 1985. Its orientation is literary, but there is excellent material on the linguistic situation in late medieval London and the author has a good sense of linguistic variation.)

+Campbell, A., *Old English Grammar* (1959) (Still the standard account in English of Old English sounds and morphology, not completely replaced by Hogg 1992a. Not for the beginner; anyone starting the study of Old English grammar is advised to approach the subject first through, for example, Hamer 1967, Prins 1972 or Mitchell and Robinson 1995. Lass 1992b is too advanced for the true beginner.)

*Chambers, J. and Trudgill, P., *Dialectology* (1980) (A standard textbook on the subject, with outlines of a number of classic descriptions and a good bibliography.)

*Clanchy, M., *From Memory to Written Record* (1993 edn) (This book, by a leading documentary historian, has excellent insights into linguistic relationships in the medieval world, and incidentally on the relationship between oral and written discourse.)

*Dawkins, R., *The Blind Watchmaker* (1986) (A now-classic account of evolutionary theory which has many implications for linguistic evolution as well. Highly readable, challenging, thought-provoking. See also Lieberman 1984.)

+Denison, D., *English Historical Syntax* (1993) (Now the standard single-volume diachronic account, with very helpful surveys of the literature and suggestions for further reading and research.)

*Dillard, J.L., *A History of American English* (1992) (A handy single-volume narrative.)

+Dobson, E.J., *English Pronunciation 1500–1700* (2 vols)(1968 edn) (Massive and authoritative; the standard study of the early spelling-reformers and writers on pronunciation during the Early Modern English period. Some scholars have from time to time complained about its idiosyncrasies, but these complaints are overstated; the book's focus on the evolution of 'standard' English is a reflection of the nature of the evidence with which it deals. There is, in fact, a surprisingly large amount of material here about 'non-standard' varieties during the period in question. Perhaps best approached through Ekwall 1974 or Prins 1972.)

*Ekwall, E. (trans. A. Ward), *A History of Modern English Sounds and Morphology* (1974) (The title is self-explanatory. A good, concise introduction to the Early Modern English period.)

*Elliott, R., *Chaucer's English* (1974) (Particularly good on Chaucer's vocabulary.)

*Gimson, A.C. (rev. S. Ramsaram), *An Introduction to the Pronunciation of English* (1989 edn) (A standard textbook on phonetics, with some historical material. Essential for anyone seriously interested in sound-change.)

+Greenbaum, S. and Quirk, R., *A Student's Grammar of the English Language* (1990) (Perhaps the standard one-volume grammar for student use, based upon, but updated from, the larger definitive work, Greenbaum *et al.* 1980. Any student working through this book will have gained a thorough understanding of the principles and stuctures of Present-Day English, and will have developed an appropriate 'metalanguage' for grammatical discussion. Some students may find it handy, however, to approach this book through the medium of a less-advanced primer using the same essential orientation; recommended is Leech *et al.* 1982, for which see below.)

*Hamer, R., *Old English Sound-Changes for Beginners* (1967) (The title is self-explanatory. A very clear, concise account, handy for the beginning student.)

+Harris, R., *The Linguistics Wars* (1993) (An hilarious, mordant account of the development of linguistics in the United States in the last thirty years. An insider's view of a world seeming at times to be hermetically sealed from the rest of us. See also Sampson 1982.)

+Hogg, R., *A Grammar of Old English,* Vol. I: *Phonology* (1992a) (An important new study; although certainly more theoretically coherent, and with many new insights based upon recent research, it complements rather than replaces Campbell 1959. Volume II is eagerly awaited.)

*Hudson, R., *Sociolinguistics* (1980) (A useful single-volume introduction to the subject, which takes a broader view of the 'social' approach to linguistic study than is sometimes the case.)

+Iordan, I. and Orr, J. (rev. R. Posner), *An Introduction to Romance Linguistics* (1970) (An updated version of a classic from 1937. Still useful for the student of ideas.)

+Jones, C., *A History of English Phonology* (1989) (An ambitious attempt to find recurring patterns in the evolution of English phonology, this book is essentially descriptive, with a useful bibliography. Not really for the beginner, for whom Prins 1972 remains more suitable. However, there are many interesting insights.)

+Jordan, R. (trans. E.J. Crook), *Handbook of Middle English Grammar: Phonology* (1974) (Although in a number of respects seriously outdated, still the only full single-volume Middle English phonology yet published in English. A replacement is needed.)

+Kastovsky, D. and Bauer, G. (eds), *Luick Revisited* (1988) (An important collection of essays, mostly on Old English but a few on the later period.)

+Keller, R., *On Language Change* (1994) (One of the most sensible accounts to date, with many references to earlier theories and a good bibliography.)

+Labov, W., *Principles of Linguistic Change*, Vol.I: *Internal Factors* (1994) (Volume II is eagerly awaited. Labov is undoubtedly the world's leading sociolinguist; this book, which 'uses the present to explain the past', is the outcome of many years' patient research. Essential reading for the serious student.)

+Laing, M. (ed.), *Middle English Dialectology* (1989) (An important collection of essays by leading scholars of Middle English.)

LALME = *Linguistic Atlas of Late Mediaeval English* (See McIntosh, Samuels and Benskin 1986.)

+Lass, R. (ed.), *Approaches to English Historical Linguistics* (1969) (An extremely useful collection of some of the most important essays on the subject up to the date of publication. Updated versions of the essays by McIntosh and Samuels appear in Laing 1989.)

*Lass, R., *Phonology* (1984) (A very useful introduction to phonology, with much historical material. Perhaps the most uncontroversial of Lass's books, but perhaps therefore the most useful for the beginning student.)

+Lass, R., *The Shape of English* (1987) (An important, highly stimulating but also highly personal account of the history of English from an essentially formalist perspective. Lass's work cannot be ignored by the serious student of the subject, although – as he freely and honestly acknowledges in his Epilogue – his orientation is still not generally accepted by other scholars. Keller 1994 and Waldron 1985 make useful philosophical supplements.)

+Lass, R., *Old English* (1992b) (A useful handbook of Old English, designed as a 'bridge' between such works as Mitchell and Robinson 1995 and Campbell 1959. Too advanced, however, for the true beginner.)

+Leech, G., *Principles of Pragmatics* (1983) (An important outline, by a leading practitioner, of a developing subdiscipline of linguistics whose implications for historical study are increasingly becoming apparent.)

*Leech, G., Deuchar, M. and Hoogenraad, R., *English Grammar for Today* (1982) (A clearly written distillation of the principles of English grammar, designed for the beginning student. This short book also makes a useful introduction to Greenbaum *et al.* 1980.)

*+Lehmann, W., *Historical Linguistics* (1992 edn) (A classic introduction to the subject, now fully updated: very clear, readable, extremely well illustrated and exemplified. A workbook to accompany this textbook is also available directly from the Summer Institute of Linguistics.)

+Lieberman, P., *The Biology and Evolution of Language* (1984) (An important study by a cognitive scientist, supplementing from a biological viewpoint the philosophical approach put forward by, for example, Waldron 1985.)

+McIntosh, A., Samuels, M.L. and Benskin, M. with Laing, M. and Williamson, K., *A Linguistic Atlas of Late Mediaeval English* (4 vols) (1986) (= *LALME*) (Absolutely essential reading and reference-book for the serious student of Middle English. The introduction to volume I is perhaps the best introduction to Middle English studies yet written.)

*Machan, T. and Scott, C. (eds), *English in its Social Contexts* (1992) (A useful one-volume survey of varieties of English, especially handy for those varieties which have emerged outside the British Isles. Useful bibliographies.)

*Millward, C., *A Biography of the English Language* (1989) (Perhaps the best single-volume history to emerge in the United States. Highly readable and full of anecdote; some useful theoretical orientation. A limitation for the European reader is that, like many American works, it does not use consistently the notations of the International Phonetics Association. An accompanying workbook is also available.)

+Milroy, J., *Linguistic Variation and Change* (1992) (Milroy is possibly the leading British sociolinguist of his generation. This comparatively short book is an important study of the social location of linguistic change, emphasising the importance of the 'actuation problem'.)

+Mitchell, B., *Old English Syntax* (2 vols) (1985) (Now the standard survey of syntax. Highly personal, but also extraordinarily thorough and learned; a mine of useful examples.)

*Mossé, F. (trans. J Walker), *A Handbook of Middle English* (1952) (Still handy as a general introduction to Middle English. Contains a useful selection of illustrative texts.)

+Mustanoja, T., *A Middle English Syntax: I* (1959) (Only one volume ever published. Orientation rather similar to that adopted by Mitchell 1985, although less personal in expression.)

*Nielsen, H.F., *The Germanic Languages* (1989) (A useful introduction to the relationships between the Germanic languages, with handy bibliographies, by a leading scholar in the area of historical–comparative Germanic philology.)

+Page, R.I., *An Introduction to English Runes* (1973) (Still the authoritative survey, with an excellent bibliography up to date of publication. Essential reading for anyone working in this area.)

*Pinker, S., *The Language Instinct* (1994) (Very well-written, popular book with many interesting anecdotes, expounding one view of the phenomenon of human language. In the opinion of this author, however, it should be read alongside Lieberman 1984 and Waldron 1985, which offer distinct and more balanced views.)

*Prins, A.A., *A History of English Phonemes* (1972) (A standard account, well-organised and easy for the student to follow.)

+Prokosch, E., *A Comparative Germanic Grammar* (1938) (Still the only handbook in English for students of this subject.)

+Sampson, G., *Schools of Linguistics* (1982) (Highly readable account of the dominant schools of linguistics since the nineteenth century. Witty, acerbic, exciting. The book makes an interesting companion to Harris 1993, if only because it places US developments in a wider context.)

+Samuels, M.L., *Linguistic Evolution, with Special Reference to English* (1972) (In the author's opinion, indispensable for the serious student of English historical linguistics. Sometimes dismissed as a 'functional' work, but a careful reading shows it to be a good deal more than that. Although Samuels's work has been challenged in detail since it was published – not always justifiably – it remains in essentials the outstanding book on the historical study of English.)

*Sandved, A.O., *Introduction to Chaucerian English* (1985) (A fairly traditional, clear outline of Chaucerian phonology and morphology. Although criticised by some reviewers for its alleged avoidance of theoretical engagement, the book is extremely useful for the students for whom it was designed.)

*Scragg, D., *A History of English Spelling* (1974) (A useful survey of the subject, although now needing updating in the light of the publication of *LALME*.)

*Simpson, J.M.Y., *A First Course in Linguistics* (1979) (A new edition is in preparation. A very thorough survey of the subject by an experienced teacher. Excellent suggestions for further reading.)

+Strang, B.M.H., *A History of English* (1972) (Still in some senses the leading single-volume history of English, although now showing its age. Its organisation – beginning with Present-Day English and going backwards in time – has always attracted criticism from students and other scholars, although intellectually entirely justifiable.)

*Waldron, R.A., *Sense and Sense Development* (1979 edn) (An excellent, clear and highly readable introduction to the study of semantics.)

+Waldron, T.P., *Principles of Language and Mind* (1985) (A philosopher's investigation into the evolution of language, described in A. Montagu's foreword as 'the sanest statement of the problems concerning the nature and function of language that I have read'. Useful as a companion to Keller 1994, Lieberman 1984.)

+Wells, J., *Accents of English* (3 vols) (1982) (The most authoritative study of Present-Day English accents, this major survey also contains much material of interest to linguistic historians. Very useful bibliographies.)

+Wyld, H.C., *A History of Modern Colloquial English* (1936 edn) (Wyld's work, though often criticised and to be treated with care, is still classic and worth rereading. Wyld was one of the few scholars of his generation *not* to treat the history of English as synonymous with the history of the evolution of Standard English and Received Pronunciation.)

+Wyld, H.C., *Studies in English Rhymes* (1923 edn) (Possibly Wyld's best book. It makes a useful supplement to Dobson 1968, although it should always be consulted alongside that work.)

JOURNALS

Most of the major journals in this field appear in the list of References. The following regularly include material useful for students of English historical linguistics: *Anglia, Anglo-Saxon England, Diachronica, English Studies, Folia Linguistica Historica, Journal of English and Germanic Philology, Journal of Linguistics, Language, Lingua, Medium Aevum, Neophilologus, Neuphilologische Mitteilungen, NOWELE, Studia Neophilologica, Transactions of the Philological Society, Word.*

References

Agard, J. (1985), ' "Stereotype" from *Mangoes and Bullets* (1985)', in Brown (1992), 147.

Agutter, A. (1989), 'Middle Scots as a literary language', in R.D.S. Jack (ed.), *The History of Scottish Literature*, Vol. I, Aberdeen: Aberdeen University Press, 13–25.

Aitchison, J. (1991), *Language Change: Progress or Decay?*, Cambridge: Cambridge University Press.

Alleyne, M. (1980), *Comparative Afro-American*, Ann Arbor: Karoma Press.

Asher, R. and Simpson, J.M.Y. (eds) (1994), *The Encyclopedia of Language and Linguistics*, Oxford: Pergamon.

Atkins, J.W.H. (ed.) (1922), *The Owl and the Nightingale*, Cambridge: Cambridge University Press.

Bailey, C.-J.N. (1973), *Variation and Linguistic Theory*, Arlington: Center for Applied Linguistics.

Baldinger, K. (1980), *Semantic Theory*, trans. W.C. Brown and ed. R. Wright, Oxford: Blackwell.

Barber, C.L. (1993), *The English Language: an Historical Introduction*, Cambridge: Cambridge University Press.

Baugh, A.C. and Cable, T. (1993), *A History of the English Language*, 4th edn, London: Routledge.

BBC English Dictionary (1992) (J. Sinclair editor-in-chief), London: HarperCollins.

Bean, M. (1983), *The Development of Word Order Patterns in Old English*, London: Croom Helm.

Bennett, J.A.W. and Smithers, G.V. (eds) (1974), *Early Middle English Verse and Prose*, Oxford: Clarendon Press.

Benskin, M. (1994), 'Descriptions of dialect and areal distributions', in Laing and Williamson (1994), 169–187.

Benskin, M. and Laing, M. (1981), 'Translations and *Mischsprachen* in Middle English manuscripts', in Benskin and Samuels (1981), 55–106.

Benskin, M. and Samuels, M.L. (eds) (1981) *So meny people longages and tonges: Philological Essays in Scots and Mediaeval English Presented to Angus McIntosh*, Edinburgh: Middle English Dialect Project.

Benson, L. (gen. ed.) (1988), *The Riverside Chaucer*, Oxford: Oxford University Press.

Black, M. (forthcoming), 'Studies in the dialect materials of medieval Herefordshire', unpublished Ph.D., University of Glasgow.

Blake, N.F. (ed.) (1992), *The Cambridge History of the English Language*, Vol. II, Cambridge: Cambridge University Press.

Bloomfield, L. (1933), *Language*, London: Allen & Unwin.

Bold, A. (1991), *A Burns Companion*, Basingstoke: Macmillan.

Bosworth, J. and Toller, T.N. (1898), *An Anglo-Saxon Dictionary*, Oxford: Clarendon Press.

Britton, D. (1991), 'On Middle English *she*, *sho*: a Scots solution to an English problem', *NOWELE* 17, 3–51.

Brown, S. (ed.) (1992), *Caribbean Poetry Now*, 2nd edn, London: Edward Arnold.

Brunner, K. (1970), *Outline of Middle English Grammar*, trans. G. Johnston, Oxford: Blackwell.

Burchfield, R. (ed.) (1994), *The Cambridge History of the English Language*, Vol. V, Cambridge: Cambridge University Press.

Burnley, J.D. (1983), *A Guide to Chaucer's Language*, Basingstoke: Macmillan.

—— (ed.) (1992), *The History of the English Language: a Source-Book*, London: Longman.

Burrow, J. and Turville-Petre, T. (eds) (1992), *A Book of Middle English*, Oxford: Blackwell.

Campbell, A. (1959), *Old English Grammar*, Oxford: Clarendon Press.

Cawley, A.C. (ed.) (1958), *The Wakefield Pageants in the Towneley Cycle*, Manchester: Manchester University Press.

Cercignani, F. (1981), *Shakespeare's Works and Elizabethan Pronunciation*, Oxford: Clarendon Press.

Chambers, J. and Trudgill, P. (1980), *Dialectology*, Cambridge: Cambridge University Press.

Chambers, R.W. and Daunt, M. (eds) (1931), *A Book of London English 1384–1425*, Oxford: Clarendon Press.

Chambers Dictionary (1993) (C. Schwarz editor-in-chief), Edinburgh: Chambers Harrap.

Cigman, G. (ed.) (1989), *Lollard Sermons*, Oxford: Early English Text Society.

Clanchy, M. (1993), *From Memory to Written Record*, 2nd edn, Oxford: Blackwell.

Clark, C. (ed.) (1970), *The Peterborough Chronicle 1070–1154*, 2nd edn, Oxford: Clarendon Press.

Concise Scots Dictionary (1985) (M. Robinson editor-in-chief), Aberdeen: Aberdeen University Press.

Crawford, B. (1987), *Scandinavian Scotland*, London: Leicester University Press.

Croft, W. (1995), 'Bringing chaos into order: mechanisms for the actuation of language change', address to the International Conference on Historical Linguistics, University of Manchester, 1995.

d'Ardenne, S.R.T.O. (ed.) (1961), *Þe Liflade ant te Passiun of Ste Iuliene*, Oxford: Early English Text Society.

Davies, C. (1934), *English Pronunciation from the Fifteenth to the Eighteenth Century*, London: Dent.

Davies, N. (1982), *The Ancient Kingdoms of Mexico*, Harmondsworth: Penguin.

Davis, N. (ed.) (1971–1976), *Paston Letters and Papers of the Fifteenth Century*, Oxford: Clarendon Press.

Dawkins, R. (1986), *The Blind Watchmaker*, Harmondsworth: Penguin.

—— (1994), 'The origins of the specious' (*sic*), *Independent* 27 July 1994, 15.

Denison, D. (1993), *English Historical Syntax*, London: Longman.

Devitt, A. (1989), *Standardizing Written English*, Cambridge: Cambridge University Press.

Dickins, B. (1932), 'A system of transliteration for Old English runic inscriptions', *Leeds Studies in English* I, 15–19.

Dickinson, A. (1977), *Scotland from the Earliest Times to 1603*, revised and edited by A.A.M. Duncan, Oxford: Clarendon Press.

Dieth, E. (1955), 'Hips: a geographical contribution to the "she" puzzle', *English Studies* 36, 209–217.

Dillard, J. (1992), *A History of American English*, London: Longman.

Dobson, E.J. (1955), 'The Hymn to the Virgin', *Transactions of the Honourable Society of Cymmrodorion*, session 1954, 70–124.

—— (1962), 'Middle English lengthening in open syllables', *Transactions of the Philological Society*, 124–148.

—— (1968), *English Pronunciation 1500–1700*, Oxford: Clarendon Press.

Donaldson, W. (1986), *Popular Literature in Victorian Scotland: Language, Fiction and the Press*, Aberdeen: Aberdeen University Press.

—— (1989), *The Language of the People: Scots Prose from the Victorian Revival*, Aberdeen: Aberdeen University Press.

Doyle, A.I. and Parkes, M.B. (1978), 'The production of copies of the *Canterbury Tales* and the *Confessio Amantis* in the early fifteenth century', in M.B. Parkes and A.G. Watson (eds), *Mediaeval Scribes, Manuscripts and Libraries: Essays Presented to N.R. Ker*, London: Scolar Press, 163–210.

Dunning, T. and Bliss, A. (eds) (1969), *The Wanderer*, London: Methuen.

Dutch, R.A. (ed.) (1962) *Roget's Thesaurus of English Words and Phrases*, London: Longman.

Ekwall, E. (1974), *A History of Modern English Sounds and Morphology*, trans. A. Ward, Oxford: Blackwell.

Eldredge, N. (1985), *Time Frames: the Rethinking of Darwinian Evolution and the Theory of Punctuated Equilibrium*, New York: Simon & Schuster.

Elliott, R. (1974), *Chaucer's English*, London: Deutsch.

Ellis, A.J. (1869–1889), *On Early English Pronunciation*, London: Early English Text Society.

English Dialect Dictionary (1898) (J. Wright ed.), London: Frowde.

Falkus, M. and Gillingham, J. (eds) (1981), *Historical Atlas of Britain*, London: Grisewood & Dempsey.

Fisher, J., Richardson, M. and Fisher J. (eds) (1984), *An Anthology of Chancery English*, Knoxville: University of Tennessee Press.

Fisiak, J. (1987), *A Bibliography of Writings for the History of the English Language*, Berlin: Mouton de Gruyter.

Fowler, H.W. (1965), *Modern English Usage*, rev. E. Gowers, Oxford: Clarendon Press.

Gimson, A.C. (1989), *An Introduction to the Pronunciation of English*, rev. S. Ramsaram, London: Edward Arnold.

Glauser, B. (1974), *The Scottish–English Linguistic Border: Lexical Aspects*, Bern: Francke.

Gleick, J. (1988), *Chaos*, London: Heinemann.

Gordon, E. (1957), *Introduction to Old Norse*, rev. A. Taylor, Oxford: Clarendon Press.

Görlach, M. (1991), *An Introduction to Early Modern English*, Cambridge: Cambridge University Press.

Gould, S.J. (1982), 'The meaning of punctuated equilibrium, and its role in validating a hierarchical approach to macroevolution', in R. Milkman (ed.), *Perspectives on Evolution*, Sunderland, Mass.: Sinauer, 83–104.

Gradon, P.O.E. (ed.) (1979), *Ayenbite of Inwyt (Vol. II: Introduction, Notes and Glossary)*, Oxford: Early English Text Society.

Grammont, M. (1933), *Traité de phonétique*, Paris: Librarie Delagrave.

Gray, M.M. (ed.) (1912), *Lancelot of the Laik*, Edinburgh: Scottish Text Society.

Greenbaum, S. and Quirk, R. (1990), *A Student's Grammar of the English Language*, London: Longman.

Greenbaum, S., Leech, G., Quirk, R. and Svartvik, J. (1980), *A Comprehensive Grammar of the English Language*, London: Longman.

Halliday, M.A.K. (1987), 'Language and the order of nature', in N. Fabb and

A. Durant (eds), *The Linguistics of Writing*, Manchester: Manchester University Press, 135–154.

Hamer, R. (1967), *Old English Sound-Changes for Beginners*, Oxford: Blackwell.

Harris, R. (1993), *The Linguistics Wars*, New York: Oxford University Press.

Haugen, E. (1976), *The Scandinavian Languages*, London: Faber & Faber.

Haugen, E., McClure, J.D. and Thomson, D.S. (eds) (1981), *Minority Languages Today*, Edinburgh: Edinburgh University Press.

Heuser, W. (1908), 'Die ältesten Denkmäler und die Dialekte des Nordenglischen', *Anglia* 31, 276–292.

Heyworth, P. (ed.) (1968), *Jack Upland, Friar Daw's Reply and Upland's Rejoinder*, Oxford: Clarendon Press.

Hines, J. (1984), *The Scandinavian Character of Anglian England in the pre-Viking period* (British Archaeology Reports, British Series 124), Oxford: British Archaeology Reports.

Hoad, T. (ed.) (1978), *Sweet's Second Anglo-Saxon Reader: Archaic and Dialectal*, Oxford: Clarendon Press.

Hogg, R. (1992a), *A Grammar of Old English*, Vol. I: *Phonology*, Oxford: Blackwell.

—— (ed.) (1992b), *The Cambridge History of the English Language*, Vol. I, Cambridge: Cambridge University Press.

Holm, J.A. (1994), 'English in the Caribbean', in Burchfield (1994), 328–381.

Hudson, A. (ed.) (1978), *Selections from English Wycliffite Writings*, Cambridge: Cambridge University Press.

Hudson, R. (1980), *Sociolinguistics*, Cambridge: Cambridge University Press.

Ihalainen, O. (1994), 'The dialects of England since 1776', in Burchfield (1994), 197–274.

Iordan, I. and Orr, J., with Posner, R. (1970), *An Introduction to Romance Linguistics*, Oxford: Blackwell.

Jespersen, O., (1922), *Language, its Nature, Development and Origin*, London: Allen & Unwin.

—— (1938), *Growth and Structure of the English Language*, 9th edn, Stuttgart: Teubner.

—— (1941), *Efficiency in Language Change*, Copenhagen: Ejnar Munksgaard.

Johnson, L.K. (1992), 'Youtman', in Brown (1992), 25.

Johnson, S. (1755 and subsequent editions) *A Dictionary of the English Language*.

Jones, C. (1988), *Grammatical Gender in English 950–1250*, New York: Croom Helm.

—— (1989), *A History of English Phonology*, London: Longman.

—— (ed.) (1991), *Sylvester Douglas: a Treatise on the Provincial Dialect of Scotland*, Edinburgh: Edinburgh University Press.

—— (1993), 'Scottish Standard English in the late eighteenth century', *Transactions of the Philological Society* 91, 95–131.

Jordan, R. (1974), *Handbook of Middle English Grammar: Phonology*, trans. E.J. Crook, The Hague: Mouton.

Kastovsky, D. and Bauer, G., with Fisiak, J. (eds) (1988), *Luick Revisited*, Tübingen: Narr.

Kay, C.J. (forthcoming), 'Homonymy revisited: a multifactorial approach'.

Keller, R. (1994), *On Language Change*, London: Routledge.

King, A. (1992a), 'You say [æ(ː)jðər], I say [æ(ː)jhwæðər]? – interpreting Old English written data', in F. Colman (ed.), *Evidence for Old English*, Edinburgh: John Donald, 20–43.

—— (1992b), 'Old English ABCs', in Rissanen *et al.* (1992), 130–143.

—— (1994), 'Runes', in Asher and Simpson (1994), 3627–3629.

Kingman, J. (1988), *Report of the Committee of Inquiry into the Teaching of English Language*, London: HMSO.

Kinsley J. (ed.) (1968), *Burns: Poems and Songs*, Oxford: Clarendon Press.

Kitson, P. (1993), 'Geographical variation in Old English prepositions and the location of Ælfric's and other literary dialects', *English Studies* 74, 1–50.

Knowles, G. (1974), 'Scouse: the urban dialect of Liverpool', unpublished Ph.D., University of Leeds.

—— (1978), 'The nature of phonological variables in Scouse', in P. Trudgill (ed.), *Sociolinguistic Patterns in British English*, London: Edward Arnold, 80–90.

Kolb, E. (1966), *Phonological Atlas of the Northern Region*, Bern: Francke.

Kuhn, S. (1945), '*e* and *æ* in Farman's Mercian Glosses', *Publications of the Modern Language Association of America* 60, 631–669.

Kuhn, T. (1970), *The Structure of Scientific Revolutions*, 2nd edn, Chicago: University of Chicago Press.

Labov, W. (1972), *Sociolinguistic Patterns*, Philadelphia: Pennsylvania University Press.

—— (1983), 'Recognizing Black English in the Classroom', in J. Chambers (ed.), *Black English: Educational Equity and the Law*, Ann Arbor: Karoma, 29–55.

—— (1994), *Principles of Linguistic Change*, Vol. I: *Internal Factors*, Oxford: Blackwell.

LAE = Linguistic Atlas of England: see Orton *et al.* (1978).

Laing, M. (ed.) (1989), *Middle English Dialectology*, Aberdeen: Aberdeen University Press.

—— (1991), 'Anchor texts and literary manuscripts in Early Middle English', in Riddy (1991), 27–52.

—— (1993), *Catalogue of Sources for a Linguistic Atlas of Early Medieval English*, Cambridge: Brewer.

Laing, M. and Williamson, K. (eds) (1994), *Speaking in our Tongues: Proceedings of a Colloquium of Medieval Dialectology and Related Disciplines*, Cambridge: Brewer.

Lakoff, G. and Johnson, M. (1980), *Metaphors We Live By*, Chicago: University of Chicago Press.

LALME = A Linguistic Atlas of Late Mediaeval English: see McIntosh *et al.* (1986).

Lass, R. (ed.) (1969), *Approaches to English Historical Linguistics*, New York: Holt, Rinehart & Winston.

—— (1976), *English Phonology and Phonological Theory*, Cambridge: Cambridge University Press.

—— (1984), *Phonology*, Cambridge: Cambridge University Press.

—— (1987), *The Shape of English*, London: Edward Arnold.

—— (1988), 'Vowel Shifts, great and otherwise: remarks on Stockwell and Minkova', in Kastovsky and Bauer (1988), 395–410.

—— (1990), 'How to do things with junk: exaptation in language evolution', *Journal of Linguistics* 26, 79–102.

—— (1992a), 'What, if anything, was the Great Vowel Shift?', in Rissanen *et al.* (1992), 144–155.

—— (1992b), *Old English*, Cambridge: Cambridge University Press.

Le Page, R.B. and Tabouret-Keller, A. (1985) *Acts of Identity: Creole-based Approaches to Language and Ethnicity*, Cambridge: Cambridge University Press.

Leech, G. (1983) *Principles of Pragmatics*, London: Longman.

Leech, G., Deuchar, M. and Hoogenraad, R. (1982), *English Grammar for Today*, Basingstoke: Macmillan.

Lehmann, W. (1992), *Historical Linguistics*, 3rd edn, London: Routledge.

Leith, D. (1983), *A Social History of English*, London: Routledge.

Lemke, J.L. (1992), 'New challenges for systemic–functional linguistics: dialect diversity and language change', *Network* 18, 1–16.

Lewis, C.T. and Short, C. (1879), *A Latin Dictionary*, Oxford: Clarendon Press.

Lieberman, P. (1984), *The Biology and Evolution of Language*, Cambridge, Mass.: Harvard University Press.

Lightfoot, D. (1979), *Principles of Diachronic Syntax*, Cambridge: Cambridge University Press.

Lowe, K.A. (1994), 'Palaeography', in Asher and Simpson (1994), 2900–2906.

—— (forthcoming a) 'On the plausibility of Old English dialectology: the ninth-century Kentish charter materials', *Anglo-Saxon England*.

—— (forthcoming b), '⟨The⟩ and ⟨ye⟩: text, typeface and tradition in Late Middle and Early Modern English'.

Luick, K. (1964), *Historische Grammatik der englischen Sprache*, Oxford: Blackwell.

Lutz, A. (1992), *Phonotaktisch gesteuerte Konsonantenveränderungen in der Geschichte des Englischen*, Tübingen: Niemeyer.

Lyons, J. (1968), *An Introduction to Theoretical Linguistics*, Cambridge: Cambridge University Press.

McClure, J.D. (1981), 'The synthesisers of Scots', in Haugen *et al.* (1981), 91–99.

—— (1988), *Why Scots Matters*, Edinburgh: Saltire Society.

McIntosh, A. (1963), 'A new approach to Middle English dialectology', *English Studies* 44, 1–11 (repr. with corrections in Laing 1989).

—— (1973), 'Word geography in the lexicography of mediaeval English', *Annals of the New York Academy of Sciences* 211, 55–66 (repr. with corrections in Laing 1989).

—— (1974), 'Towards an inventory of Middle English scribes', *Neuphilogische Mitteilungen* 75, 602–624 (repr. with corrections in Laing 1989).

McIntosh, A., Samuels, M.L. and Benskin, M., with Laing, M. and Williamson, K. (1986), *A Linguistic Atlas of Late Mediaeval English*, Aberdeen: Aberdeen University Press.

Machan, T. and Scott, C. (eds) (1992), *English in its Social Contexts*, New York: Oxford University Press.

Manly, J. and Rickert, E. (eds) (1940), *The Text of the Canterbury Tales*, Chicago: University of Chicago Press.

Menner, R. (1934), 'Farman Vindicatus', *Anglia* 58, 1–27.

A Microfiche Concordance to Old English (1980) (A. Healey and R. Venezky eds), Toronto: Centre for Medieval Studies, University of Toronto.

Middle English Dictionary (1952–) (= MED), (H. Kurath founding ed.), Ann Arbor: University of Michigan Press.

Millward, C. (1989), *A Biography of the English Language*, Fort Worth: Holt, Rinehart & Winston.

Milroy, J. (1992), *Linguistic Variation and Change*, Oxford: Blackwell.

Milroy, J. and Milroy, L. (1993), *Real English*, London: Routledge.

Mitchell, B. (1985), *Old English Syntax*, Oxford: Clarendon Press.

Mitchell, B. and Robinson, F. (1991), *A Guide to Old English*, 5th edn, Oxford: Blackwell.

Morris, R. (ed.) (1876), *Cursor Mundi*, London: Early English Text Society.

Mossé, F. (1952), *A Handbook of Middle English*, trans. J. Walker, Baltimore: Johns Hopkins University Press.

Moulton, W.G. (1962), 'Dialect geography and the concept of phonological space', *Word* 18, 23–32.

Mugglestone, L. (1991), 'The fallacy of the Cockney rhyme: from Keats and earlier to Auden', *Review of English Studies*, n.s. 42, 57–66.

Munro, M. (1985), *The Original Patter: a Guide to Current Glasgow Usage*, Glasgow: Glasgow District Libraries.

Murison, D. (1977), *The Guid Scots Tongue*, Edinburgh: Blackwood.

Mustanoja, T. (1959), *Middle English Syntax*, Helsinki: Société Néophilologique.

Needham, R. (1971), *About Chinese*, Harmondsworth: Penguin.

Nerlich, B. (1990), *Change in Language: Whitney, Bréal and Wagener*, London: Routledge.

Nielsen, H.F. (1989), *The Germanic Languages*, Tuscaloosa: University of Alabama Press.

Oftedal, M. (1981), 'Is Nynorsk a minority language?', in Haugen *et al.* (1981), 120–129.

Orton, H., Sanderson, S. and Widdowson, J. (eds) (1978) *The Linguistic Atlas of England*, London: Croom Helm.

Ower, C. (forthcoming), 'A diachronic study of the semantic field "death" ', unpublished M.Phil., University of Glasgow.

Oxford Dictionary of English Etymology (1966) (= ODEE), (C.T. Onions editor-in-chief), Oxford: Oxford University Press.

Oxford English Dictionary (1989) (= OED), (J.A. Simpson and E. Weiner eds), 2nd edn, Oxford: Oxford University Press.

Page, R.I. (1973), *An Introduction to English Runes*, London: Methuen.

Parkes, M.B. (1979), *English Cursive Book Hands*, London: Scolar Press.

—— (1992), *Pause and Effect: an Introduction to the History of Punctuation in the West*, Aldershot: Scolar.

Paul, H. (1888), *Principles of the History of Language*, trans. H.A. Strong, London: Swan Sonnenschein.

Pinker, S. (1994), *The Language Instinct*, Harmondsworth: Penguin.

Postal, P. (1968), *Aspects of Phonological Theory*, New York: Harper & Row.

Prigogine, I. and Stengers, I. (1984), *Order Out of Chaos*, London: Heinemann.

Prins, A.A. (1972), *A History of English Phonemes*, Leiden: Leiden University Press.

Prokosch, E. (1938), *A Comparative Germanic Grammar*, Baltimore: Linguistic Society of America.

Reay, I.E. (1994), 'Sound symbolism', in Asher and Simpson (1994), 4064–4070.

Riddy, F. (ed.) (1991), *Regionalism in Late Medieval Manuscripts and Texts*, Cambridge: Brewer.

Rissanen, M., Ihalainen, O., Nevalainen, T. and Taavitsainen, I. (eds) (1992), *History of Englishes: New Methods and Interpretations in Historical Linguistics*, Berlin: Mouton de Gruyter.

Roberts, J. and Kay, C.J., with Grundy, L. (1995), *A Thesaurus of Old English*, London: King's College London.

Rodby, J. (1992), 'A polyphony of voices: the dialectics of linguistic diversity and unity in the twentieth-century United States', in Machan and Scott (1992), 178–203.

Sampson, G. (1982), *Schools of Linguistics*, London: Hutchinson.

Samuels, M.L. (1963), 'Some applications of Middle English dialectology', *English Studies* 44, 81–94 (repr. with corrections in Laing 1989).

—— (1972), *Linguistic Evolution, with Special Reference to English*, Cambridge: Cambridge University Press.

—— (1985), 'The Great Scandinavian Belt', in R. Eaton, O. Fischer, W. Koopman and F. van der Leek (eds), *Papers from the Fourth International Conference on English Historical Linguistics*, Amsterdam: Benjamins, 269–281 (repr. in Laing 1989).

—— (1987), 'The status of the functional approach', in W. Koopman, F. van der Leek, O. Fischer and R. Eaton (eds), *Explanation and Linguistic Change* (Current Issues in Linguistic Theory 45), Amsterdam: Benjamins, 239–250.

Samuels, M.L. and Smith, J.J. (1981), 'The language of Gower', *Neuphilologische Mitteilungen* 82, 294–304 (repr. with corrections in Samuels and Smith 1988).

—— (1988) *The English of Chaucer*, Aberdeen: Aberdeen University Press.

Sandved, A. (1981), 'Prolegomena to a renewed study of the rise of Standard English', in Benskin and Samuels (1981), 31–42.

—— (1985) *Introduction to Chaucerian English*, Cambridge: Brewer.

Saussure, F. de (1974), *Course in General Linguistics*, trans. W. Baskin, Glasgow: Collins.

Scottish National Dictionary (1976) (= SND), (W. Grant and D. Murison eds), Edinburgh: Scottish National Dictionary Association.

Scragg, D. (1974), *A History of English Spelling*, Manchester: Manchester University Press.

Sebba, M. (1993), *London Jamaican*, London: Longman.

Serjeantson, M. (1935), *A History of Foreign Words in English*, London: Kegan Paul, Trench & Trübner.

Simpson, J.M.Y. (1979), *A First Course in Linguistics*, Edinburgh: Edinburgh University Press.

Sisam, K. (1953), *Studies in the History of Old English Literature*, Oxford: Clarendon Press.

Smith, J. (1971), 'Word order in the older Germanic dialects', unpublished dissertation, University of Illinois (Urbana-Champaign).

Smith, J.J. (1986), 'Some spellings in Caxton's Malory', *Poetica* 24, 58–63.

—— (1988a), 'Spelling and tradition in fifteenth-century copies of Gower's *Confessio Amantis*', in Samuels and Smith (1988), 96–113.

—— (1988b), 'The Trinity Gower D-scribe and his work on two early *Canterbury Tales* manuscripts', in Samuels and Smith (1988), 51–69.

—— (1991), 'Tradition and innovation in South-West Midland Middle English', in Riddy (1991), 53–65.

—— (1992), 'A linguistic atlas of Early Middle English: tradition and typology', in Rissanen *et al.* (1992), 582–591.

—— (1993), 'Dialectal variation in Middle English and the actuation of the Great Vowel Shift', *Neuphilologische Mitteilungen* 94, 259–277.

—— (1994a) 'A philologist's view', in Laing and Williamson (1994), 99–105.

—— (1994b), 'Norse in Scotland', *Scottish Language* 13, 18–33.

—— (1995), 'The Great Vowel Shift in the North of England, and some spellings in manuscripts of Chaucer's *Reeve's Tale*', *Neuphilologische Mitteilungen* 95, 433–437.

—— (forthcoming a), 'Ear-rhyme, eye-rhyme and traditional rhyme: English and Scots in Robert Burns's *Brigs of Ayr*', *The Glasgow Review*.

—— (forthcoming b), 'Dialect and standardisation in the Waseda manuscript of Nicholas Love's *Mirror of the Blessed Life of Jesus Christ*', in S. Ogura, M. Sargent and P. Snowden (eds), *Papers from the Nicholas Love Conference at Waseda*.

Stockwell, R. and Minkova, D. (1988a), 'The English Vowel Shift: problems of coherence and explanation', in Kastovsky and Bauer (1988), 355–394.

—— (1988b), 'A rejoinder to Lass', in Kastovsky and Bauer (1988), 411–417.

Strang, B. (1972), *A History of English*, London: Methuen.

Survey of English Dialects: the Dictionary and Grammar (1994) (C. Upton, D. Parry and J. Widdowson eds), London: Routledge.

Tajima, M. (1988), *Old and Middle English Language Studies: a Classified Bibliography*, Amsterdam: Benjamins.

Taylor, J. (1995), *Linguistic Categorization*, Oxford: Clarendon Press.

Tolkien, J.R.R. (1929), '*Ancrene Wisse* and *Hali Meiðhad*', *Essays and Studies* 14, 104–126.

—— (1934), 'Chaucer as a philologist: *The Reeve's Tale*', *Transactions of the Philological Society*, 1–70.

Toon, T. (1983), *The Politics of Early Old English Sound Change*, New York: Academic Press.

Ullmann, S. (1962), *Semantics*, Oxford: Blackwell.

Vennemann, T. (1994), 'Linguistic reconstruction in the context of European prehistory', *Transactions of the Philological Society* 92, 215–284.

Wahlén, N. (1925), 'The Old English impersonalia', diss. University of Göteborg.

Wakelin, M. (1972), *Patterns in the Folk Speech of the British Isles*, London: Athlone.

Waldron, R.A. (1979), *Sense and Sense Development*, 2nd edn, London: Deutsch.

Waldron, T.P. (1985), *Principles of Language and Mind*, London: Routledge.

Wallace, W. (ed.) (1990), *Poetical Works of Robert Burns*, Edinburgh: Chambers.

Warner, A. (1993), *English Auxiliaries, Structure and History*, Cambridge: Cambridge University Press.

Weinreich, U., Labov, W. and Herzog, M. (1968), 'Empirical foundations for a theory of language change', in W. Lehmann and Y. Malkiel (eds), *Directions for Historical Linguistics*, Austin: University of Texas Press, 95–188.

Wells, J.C. (1973), *Jamaican Pronunciation in London*, Oxford: Blackwell.

—— (1982), *Accents of English*, Cambridge: Cambridge University Press.

Whitelock, D. (ed.) (1971), *Sweet's Anglo-Saxon Reader*, Oxford: Clarendon Press.

Wilson, E.O. (1978), *On Human Nature*, Harmondsworth: Penguin.

Wittig, K. (1958), *The Scottish Tradition in Literature*, Edinburgh: Oliver & Boyd.

Wyld, H.C. (1923), *Studies in English Rhymes*, Oxford: Blackwell.

—— (1936), *A History of Modern Colloquial English*, Oxford: Blackwell.

Zupitza, J. and Furnivall, F. (eds) (1892–1898), *Specimens of all the Accessible Unprinted Manuscripts of Chaucer's Canterbury Tales*, London: Kegan Paul, Trench & Trübner.

Index

To save space, this Index does not include references to persons whose names occur only in the 'Suggestions for further reading'. Where topics are covered very frequently, an initial definition only is referred to.